THE PMP® EXAM
How To Pass On Your First Try

Andy Crowe, PMP

Velociteach Press

All inquiries should be addressed to:

e-mail: info@velociteach.com

First printing, second printing. third printing, fourth printing, 2003. fifth printing, 2003, sixth printing, 2004.

Printing: February, 2004

International Standard Book No. ISBN 0-9729637-0-3

ATTENTION CORPORATIONS, UNIVERSITIES, COLLEGES, AND PROFESSIONAL ORGANIZATIONS. Quantity discounts are available on bulk purchases of this book. For information, please contact info@velociteach.com.

To Karen for all of your help in this. You went above and beyond.

To the hundreds of students and readers who have shared comments and suggestions and have helped to hone this material to an edge. Thank you all.

Contents

Foreword

The idea behind this book was born many years ago when I began studying to become a Project Management Professional (PMP). Preparation for the exam is never trivial, nor does the project management community want it to be; however, the process of determining what to learn, and more importantly, *why* I should learn it, was maddening. I wanted to understand where the information came from, and in many instances I wanted to dive deeper into the subject matter.

Studying for PMP Certification takes a significant amount of commitment and effort, but knowing *what to study* should be effortless.

Another problem I encountered was a lack of focus in many test preparation resources. These resources go into great detail on certain subjects that are only tangentially related to the PMP Exam. For example, one resource listed over thirty different types of contract terms and conditions with which it claimed the reader needed to be familiar. Not only is this incorrect, but many students probably spent the better part of an hour learning something that they did *not* need to know in order to pass the PMP Exam. The latest edition of another test prep resource spent several pages explaining complex financial analysis techniques that are no longer even used on the exam.

This massive volume of unnecessary material can have the effect of not only distracting, but completely overwhelming people who want to know what to study and what to memorize. An additional obstacle for some is that they study for the PMP exam, memorizing lists and formulae ad nauseam, without ever really understanding how or why the information is included or structured the way it is.

PMI's processes are not arbitrary. They are derived from a compilation of generally accepted best practices, industry knowledge, and wisdom that has taken decades to evolve into its current form. Those who pass the exam without truly understanding the driving philosophy and reasons behind the material are doing themselves and the project management profession a great disservice.

Several resources exist for PMP exam preparation, so why should this be the one volume you use? This book represents the only one of its kind, in that it is focused on helping people to pass the PMP Exam on their first try. It also explains the philosophies underlying the test and provides references and sources so that prospective PMPs may explore subjects deeper. Special attention is paid to helping readers gain a context for the information so that it is not merely memorized, but understood.

The philosophies that underpin this book are simple:

1. Provide current and relevant information on all test topics.
2. Cite original sources, informing the reader where to go to find out more.
3. Focus on the essential information that must be learned.
4. Provide tools and exercises that help with the parts that must be memorized in order to pass the PMP Exam, as opposed to merely telling you what to learn.

I believe you will find this end result to be the most complete, concise, and up to date study resource for the PMP Exam.

Here's to your success!

Andy Crowe, PMP

About the Author

Andy Crowe is a Project Management Professional, a Six Sigma Black Belt, and a founder of Velociteach. He is a sought-after speaker, corporate trainer, and writer, instructing people around the world in theory and best practices for project management.

In addition to delivering PMP and project management instruction, Andy has led training for numerous private sector, government, and industry entities. He has taught classes in C++ for Microsoft University and advanced technology courses for the United States Government, as well as designing and leading courses in high-impact project management for Fortune 50 companies.

Prior to Velociteach, Andy founded and built two successful consulting companies and directed the software development practice of Intellinet, one of the most successful information technology consultancies in the southeastern United States, through a period of unprecedented growth. Additionally, he has managed several high-profile domestic and international projects, including the creation of Europe's largest Internet e-commerce site. He recently served on Microsoft's .NET Advisory Committee as one of 21 people worldwide representing the six populated continents.

Andy specializes in information technology management and the synthesis of PMI's processes with organizational methodologies. He holds a degree in Business Management from Kennesaw State University.

About Velociteach

Velociteach, an Atlanta, GA – based company, is the recognized leader in PMP Certification preparation and Project Management training.

As a Registered Education Provider (R.E.P.) with the Project Management Institute, Velociteach offers consulting and training around the world, teaching certification and advanced project management theory and practice.

Velociteach offers a three day accelerated learning course that guarantees passing of the PMP Exam. Full details on this and other course offerings are available online at www.velociteach.com.

Introduction

Everyone who has worked in or around project management for any length of time understands that project failures can have consequences that extend far beyond the financial and organizational impact.

As an example, on March 18, 1937, the community of New London, Texas, was devastated by news of a disaster. The main school building, heated by odorless and colorless natural gas, exploded due to a leaky pipe in the boiler room. Along with their teachers, over 300 children died instantly in the massive explosion. Many others were buried alive under tons of rubble and debris.

This tragedy ultimately led to two significant developments. First, methyl mercaptan was added to the natural gas to give it an identifiable sulfuric odor so that people could know of impending danger. Second, the state of Texas decided to license its engineers. No longer would just anyone be allowed to work on projects like this one. They would be required to demonstrate a high level of understanding and proficiency and the ability to apply that knowledge.

Until recently, licensure in the field of project management has lagged behind other industries such as engineering, medicine, transportation, and real-estate. However, as companies put more of an emphasis on projects, they are requiring a greater understanding of the process of project management and of the many areas of expertise it touches.

There is an old saying, "If it were easy, everyone would do it." Among the many certifications available today, the PMP stands out as the most prestigious, in part because it is considered highly difficult to attain. The fact that the vast majority of project managers never even take the first steps toward earning PMI's certification is evidence that the process is not an easy one.

This book will cut down on the difficulty factors and demystify the material. In the following chapters, you will find exactly what you need to study for the test, how to learn it, how to apply it, and why it is important. *The PMP Exam: How to Pass on Your First Try* is a complete resource to help you prepare fully for the PMP Certification Exam.

In order to get the most from your efforts, you should read the material in this book, practice the examples, and then take and re-take the sample exam, reading the explanations that accompany each question. Additionally, Chapter 14 was written to help you know when you are ready to take the exam.

All in all, you should find your preparation for PMP Certification a highly rewarding experience. Aside from the financial and career benefits that accompany it, PMP Certification is a very worthy goal. The PMP is one of the most fungible certifications you can earn, recognized by nearly every industry and in over 120 countries around the world.

Conventions Used in this Book

The PMP Exam: How to Pass on Your First Try is structured differently than other exam preparation materials. Some of the key features that will help you get the most from this book are listed below:

- The temptation simply to follow the structure of the PMBOK[1] chapter by chapter was avoided. The topic of Integration Management was addressed near the end of the book, unlike in the PMBOK (and other test prep books), where it is located near the very beginning. The reasoning behind this change is simple: You need a solid understanding of the parts before you can fully appreciate how they work together. Studying long lists right at the beginning, or trying to understand how all of the pieces fit together when you may not understand what the pieces are, only serves to frustrate and discourage many prospective PMPs. Integration is considered by many to be the hardest part of the test; however, those who study from this book do far better on that section than the average test taker!

- While it is true that no two people ever have the same PMP Exam due to randomization of the questions, there is a structure and priority to the material. By studying the right information with the proper emphasis, you can be confident of passing. You will also find many topics not even mentioned in the PMBOK expanded on quite heavily in this book. These come from recognized industry sources and volumes on which PMI relies heavily.

- The philosophy behind each knowledge area and many of the sub-topics is explained. Because a significant number of questions on the PMP Exam require you to *apply* the information instead of simply regurgitating it, it is essential to understand "why" the information is structured the way it is instead of merely memorizing it.

- A large portion of the PMP Exam relies on understanding key terms related to project management. Many test takers go wrong by relying on their own experience to interpret terminology instead of understanding PMI's definitions. PMI's use of a term or concept may be very different than that of someone who has not had exposure to PMI's philosophy. Key terms are given special attention where necessary to help readers become acquainted with PMI's usage of project management terms and concepts.

- Instead of making the book gender neutral (he/she), the masculine pronoun was generally used. The use of this convention was not intended to diminish the role of female project managers. Rather, this choice was made to improve the readability of the book.

- Finally, one of the best features of this book is that it is annotated. Instead of keeping the material arcane and shrouded in mystery, the reader is provided with the sources from which it came. Combined with the bibliography included with chapters 3 - 12 under the heading "Going Deeper", you can delve into any given topic covered here to get a more thorough understanding of the material than would be practical or necessary to present here. For project managers looking to build their library of quality project management books, this will be a very valuable resource.

In a Hurry?
Take the Velociteach 3 Day PMP Study Course

Better

You will pass the PMP Exam. In fact, we guarantee it! Before you sign up with anyone, read the fine print on their guarantee. Most places only "guarantee" that you can take their class again. **Velociteach guarantees you will pass the exam or you get your money back.**

Smarter

Velociteach is unique. Instead of just telling you what to learn, we help you memorize the essential material *in class*. When you finish with the Velociteach 3 Day PMP Course, you will be ready to pass the PMP Exam.

Faster

Velociteach prepares you to pass the PMP exam after only 3 days. No one else promises or delivers that!

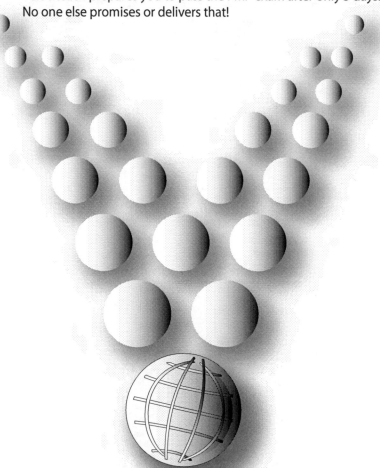

Registration information, schedule, and guarantee details available at:

www.velociteach.com

The Exam

This chapter will explore the PMP Certification Exam, what it is like, and the material it covers. It will help you understand what the test is, how it is structured, and an overview of the contents. Specific strategies on how to pass the exam will be discussed in Chapter 14 – How to Pass the PMP on Your First Try.

What the Exam Tests

Before we discuss what the PMP Certification Exam does test, let's clear up a few misconceptions about the exam.

The PMP Certification Exam *does not* test:

- Your project management experience
- Your common sense
- Your knowledge of industry practices
- Your knowledge of how to use software tools
- What you learned in management school
- Your intelligence

The PMP Certification Exam *does* test:

- Your knowledge of PMI's processes
- Your understanding of the many terms that are used to describe the processes
- Your ability to apply those processes in a variety of situations
- Your ability to apply key formulae to scheduling, costing, estimating, and other problems
- Your understanding of professional responsibility as it applies to project management

A Passing Grade

Not to scare you right away, but the cold, hard truth is that many who take the PMP Exam do not pass. In fact, the number of people who take the test for the *first* time and do not pass is estimated at around 47%.

This includes a broad cross section of people, ranging from those who have approached the exam with extensive preparation, including books and training classes, to those who have barely expended any effort.

Still, if there is a bright side to this otherwise bleak statistic, it is that more first time test takers pass the PMP than fail, so you begin with the odds on your side. By using this book, you are tilting the scales decidedly in your favor!

Now for another piece of good news: The exam is pass/fail, and to pass the PMP Exam, you only have to answer 137 questions correctly out of the 200 on the test. That translates to 68.5%, so there is quite a margin for error.

Some people find it very difficult to understand why they cannot study and make a perfect score on the PMP. It is a good thing to want to do well on the exam, but considering the incredible breadth of material, simply passing it is a terrific accomplishment!

Experts disagree over some of the questions, and there will be a few that you will be absolutely certain you got right that you actually missed. This has more to do with the way the questions are constructed and worded than it does with the study effort you put in, your intellectual powers, or your test taking abilities.

Your goal in taking the PMP should be to do your absolute best, and to make sure that your best effort falls within PMI's passing score limits.

The Exam Material

Your PMP Exam will be made up of exactly 200 questions, covering a broad variety of material. The questions are chosen from an extensive test bank, and because the process is randomized, no two people should ever have the same exact exam.

PMI does provide some guidelines as to how the material will be presented. The exam was significantly updated in March of 2002, and the updated material and questions are allocated as follows:

Question Allocation on the PMP[1]

Process	Number of Questions	% of Exam
Initiating	17	8.5%
Planning	47	23.5%
Executing	47	23.5%
Control	46	23%
Closing	14	7%
Professional Responsibility[2]	29	14.5%

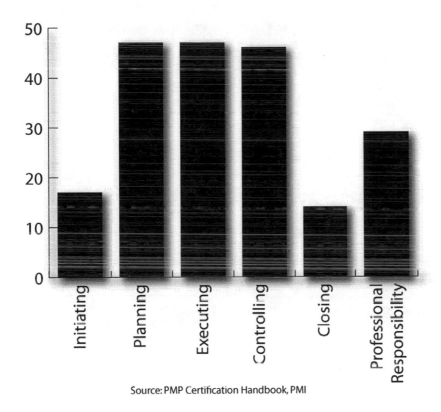

Source: PMP Certification Handbook, PMI

The terms above - initiating, planning, executing, controlling, and closing - will be explained in Chapter 3 – Project Framework.

This fact shocks many people preparing for the exam, but the PMBOK (pronounced "pim-bock"), which stands for a Guide to the Project Management Body of Knowledge, is not a single study source for the exam. The PMBOK does provide an excellent definition and presentation of the overall processes, but it does not give you much help in knowing how that material will translate to the exam. Many of those who do not pass the PMP Exam tried to use the PMBOK as their study guide and were surprised at the way questions were worded or the actual questions that were asked. In fact, the entire section of professional responsibility (covered in Chapter 13 of this book) is not even discussed in the PMBOK, and 29 of your exam questions will come straight from this section!

Getting to the Test (Application)

It is highly recommended that you join the Project Management Institute prior to signing up to take the test. At publication time, the new member fee was $129.00 ($119.00 membership + $10.00 new member activation fee). Application may be made online at www.pmi.org, or you may obtain an application from PMI by calling (610) 356-4600.

After joining PMI, you will receive a membership number that you can use to receive a $150.00 discount on the exam's non-member fee, so you instantly save money by joining. The Examination Fee will be $405.00 for a member in good standing. If you elect not to join PMI, it will cost $555.00 to apply to take the test.

In addition to the financial advantage, there are many other benefits that come with joining PMI, including a subscription to PMI's publications, PM Network, and PM Journal, discounts on books and PMI-sponsored events, and access to a wealth of information in the field of project management.

When you get ready to apply for eligibility for PMP Certification, you can apply online or use printed forms. If at all possible, you should apply online. Depending on the time of year, wait times have been known to stretch out for weeks when using printed forms through the mail, while online applicants usually report turnaround times within one to two weeks. The length of time can vary, depending on the volume of applications that PMI is processing. In any case, you must have your letter of eligibility from PMI to sit for the PMP Certification Exam.

To be eligible for PMP Certification, you will need to demonstrate that you meet certain minimum criteria. The current qualifications that PMI requires include:

Requirements to Apply Under Category 1

- A University Degree
- 4,500 hours of project management experience covering the 5 process groups
- 3 years of project management experience within the last 6 years
- 36 continuous calendar months of project management experience
- 35 hours of project management education

Requirements to Apply Under Category 2

- A High school diploma or equivalent
- 7,500 hours of project management experience covering the 5 process groups
- 5 years of project management experience within the last 8 years
- 60 continuous calendar months of project management experience
- 35 hours of project management education

In short, if you hold a university degree, you should apply under Category 1. If not, you should apply under Category 2. See PMI's official guide, available online, for more details on this point.

Ongoing Education

PMPs are expected to demonstrate not only knowledge and experience but also their ongoing commitment to the field of project management. To promote such commitment, PMI requires that all PMPs maintain their certification status by completing at least 60 Professional Development Units (PDUs) every 36 months. The requirements for PDUs are defined in further detail in the PMI Continuing Certification Requirements Program Handbook given to all PMPs, and these requirements are similar in nature to requirements that legal, medical, and other professions have adopted. In order to maintain the value of this certification, PMI requires its PMPs to maintain a project management focus and a continued commitment to the field of project management.

The Testing Environment

The PMP Certification Exam is administered in a formal environment. There is no talking during the exam, and you cannot bring notes, books, paper, cell phones, PDAs, or even many types of calculators into the examination room with you. The PMP is considered a "high-stakes" or "high-security" exam and is very carefully monitored. Test takers are constantly observed by the test proctor and are under recorded video and audio surveillance. This can be distracting as well as unnerving, so it is important to be mentally prepared as you walk into the exam.

The test is delivered on a standard Windows-based PC that runs a secure, proprietary testing application. The computer setup is very straightforward, with a mouse and keyboard and a black and white graphical user interface used to display the test. PMI can arrange special accommodations for those test takers who have special physical needs.

The exam ends either when your 4-hour time limit has been reached (more on this in a moment) or when you choose to end the exam. Once the exam is over, you will know your score within a few seconds, and those results are electronically transmitted to PMI. If you passed, you are immediately a "PMP" and you may start using that designation after your name. PMI will mail you all of the official information, including your PMP lapel pin and certificate, within a few weeks. If you did not pass, you may immediately apply with PMI to retake the exam at a discounted rate.

The Time Limit

Taking a test while the clock is ticking can be unnerving. The PMP is a long exam, but you are given a significant block of time to complete the test. From the time you begin the exam, you will have 240 minutes (4 hours) to finish. For most people, this is enough time to take the test and review the answers. The allocation works out to 72 seconds per question if no breaks are taken. While a few of the more complicated questions will certainly require more than 72 seconds, most will take much less time.

The subject of time management for the exam, along with a suggested strategy for managing your time, is covered later in Chapter 14 – How to Pass the PMP on the First Try.

Question Format

Exam questions are given in a multiple choice format, with four possible answers, marked A, B, C, and D, and only one of those four answers is correct. Unlike in some exams, there is no penalty for guessing, so it is to your advantage to answer every question on the PMP exam, leaving none of them blank.

Many of the PMP questions are quite short in format; however, the PMP Exam is famous (or infamous) for its long, winding questions that are difficult to decipher. To help you prepare, you will see different question styles represented in this book. Going through all the sample questions provided in this volume is an excellent way to prepare for the types of questions you will encounter on the actual exam.

Foundational Concepts

Difficulty	Memorization	Exam Importance	Corresponding PMBOK Chapter
Medium	Medium	High	Chapters 1,2,3

What is a project? How is it different from operations or a program? What is a project manager, and how do different organizational structures change the role and power of a project manager? In order to understand PMI's approach to project management, you need a solid overview to these and other topics.

While much of the rest of this book is focused on PMI's processes, inputs, tools, techniques, outputs, and formulae, this chapter lays the foundation on which those knowledge areas are built.

Philosophy

PMI's philosophy of project management does not disconnect projects from the organizations that carry them out. Every project has a context and is heavily influenced by the type of organization in which the project is performed.

Another aspect to be considered in the context of the project is the roles of the different stakeholders. An effective project manager must identify the different types of project stakeholders (such as customers, the project sponsor, senior management, etc.), understand their needs, and help them all work together to create common and realistic goals that will lead to a successful project.

Importance

Because this chapter is foundational, it is highly important! There will be many questions on the PMP Exam that test your understanding of a project manager, stakeholder, and sponsor. You must also be able to identify the different types of organizations, and to recognize a project as compared to other types of related endeavors. Spend time making certain you understand these terms and definitions.

Preparation

The volume of material here is less than in later chapters. Test preparation should be focused on memorization of the terms and your ability to apply them. Word for word memorization is not essential, but a solid understanding is.

Essential Terms

Begin your PMP exam study by cementing your understanding of the following terms:

Process

Processes are encountered regularly when studying for the PMP Exam. For purposes of the test, think of a process as a package of inputs, tools, and outputs used together to do something on the project. For instance, schedule development is the process in which the project schedule is created. Risk identification is the process in which the list of risks is created, etc. There are 39 unique processes you will need to understand for the exam, all of which are covered in this book.

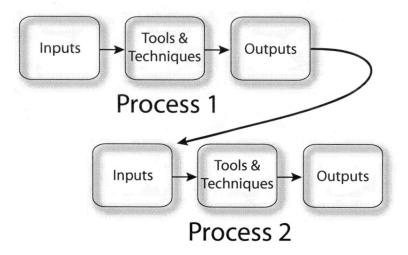

Interactions within a Process

As the preceding diagram illustrates, the outputs from one process are often used as inputs into other processes.

Phases

Many organizations use project methodologies that define project phases. These phases may have names like "requirements gathering," "design," "development," "testing," and "implementation." Each phase of a project produces one or more deliverables.

One of the major problems test takers have when encountering PMI's material is to understand that all of the processes in the PMBOK may take place within each phase of the project. In other words, if your organization's methodology specifies a phase for product design, some or all of the 39 processes (described in chapters 2-13 of this book) may take place in that phase alone, only to be repeated in the subsequent project phases. Keep this fact in mind while reading the remaining chapters.

It is important to understand that PMI does not define what phases you should use on your project. That is because *the PMBOK does not describe a project methodology*. Instead, *processes* are defined that will fit into your project methodology.

The example below shows how deliverables are usually associated with each phase. The deliverables are reviewed to determine whether the project should continue. This decision point is known as an exit gate or a kill point, and the decision on whether to proceed with the project is usually made by a person external to the project.

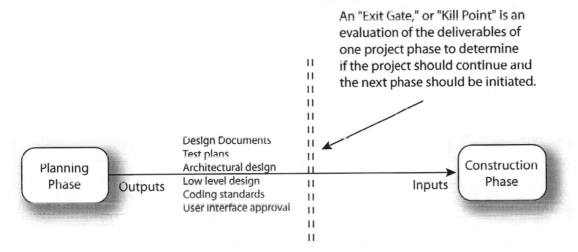

An "Exit Gate," or "Kill Point" is an evaluation of the deliverables of one project phase to determine if the project should continue and the next phase should be initiated.

Project

A project is a temporary (finite) group of related tasks undertaken to create a unique product, service, or result. You may encounter a question on the exam that describes a situation and asks you whether that situation represents a project. If you see such a question, remember that you are looking for the following characteristics:

- A project is time-limited (it has a definite beginning and end).
- A project is unique (it has not been attempted before by this organization).
- A project is comprised of interrelated activities.
- A project is undertaken for a purpose (it will yield a specific product, service, or result).

As the above diagram illustrates, companies set strategic goals for the entire organization. A company's project portfolio represents all of the project and program investments they make.

Programs represent a group of projects managed together in order to gain efficiencies on cost, time, technology, etc. For instance, by managing three related technology projects as a program, an organization might be able to save time and money by developing several common components only once and leveraging them across all of the projects that use those components.

Project management is the application of resources, time, and expertise to meet the project requirements. Project management usually applies to individual projects.

Program

A program is a larger effort than a project, because it is a group of related projects coordinated together. Programs may also include operations. Organizations often group projects into programs in order to realize some benefit that could not be achieved if those projects were not undertaken in concert.

Portfolio

A company's project portfolio represents the entire investment in projects and programs. Project portfolios should be aligned to the organization's strategic goals.

Ideally, the benefit of all project investments should be expressed in how they meet or assist the organization's strategic goals.

Progressive Elaboration

The term "progressive elaboration" simply means that you do not know all of the characteristics about a product when you begin the project. Instead, they may be revisited often and refined. For instance, you may gather some of the requirements, perform preliminary design, take the results to the stakeholders for feedback, and then return to gather more requirements. The characteristics of the product emerge over time, or "progressively."

Project Management

Project management is using skills, knowledge, and resources to satisfy project requirements.

Historical Information

Historical information is found many places on the exam, and it is important to know that it is always used as an input to processes wherever it is found. (*Inputs* and *processes* will become clearer in the next chapter.) Historical information is found in the records that have been kept on previous projects. These records can be used to help benchmark the current project. They may show what resources were previously used and what lessons were learned. More than anything, historical information is used to help predict trends for the current project and to evaluate the project's feasibility.[1] Historical records are always created or updated during the project's closing processes.

Because PMI advocates constant improvement and continuous learning, historical records are extremely important in project management, and they are used heavily during planning activities. They can provide useful metrics, be used to validate assumptions, and help prevent repeated mistakes.

Baseline

The term baseline is used for the project plan, time, scope, and cost. The baseline is simply the original plan plus any approved changes. Many people who take the exam do not understand that the baseline includes all approved changes, but baselines are used as tools to measure how performance deviates from the plan, so if the plan changes, the new plan becomes the baseline.

Suppose you were running a one mile race, and you considered that distance as your baseline. Your plan was to run at the healthy pace of six minutes per mile. Now suppose that the race length was changed to a three mile race. You ran the race and still finished in a respectable twenty minutes. Would you want your progress measured against the original distance or the updated one? If you did not update your baseline to three miles, your pace of twenty minutes against the original distance of one mile would not be very impressive at all. Your performance measurements would only be meaningful if you had an accurate baseline.

Remember - your project's baseline is defined as the original plan plus all approved changes. Even though the baseline changes as the plan changes, it is a good idea to keep records that show how the plan has progressed and changed over time.

Lessons Learned

Lessons learned are documents focused on variances created at the end of each process that detail what lessons were learned that should be shared with future projects. Lessons learned from past projects are an input into many planning processes. It is important that lessons learned put a special emphasis on variances that occurred on the project between what was planned to happen and what actually happened.

Regulation

A regulation is an official document that provides guidelines that must be followed. Compliance with a regulation is mandatory (e.g., in the United States, wheelchair ramps are required for ADA compliance). Regulations are issued by government or another official organization.

Standard

A standard is a document approved by a recognized body that provides guidelines. Compliance with a standard is not mandatory but may be helpful. For example, the size of copy paper is standardized, and it would probably be a very good idea for paper manufacturers to follow the standard, but there is not a law in most countries requiring that copy paper be made the standard size. The PMBOK provides a standard for project management.

System

There are several instances of "systems" in the PMBOK. A system incorporates all the formal procedures and tools put in place to manage something. The term "system" does not refer simply to computer systems, but to procedures, checks and balances, processes, forms, software, etc. For instance, the project management information system (discussed in chapter 13 – Project Integration Management), may include a combination of high-tech and low-tech tools such as computer systems, paper forms, policies and procedures, meetings, etc.

Project Roles

Another area of study regarding the project context is that of the roles and responsibilities found on projects. You should be familiar with the following terms related to project roles:

Project Manager

The project manager is the person ultimately responsible for the outcome of the project. The project manager is:

- Formally empowered to use organizational resources
- In control of the project
- Authorized to spend the project's budget
- Authorized to make decisions for the project

Project managers are typically found in a matrix or projectized organization (more about types of organizations shortly). If they do exist in a functional organization, they will often be only part-time and will have significantly less authority than project managers in other types of organizations.

Because the project manager is in charge of the project, most of the project's problems and responsibilities belong to him. It is typically a bad idea for the project manager to escalate a problem to someone else. The responsibility to manage the project rests with the project manager, and that includes fixing problems.

Project Coordinator

In some organizations, project managers do not exist. Instead, these organizations use the role of a project coordinator. The project coordinator is weaker than a project manager. This person may not be allowed to make budget decisions or overall project decisions, but they may have some authority to reassign resources. Project coordinators are usually found in weak matrix or functional organizations.

Project Expeditor

The weakest of the three project management roles, an expeditor is a staff assistant who has little or no formal authority. This person reports to the executive who ultimately has responsibility for the project. The expeditor's primary responsibility lies in making sure things arrive on time and that tasks are completed on time. An expeditor is usually found in a functional organization.

Senior Management

For the exam, you can think of senior management as anyone more senior than the project manager. Senior management's role on the project is to help prioritize projects and make sure the project manager has the proper authority and access to resources. Senior management issues strategic plans and goals and makes sure that the company's projects are aligned with them. Additionally, senior management may be called upon to resolve conflicts within the organization.

Functional Manager

The functional manager is the departmental manager in most organizational structures, such as the manager of engineering, director of marketing, or information technology manager. The functional manager usually "owns" the resources that are loaned to the project, and has human resources responsibilities for them. Additionally, he may be asked to approve the overall project plan. Functional managers can be a rich source of expertise and information available to the project manager and can make a valuable contribution to the project.

Stakeholder

Stakeholders are individuals who are involved in the project or whose interest may be positively or negatively affected as a result of the execution or completion of the project. They may exert influence over the project and its results. This definition can be very broad, and it can include a vast number of people! Often when the term "stakeholders" appears on the exam, it may be referring to the key stakeholders who are identified as the most important or influential ones on the project.

Sponsor

The sponsor is the person paying for the project. He may be internal or external to the company. In some organizations the sponsor is called the project champion. Also, the sponsor and the customer may be the same person, although the usual distinction is that the sponsor is internal to the performing organization and the customer is external.

The sponsor may provide valuable input on the project, such as due dates and other milestones, important product features, and constraints and assumptions. If a serious conflict arises between the project manager and the customer, the sponsor may be called in to help work with the customer and resolve the dispute.

Project Office

This term refers to a department that can support project managers with methodologies, tools, training, etc., or even ultimately control all of the organization's projects. Usually the project office serves in a supporting role, defining standards, providing best practices, and auditing projects for conformance.

Project Context

Another major area of study for the PMP exam is the concept of a project context, or organizational environment, in which a project is carried out. A large part of the project context is determined by the organization's structure, which PMI refers to as the type of organization.

Types of Organizations

The type of organization that undertakes a project will have an impact on the way the project is managed and even its ultimate success. There are three major types of organizations described by PMI: functional organizations, projectized organizations, and a blend of those two

Project Roles

called matrix organizations. Furthermore, matrix organizations can be characterized as weak, strong, or balanced.

The chart that follows summarizes essential information regarding these three types of organizations. You should be very familiar with this information before taking the exam, as you may see several questions that describe a project or situation and require you to identify what type of organization is involved.

Project Context

Organizational Structures[2]

Type	Description	Who is in Charge?	Benefits	Drawbacks
Functional	Very common organizational structure where team members work for a department, such as engineering or accounting, but may be loaned to a project from time to time. The project manager has low influence or power.	Functional (Departmental) manager	• Deeper company expertise by function. • High degree of professional specialization . • Defined career paths.	• Project manager is weak. • Projects are prioritized lower. • Resources are often not dedicated to a project.
Projectized	The organization is structured according to projects instead of functional departments. The project manager is both the manager of the project and of the people. He is highly empowered and has the highest level of control.	Project manager	• Project manager has complete authority. • Project communication is easiest since everyone is on a single team. • Loyalty is strong, to both the team and the project. • Contention for resources does not exist.	• Team members only belong to a project – not to a functional area . • Team members "work themselves out of a job" – they have nowhere to go when the project is over • Professional growth and development can be difficult.
Matrix	A hybrid organization where individuals have both a functional manager and a project manager for projects. In a strong matrix, the project manager carries more weight. In a weak matrix, the functional manager has more authority. In a balanced matrix, the power is shared evenly between the functional and project managers.	Power shared between project manager and functional manager	• Can be the "best of both worlds." Project managers can get the deep expertise of a functional organization, while still being empowered to manage resources on the project.	• Higher overhead due to duplication of effort on some tasks. • Resources report to a functional manager and they have a "dotted line" to a project manager, sometimes causing conflict and confusion. • High possibility for contention between project managers and functional managers. • Because resources do not report to the project manager, they may be less loyal to him.

Organizational Structures

Project Manager's Power

Once you are comfortable in your understanding of types of organizations and the roles that different stakeholders play in a project, you can see that the organizational context in which a project is carried out will have a great deal of influence on that project. One way that the type of organization affects the project manager in particular is in how much power he is given. The chart below illustrates the relationship between a project manager's level of empowerment and the type of organization in which he works.

The Project Manager's Power by Organization Type

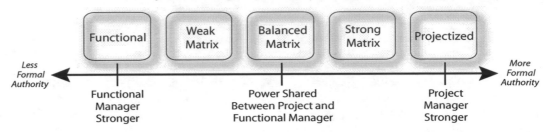

Project Manager's Management Skills

The practice of project management overlaps many other disciplines. Since most projects are performed within an organization, there are other management skills that make up the foundation of project management. These skills will probably have a significant effect on projects. The project manager should have experience in:

Leading

Motivating people and inspiring them to commit.

Communicating

Exchanging information clearly and correctly. Although communication skills are not emphasized on the exam, they are important to the project manager and critical to the success of the project.

Negotiating

Working to reach a mutual agreement. Negotiations may happen with groups or individuals inside and outside the organization.

Problem Solving

Defining the problem and dealing with the factors that contribute to or cause the problem.

Influencing

Accomplishing something without necessarily having formal power. Influencing the organization requires a keen understanding of the way the organization is structured, both formally and informally.

Management Skills

Project Life Cycle

The project life cycle is simply a representation of the phases that a project typically goes through. These phases are general, but they are representative of the general flow of activities on a project.

The six phases represented at the bottom of the graphic below describe the way in which a project typically progresses. It should be noted, however, that this depiction is very general, and different phases and phase names are used by different industries and projects.

The image also shows some other facts about the project life cycle that often appear on the PMP exam in the form of questions. These questions typically focus on the fact that resource and cost levels rise early in the project and drop over time, or how risk and stakeholders' ability to influence the project are highest early in the project and decrease as the project progresses.

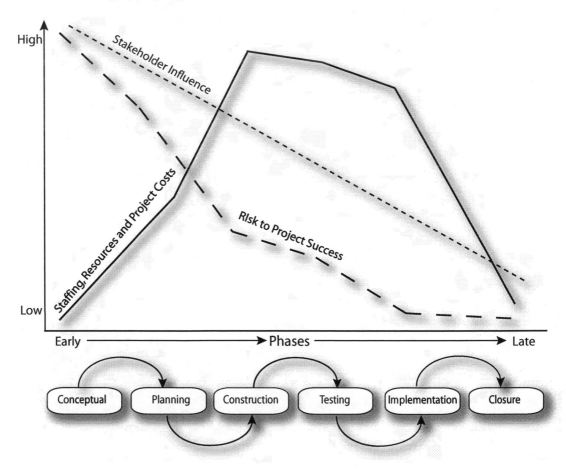

The Triple Constraint

Another fundamental topic in project management is commonly referred to as "the triple constraint." It is based on the realization that while changes do occur during a project, they do not happen in a vacuum. When the scope of a project is changed, time and cost are also affected. Of course, the same is true when changes are made to cost or time. Those changes will have some impact on the other two areas.

As many different types of changes will be requested in most projects, it is essential in project management to be mindful of the triple constraint and to help keep others aware of it. The project manager should not simply accept all changes as valid; rather, the project manager should evaluate how those changes affect the other aspects of the project.

The triple constraint, or as some know it, the iron triangle, is simply the concept that scope, time, and cost are closely interrelated. Just as you cannot affect one side of a triangle without changing one or both of the other lengths, you cannot simply change one part of the triple constraint without affecting other parts.[3]

However common a practice it may be in some organizations to slash a budget without revisiting the scope or the schedule, the project manager should not simply accept these mandates. The triple constraint is in place whether the organization recognizes and accepts it or not.

The classic approach to the triple constraint is represented in the following diagram:

The triple constraint, also called the iron triangle

But as many topics are interrelated in project management, an expanded view of the "triple" constraint could be represented not as a triangle but as a hexagon as shown below:

Expanded view of the "triple" constraint

Triple Constraint

Going Deeper

For further exploration on the topics presented in this chapter, the following resources are suggested:

Knutson, Joan. *Project Management for Business Professionals: A Comprehensive Guide.* New York: John Wiley & Sons, Inc., 2001.

Knutson, Joan; Bitz, Ira. *Project Management: How to Plan and Manage Successful Projects.* New York: NY AMACOM Books, 1991.

Lewis, James P. *Fundamentals of Project Management.* New York: AMACOM Books, 1995.

Taylor, James, *A Survival Guide for Project Managers.* New York: AMACOM Books, 1998.

Project Framework

Difficulty	Memorization	Exam Importance	Corresponding PMBOK Chapter
Low	High	High	Chapter 3

3

The project framework is the structure on which all of PMI's process material is built. The PMI processes are organized into nine knowledge areas and based on five foundational process groups: Initiating, Planning, Executing, Controlling, and Closing.

Every PMI process performed as part of a project may be categorized into one of these process groups. Additionally, every question on the exam will tie back to one of these five areas or to professional responsibility, discussed in Chapter 13.

This chapter describes what the processes and knowledge areas are, explains how they are structured, and provides an overview of the project management framework.

Importance

This chapter is essential to your understanding of how this material is organized and structured. Do not be discouraged if you find the material in this chapter somewhat confusing at first. The more you read and study from this book, the better you will understand these terms and how they are applied.

Preparation

There is significant memorization that accompanies this chapter. Terms must be learned, and more importantly the overall organization of the material needs to be understood. This chapter contains only a little that will actually show up on the exam, but it has to be mastered before chapters 4 – 12 can be comprehended in full.

Essential Terms

The essential information here begins with some key terms that you will need to understand. It is not necessary to memorize all the definitions, but make sure that you do understand them. They are not only foundational to this book, but they are highly important for the exam.

Processes

The term "process" is one of the most important and frequently used terms you will encounter when studying for the PMP. Processes are composed of three elements: inputs, tools and techniques, and outputs.

The different inputs, tools and techniques, and outputs are combined to form processes, which are performed for a specific purpose. For instance, schedule development is a process, and as its name implies, it is performed to develop the schedule. Risk identification is another process, with different inputs, tools, techniques, and outputs. There are 39 unique processes identified and described in the Guide to the PMBOK.

Inputs

The inputs are the starting points for the processes. Just as food is a basic building block for the production of energy in living creatures, there are specific and unique inputs into each project management process that are used as building blocks for that process. You might think of inputs as your raw materials.

Tools and Techniques

Tools are the actions or methods that are used to transform inputs into outputs. Tools can be many things, such as software, which can be used as a tool to help plan the project and analyze the schedule. Techniques are methods, such as flowcharting, which help us to frame, approach, and solve the problem. PMI combines tools and techniques since they are both used to solve problems and create outputs.

Outputs

Every process contains at least one output. The outputs are the ends of our efforts. The output may be a product, a service, or a result. Usually the outputs from one process are used as inputs to other processes or as part of a broader deliverable, such as the project plan.

Knowledge Areas

The knowledge in PMI's methodology has been organized into nine areas. Each of the 39 project management processes defined in the PMBOK fit into one of these nine knowledge areas. They are:

1. Integration Management

2. Scope Management

3. Time Management

4. Cost Management

5. Quality Management

6. Risk Management

7. Human Resources Management

8. Communications Management

9. Procurement Management

Like the Guide to the PMBOK, this book also has a chapter for each of the knowledge areas as listed above; however, it is organized slightly differently than the chapters of the PMBOK. The reason for this is that when studying for the exam, integration management fits better at the end since it brings together the other processes.

Process Groups

The project management processes defined and described in the PMBOK are not only presented according to the nine different knowledge areas; they are also arranged according to process groups. The same 39 processes that are included in the knowledge areas are included in the 5 process groups.

Process Groups

The five process groups are:

1. Initiating

2. Planning

3. Executing

4. Controlling

5. Closing

Every PMI-defined process that takes place on the project fits into one of those groups.

Organization

As hinted at in the previous paragraphs, each process has two homes. It fits into a process group *and* a knowledge area. As the chapters in this book are aligned to knowledge areas, you will be able to see how process are associated with different knowledge areas.

Understanding the Flow

Do not fall into the trap of thinking that the first step is to do the processes in initiation, the second step is to do the processes in planning, and so on. Although projects may flow very roughly that way, PMI stresses the point that the scope of a project is "progressively elaborated," which means that some processes are performed iteratively. Some planning must take place, then some executing, then some controlling processes. Further planning may be performed, further executing, and so on. The five process groups are by no means completely linear.

Illustration of the way in which process groups interrelate

Process Group 1 - Initiating

Integration	Scope	Time	Cost	Quality	HR	Communication	Risk	Procurement
	✓							

The Initiating Process Group is one of the simpler groups in that it is only made up of a single process. The sole process under the initiating group is initiation, described in further detail in Chapter 4 – Project Scope Management. This is the process group that gets the project officially authorized and underway.

The way in which a project is initiated, or begun, can make a tremendous difference in the success of subsequent processes and activities.

Although most processes are not performed in a strict order, the initiating process should be performed first or at least very early on. In initiation, the project is formally begun, and the project manager is named.

If a project is not initiated properly, the end results could range from a lessened authority for the project manager to unclear goals or uncertainty as to why the project was being performed. Conversely, a project that is initiated properly would have the business need clearly defined and would include information on why this project was chosen over other possibilities.

Initiation may be performed more than once during a single project. If the project is being performed in phases, each phase could require its own separate initiation, depending on the company's methodology, funding, and other influencing factors.

Initiating Processes

Process Group 2 - Planning

Integration	Scope	Time	Cost	Quality	HR	Communication	Risk	Procurement
✓	✓	✓	✓	✓	✓	✓	✓	✓

Planning

- Scope Planning
- Scope Definition
- Activity Definition
- Activity Sequencing
- Activity Duration Estimating
- Schedule Development
- Resource Planning
- Cost Estimating
- Cost Budgeting
- Quality Planning
- Organizational Planning
- Staff Acquisition
- Communication Planning
- Risk Mgt Planning
- Risk Identification
- Risk Qualification
- RiskQuantification
- Risk Response Planning
- Procurement Planning
- Solicitation Planning
- Project Plan Development

Planning is the largest process group, because it has the most processes, but do not make the leap that it also involves the most work. Although this is not a hard and fast rule, most projects will perform the most work and use the most project resources during the executing processes.

Project planning is extremely important, both in real life and on the PMP Exam. The processes from planning touch every one of the knowledge areas! You should be familiar with the 21 processes that make up project planning as shown in the graphic on the left of this page.

The order in which the planning processes are performed is primarily determined by how the outputs of those planning processes are used. The outputs of one process are often used as inputs into a subsequent planning process. This dictates a general order in which they must take place. For instance, the scope statement (created during scope planning) is used as an input to feed the work breakdown structure (created duing scope definition). The work breakdown structure is then used as an input to create the activity list (created during activity definition).

You may, for example, encounter a question similar to the one below:

Q: **What is the correct sequence for the following activities?**

A. Create scope statement. Create work breakdown structure. Create activity list.

B. Create scope statement. Create activity list. Create work breakdown structure.

C. Create work breakdown structure. Create scope statement. Create activity list.

D. Create activity list. Create scope structure. Create work breakdown structure.

Planning Processes

In this example, the correct sequence is represented by choice 'A'. This question ties back to the preceeding graphic showing how scope items (the work breakdown structure) are created first, time-related planning processes (the activity durations) are performed second, and cost planning processes (the budget baseline) are performed third. This particular question is discussed in more detail in the chapter on Scope Management, while this topic of planning process order is discussed under the topic of core vs facilitatating processes, covered later in this chapter.

Process Group 3 - Executing

Integration	Scope	Time	Cost	Quality	HR	Communication	Risk	Procurement
✓				✓	✓	✓		✓

As alluded to earlier, executing processes typically involve the most work.[1] You do not need to memorize a list of executing processes like the one for planning, but you should know that the executing process group is where the work actually gets carried out. In this group of processes, parts are built, planes are assembled, code is written, and houses are constructed. Other elements are also included here, such as procurement, team development, and information distribution. These all happen as part of the executing processes.

Some of the processes in the executing process group are intuitive, such as project plan execution. Others, such as quality assurance and information distribution often catch test takers by surprise because they had a different definition than was expected.

As Chapter 1 disclosed, there are currently 47 questions on the exam covering these 7 processes, so it is important to learn them well. The key to understanding the executing processes is that you are carrying out the plan.

Process Group 4 - Controlling

Integration	Scope	Time	Cost	Quality	HR	Communication	Risk	Procurement
✓	✓	✓	✓	✓		✓	✓	

Controlling

- Scope Verification
- Scope Change Control
- Schedule Control
- Cost Control
- Quality Control
- Performance Reporting
- Risk Monitoring and Control
- Integrated Change Control

Controlling processes are some of the more interesting processes. These processes touch most of the knowledge areas. Activities that relate to controlling simply ensure that the plan is working. If it is not, the processes should be adjusted to correct future results. In controlling processes, things are measured, inspected, reviewed, compared, monitored, verified, and reported. If you see one of those key words on a question, there is a good chance it is related to a controlling process.

Planning processes are easy enough to grasp for most people. Executing processes are simply carrying out the plan, and controlling processes are taking the results from the executing processes and comparing them against the plan. Then corrective action is taken, either to the plan or to the way in which it is being executed (or both) in order to ensure that the work results line up with the plan.

Keep in mind that controlling processes look backward over previous work results and the plan, but controlling actions are looking forward. In other words, controlling is about influencing future results and not so much about fixing past mistakes. It is important that you understand the previous statement for the exam, and the concept is reinforced throughout the next several chapters.

Controlling Processes

Process Group 5 - Closing

Integration	Scope	Time	Cost	Quality	HR	Communication	Risk	Procurement
						✓		✓

Closing

Administrative Closure

Contract Closure

The closing group is comprised of two very important processes. They are contract closeout (covered in Chapter 11 – Procurement Management), and administrative closure (covered in Chapter 9 – Communications Management). These two processes are sometimes difficult for people to master because in their work experience, once the customer signs off and accepts the product, the project is over.

The project does not end with customer acceptance. After the product has been checked against the scope and delivered to the customer's satisfaction, the contract must be closed out (contract closeout), and the project records must be updated, the team must be released, and the project archives and lessons learned need to be updated (administrative closure).

These processes need to be considered as part of the project, since the files, lessons learned, and archives will be used to help plan future projects.

Although there are only 2 processes in the closing process group, the questions about them make up are 7% of the exam, so you would do well to build a thorough understanding of what they are, how they work, and how they interrelate to the other processes.

If you find that you need more help in understanding the content of this chapter, read through it a couple of times before you go on. You can wait to memorize the planning steps until after you've read about them in more detail in the Knowledge Areas. You can also read through chapter 3 of the Guide to the PMBOK after you have read this chapter. It will be much easier to comprehend now that you have an understanding of its underlying structure.

Core and Facilitating Processes

As this chapter has demonstrated, processes can organized in different ways. Every process belongs to a knowledge area and a process group. This organization should become much more intuitive as you progress through this book. One other organizational concept that needs to be mentioned is the division between core processes and facilitating processes, as is illustrated in the diagram below.

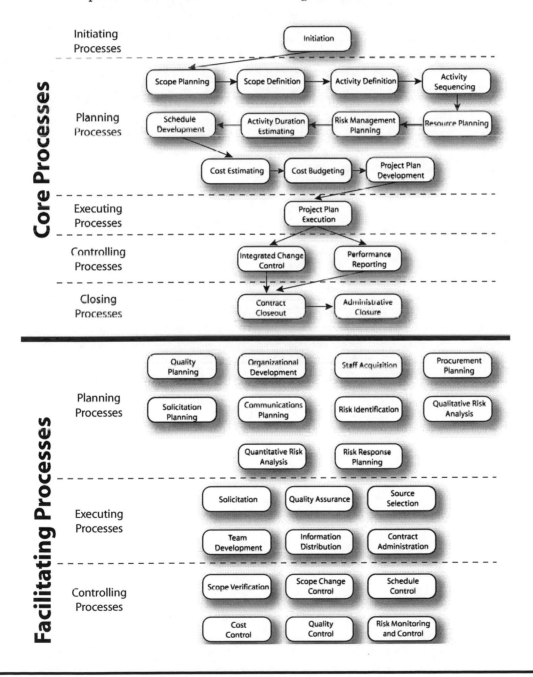

Core processes are those processes at the heart of the project. The outputs of core processes typically become inputs into other processes, and this dictates a rough order in which these processes must be performed. Non-core processes are known as facilitating processes.

Two common mistakes are made when approaching core and facilitating processes. First, you may be tempted to believe that core processes are essential and facilitating processes are optional. This is not the case, since all of the processes are essential. Second, you may fall into the trap of thinking that the core processes are performed first and then the facilitating processes are performed. This, too, is incorrect. As mentioned earlier, there is a basic order to the core processes; however, it is not firm, and as is discussed thought this book, any process may be performed over and over on a single project.

The best way to approach this material for the exam is to be able to recognize which of the 39 processes are categorized as core processes. After spending some time in this book, this will probably become intuitive.

Core Processes

Going Deeper

The best source for the way PMI has structured their material is from PMI. For a deeper treatment of the material in this chapter, two references are suggested:

A Guide to the Project Management Body of Knowledge (PMBOK® guide), North Carolina, PMI Publishing, 2000.

Pinto, Jeffrey K. *The Project Management Institute: Project Management Handbook.* Jossey-Bass Business & Management Series, 1998.

Going Deeper

Chapter 3

Scope Management

Difficulty	Memorization	Exam Importance	Corresponding PMBOK Chapter
Low	Medium	High	Chapter 5

A solid grasp of project scope management is foundational to your understanding of the material on the PMP. While none of the topics in this book are particularly easy, scope management presents fewer difficulties than most other areas of the test. Most people find scope management to be more intuitive than other areas. It has no complex formulae to memorize and no particularly difficult theories. Instead, scope management is a presentation of processes to plan, define, and control the scope of the project.

Philosophy

The philosophy behind PMI's presentation of scope management can be condensed down to this: The project manager should always be in control of the scope through rigid management of the details and the processes. Scope changes are to be handled in a structured, procedural, and controlled manner.

Good scope management focuses on making sure that the scope is well defined and clearly communicated, and that the project is carefully managed to limit unnecessary changes. The work is closely monitored to ensure that when change does happen on the project, it is evaluated, captured, and documented. Project managers should also work proactively to identify and influence the factors that cause change.

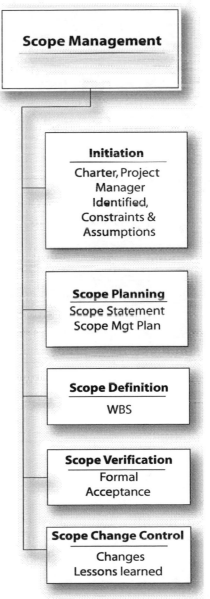

The processes of Project Scope Management with their *primary* outputs

Scope Management

Initiation
Charter, Project Manager Identified, Constraints & Assumptions

Scope Planning
Scope Statement
Scope Mgt Plan

Scope Definition
WBS

Scope Verification
Formal Acceptance

Scope Change Control
Changes
Lessons learned

Importance

The topic of scope is very important on the PMP exam. When PMI refers to the project "scope," they are referring to the work needed to successfully complete the project and *only* that work. Many companies have a culture in which they try to exceed customer expectations by delivering more than was agreed upon; this practice, often referred to as "gold plating," increases risk and uncertainty and may inject a host of potential problems into the project.[1]

Preparation

While this section requires less actual memorization than some other knowledge areas, many of the test questions can be very tricky, requiring a solid and thorough understanding of the theories and practices of scope management.

Scope Management Processes

It is essential that you understand that the topic of scope management consists of the following elements:

- Initiating the project
- Creating a plan for how scope and changes to the scope will be managed
- Defining and documenting the deliverables that fall within the project (the scope)
- Checking the work being done against the scope to ensure that is complete and correct
- Ensuring that *all* of what is "in scope" and *only* what is "in scope" is completed

There are 5 processes included in the scope management knowledge area. These are initiation, scope planning, scope definition, scope verification, and scope change control. Below are the break-outs that show to which process group each item belongs:

Process Group	Scope Management Process
Initiation	Scope initiation
Planning	Scope planning, Scope definition
Executing	(none)
Controlling	Scope verification, Scope change control
Closing	(none)

In the scope management knowledge area, it is also essential that you know the main outputs that are produced during each process. The different tasks that are performed in each process are summarized in the chart below. Included in this chart are some suggested memory "triggers" to help you make key associations.

Process	Key Outputs	Memory Trigger
Scope Initiation	Project Charter	Think of a private club: A charter member gets initiated into it.
Scope Planning	Scope Statement Supporting Detail Scope Management Plan	SP = PS (Scope Planning leads to a planned scope, consisting of the scope statement and the scope management plan).
Scope Definition	Work Breakdown Structure	Just like a dictionary definition breaks down a word into individual meanings, scope definition breaks down work into small, manageable pieces.
Scope Verification	Formal Acceptance	"Trust, but verify" – verification leads to formal acceptance, as in political treaties.
Scope Change Control	Changes to the Scope Corrective Action	CCC – The C's go together. Change control – changes – corrective action.

Scope Mgt Processes

Initiation

The process of scope initiation is where the project begins. Consider for a moment a company that is considering constructing a new office building. The management may have several options available, but resources are limited, and they can only construct one building at this time. One potential project must win out over the others.

Organizations initiate projects for several reasons. These reasons may be broadly categorized as follows:

• A problem. Consider a business that has lost its lease for a building that houses its data center. In this case, a project may be initiated to solve the problem of site selection and relocation for the data center.

• A business requirement. A business may need to initiate a project in order to continue operating smoothly. For example, many healthcare companies have initiated projects that are necessary in order to meet recent government reporting requirements.

• An opportunity. Perhaps the most common reason to initiate a project is to capitalize on an identified opportunity. The project is initiated to create a new product, service, or result.

Management may use several techniques in order to pick only one project. They may use project selection methods to measure the value or benefit of the project. These include benefit measurement methods that seek to quantify the expected benefits and the costs of the project. They may also use constrained optimization methods, which are complex mathematical decision models, to determine which project is the most attractive. Almost always they will use the technique of expert judgment to select which project would be the best one. Expert judgment simply refers to the knowledge and expertise of the key project stakeholders as applied to the current project choices.

The different types of project selection methods that often appear on the PMP exam are discussed below.

Project Selection Methods

Companies select projects using a variety of methods. The most common methods seek to quantify the monetary benefits and expected costs that will result from a project and compare them to other potential projects to select the ones which are most feasible and desirable. Such methods are called "benefit measurement methods" in the PMBOK.

Other methods apply calculus to solve for maximizations using **constrained optimization**. Constrained optimization methods are mathematical and use a variety of programming methods. If you see the terms *linear programming*, or *non-linear programming*, on the exam, you'll know they refer to a type of constrained optimization method and that the question is referring to techniques of project selection. You do not need to know how to calculate values for constrained optimization or linear programming for the exam, but you do need to know that they are project selection methods.

There are additional terms in the fields of economics, finance, managerial accounting, and cost accounting that are sometimes used as tools for project selection. These are not listed in the PMBOK, but they may show up on the exam. It is not necessary to memorize these definitions word for word; however, it is important to understand what they are and how they are used.

Benefit Cost Ratio (BCR)

The BCR is the ratio of benefits to costs. For example, if you expect a construction project to cost $1,000,000, and you expect to be able to sell that completed building for $1,500,000, then your BCR is 1,500,000 ÷ 1,000,000 = 1.5

In other words, you get $1.50 of benefit for every $1.00 of cost. A ratio of greater than 1 indicates that the benefits are greater than the costs.

Internal Rate of Return (IRR)

IRR, or "Internal Rate of Return," is a finance term used to express a project's returns as an interest rate. In other words, if this project were an interest rate, what would it be? Calculation of the IRR is no longer required on the exam, but you should understand that just like the interest rate on a savings account, bigger is better when looking at IRR.

Net Present Value (NPV)

See Present Value definition below for an explanation of Net Present Value (NPV) and Present Value (PV).

Opportunity Cost

Based on the theory that a dollar can only be invested at one place at a time, opportunity cost asks "What is the cost of the other opportunities we missed by investing our money in this project?" For project selection purposes, the smaller the opportunity cost, the better, because it is not desirable to miss out on a great opportunity!

Payback Period

The payback period is how long it will take to recoup an investment in a project. If someone owed you $100, you would prefer that they pay it to you immediately rather than paying you $25 per month for 4 months. As you want to recoup your investment as quickly as possible, a shorter payback period is better than a longer one.

Present Value (PV) and Net Present Value (NPV)

PV is based on the "time value of money" economic theory that a dollar today is worth more than a dollar tomorrow. If a project is expected to produce 3 annual payments of $100,000, then the present value (how much those payments are worth right now) is going to be *less* than $300,000. The reason for this is that you will not get your entire $300,000 until the 3rd year, but if you took $300,000 cash and put it in the bank right now, you would end up with more than $300,000 in 3 years.

PV is a way to take time out of the equation and evaluate how much a project is worth right now. It is important to understand that with PV, bigger is better.

Net Present Value (NPV) is the same as Present Value except that you also factor in your costs. For example, you have constructed a building with a PV of $500,000, but it cost you $350,000. In this case, your NPV would be $500,000 - $350,000 = $150,000.

Note that you are no longer required to calculate Present Value or Net Present Value for the exam. All you need to remember is that a bigger PV or NPV makes a project more attractive, and that NPV calculations have *already* factored in the cost of the project.

Return On Investment (ROI)

Return On Investment is a percentage that shows what return you make by investing in something. Suppose, for example, that a company invests in a project that costs $200,000. The benefits of doing the project save the company $230,000 in the first year alone. In this case, the ROI would be calculated as the (benefit – cost) ÷ cost, or $30,000 ÷ $200,000 = 15%. Note that you no longer need to perform this calculation on the exam, but you do need to understand that for ROI, bigger is better.

Ultimately, the process of scope initiation creates the project by issuing a project charter and identifying the project manager who will be in charge of the project.

The Project Charter

Once an organization has selected the project, the next step in the initiation process is the creation of the project charter. Following are the key facts you need to remember about the project charter.

The Project Charter

- It is created during initiation. (Initiation is the only process from the initiating process group.)
- It is created based on a business need, a customer request, or market force within the economy or society.
- It is signed by the performing organization's senior management.
- It names the project manager and gives him the authority to direct the project.
- It should include the product description and a description of the business need that underlies the project.
- It is a high-level document that does not include project details; the specifics of project activities will be developed during the planning processes, which are carried out *after* scope initiation is complete.

Scope Planning

Scope planning is the process in which the project scope is documented. This process usually begins shortly after the project charter has been issued. The two important outputs of scope planning are:

The Scope Statement

The scope statement is a document that outlines a common understanding of the project among stakeholders. It is used to ensure that when people talk about the project they are all speaking about the same thing. The scope statement should provide deliverables, objectives, and a description of the product of the project. It should also include the business justification for the project.

Don't forget about progressive elaboration in project processes! The scope statement created in scope planning will be revisited and updated as the project progresses.

The Scope Management Plan

The scope management plan is also created during the scope planning process. It describes how the scope will be defined and managed and also how changes to the scope will be handled. For instance, if you are going to interview users or hold requirements sessions to define the scope, that should be reflected in the scope management plan. If a change control board will be used to help evaluate scope change requests, that too should be reflected in the scope management plan.

The scope management plan makes up part of the project plan (discussed further in Chapter 14 – Project Integration Management).

Scope Definition

The Work Breakdown Structure

The Work Breakdown Structure (WBS) contains a detailed description of all of the project's deliverables. It is created during scope definition.

The WBS is a graphical depiction of the work that must be performed. What many do not understand is that this describes the work in terms of the project deliverables, whether those deliverables are products or services.[2] It should have a hierarchical structure.[3] This means simply that the WBS is presented in chart format and includes progressively detailed levels of information, beginning with the top-level deliverable of the project as the first and highest level. The lowest levels of the WBS are called work packages.

A good WBS will be mutually exclusive and cumulatively exhaustive,[4] meaning that every piece of work will be included and included only once on the WBS. There are neither duplications nor omissions in the content. Everything is logically arranged.

The WBS is foundational to the project management planning processes covered throughout this book. This document serves as one of the key inputs to other planning processes that you will see throughout PMI's materials. Among other things, the WBS is used as an input to create the schedule and budget plans, to create activity lists, and most importantly, to define all of the work that will be done on the project. A good rule to remember is that if it is not found on the WBS, it will not be deliverable on the project.

Elements of a Good Work Breakdown Structure (WBS):

- It must be detailed down to a low level. The lowest level of the WBS is made up of work packages that define every deliverable on the project.[5]
- It is graphical, arranged in a pyramid, hierarchical shape, where each sub-level rolls up to the level above it.[6]
- It numbers each element, and the numbering system should allow anyone who reads the WBS to find individual elements quickly and easily.[7]
- It should be detailed enough to provide sufficient information to drive the subsequent phases of planning.[8]
- It may often be borrowed from other projects in the organization as a starting point. These starting points are known as templates.
- It is thorough and complete. If an item is not in the WBS, it does not get delivered with the project.
- It is central to the project.
- The project team creates the WBS, not just the project manager. It is also a means of team-building.[9]
- It is an integration tool, allowing you to see where the individual pieces of work fit into the project as a whole.
- It helps define responsibilities for the team.
- It is a communication tool.[10]

Decomposition

Decomposition is one of the tools used in scope definition to create the WBS. Decomposition involves breaking down the project into progressively smaller components. In a WBS, the top layer is very general (perhaps as general as the deliverable or product name), and each subsequent layer is more and more specific. The key to reading the WBS is to understand that every level is the detailed explanation of the level above it.[11]

Decomposition may be thought of as similar to the arcade game Asteroids™ from years ago. Large pieces are progressively broken down into smaller and smaller pieces.

So, how do you know when you have decomposed your WBS far enough? As you have probably realized, the nodes can be decomposed to ridiculously low levels, wasting time and actually making the project difficult to understand and change. There are many things to consider when deciding how far to decompose work, but perhaps the two best questions to ask are:

1. Are your work packages small enough to be estimated for time and cost?
2. Are the project manager and the project team satisfied that the current level of detail provides enough information to proceed with subsequent project activities?

If you can answer "yes" to those two questions, your work packages are probably decomposed far enough.

Templates

As you might guess, the WBS on any sizable project can grow very large. This is a good thing, as it shows that you are in control of the planning and have accounted for the activities that must take place on the project.

One of the scope definition tools that helps with the creation of a substantial WBS is the use of templates. Quite often, the organization's project office will have templates that may be used to "jump start" the WBS. These templates may be examples of other WBSs used on previous projects, or they may simply include the standard items that must be considered on all projects. Either way, templates provide a starting point so that you are not forced to begin from scratch every time you begin a project.

Work Breakdown Structure Dictionary

Often included with a WBS is a work breakdown structure dictionary. This dictionary is a collection of the lowest levels in the WBS. The work packages are collected in the WBS dictionary and additional information is often included. A sample WBS dictionary entry is represented in the following table.

Work Package ID: 4221	
Work Package Name: Gather Torque Requirements	
Work Package Description: Determine torque requirements for external fasteners, for both composite materials and metallic surfaces. Wherever possible, torque requirements should conform to existing company standards.	
Assigned to: Ramiro Ortiz	*Department*: Materials Engineering
Date Assigned: January 5, 2003	*Date Due*: February 2, 2003
Estimated Cost: $1,200	*Accounting Code*: ME214PE

Scope Verification

Scope verification is a controlling process in which the project manager verifies that the product of the project is acceptable. Typically, acceptance of the product is given by the sponsor, key stakeholders, and the customer. In scope verification, the product is inspected and compared with the scope to make sure that the correct things were done correctly.

For the exam, be sure that you know that formal acceptance of the product (not the entire project) is an output of scope verification.

Scope Change Control

Scope change control is the process that evaluates and tracks changes to the product's scope. Tools used in this process may include software tools that track changes, change control boards that consider and evaluate changes, templates and forms for copying down changes, and corporate and project policies for tracking changes.

The process of scope change control may be thought of as the controlling process that keeps the scope focused and on track, and one of the most important inputs into this process is the scope management plan. The scope management plan provides the blueprint as to how the scope will be managed, as well as how changes to the scope will be managed.

Every project manager has encountered "scope creep" on projects. Scope change control is the process that aids the project manager in preventing scope creep.

Scope Change Control

Summary of Key Ideas and Terms

Inputs, Tools, and Outputs

While it is not necessary to memorize every input, tool, and output to every process in order to pass the PMP Exam, it is necessary to understand them and know why they fall in to the processes they do. Following is a table providing an overview of the processes and the inputs, tools, and outputs for Project Scope Management.

Process	Inputs	Tools/Techniques	Outputs
Scope Initiation	• Product description • Strategic plan • Project selection criteria • Historical information	• Project selection methods • Expert judgment	• Project charter • Project manager identified and assigned • Constraints • Assumptions
Scope Planning	• Product description • Project charter • Constraints • Assumptions	• Product analysis • Benefit/cost analysis • Alternatives identification • Expert judgment	• Scope statement • Supporting detail • Scope management plan
Scope Definition	• Scope statement • Constraints • Assumptions • Other planning outputs	• Work breakdown structure templates • Decomposition	• Work breakdown structure • Scope statement updates
Scope Verification	• Work results • Product documentation • Work breakdown structure • Scope statement • Project plan	• Inspection	• Formal acceptance
Scope Change Control	• Work breakdown structure • Performance reports • Change requests • Scope management plan	• Scope change control system • Performance measurement • Additional planning	• Scope changes • Corrective action • Lessons learned • Adjusted baseline

Key Terms:

Assumptions – Anything considered true for the purpose of planning that may or may not be true in reality. Assumptions should be documented along with the risks they present.

Constraints – Limiting factors on a project such as available time, budget, people, and resources.

Work Breakdown Structure – (WBS) A detailed graphical breakdown, created in scope definition, where every deliverable that will be produced as part of the project is represented.

Decomposition – Breaking down the functional deliverables into work packages that are represented on the work breakdown structure.

Work Package – The lowest level of deliverable described on the WBS. Work packages should be decomposed to the point where they can be estimated for cost and time.

Scope Statement – A statement of the project scope, used to foster a common understanding of the project among stakeholders. It includes the justification for the project, a brief product description, a summary of deliverables, and the project objectives.

Scope Management Plan – A document describing how the project scope will be managed, and how changes will be identified, evaluated, and integrated into the project. It may be formal or informal.

Scope Change Control System - A system for controlling changes to the project scope. This system may consist of a formal change control board, a computerized change tracking system, or a simple, paper-based system.

Going Deeper

For further study in the area of Scope Management, the following books and resources are suggested:

Project Management Institute. *Practice Standard for Work Breakdown Structures*. Project Management Institute, 2001.

Knutson, Joan. *Project Management for Business Professionals : A Comprehensive Guide*. New York: John Wiley & Sons, Inc. (US), 2001.

Pinto, Jeffrey K. *The Project Management Institute: Project Management Handbook*. Jossey-Bass Business & Management Series, 1998.

Going Deeper

Scope Management Questions

1. Your project team is executing the work packages of your project when a serious disagreement regarding the interpretation of the scope is brought to your attention by two of your most trusted team members. How should this dispute be resolved?

   A. The project team should decide on the resolution.
   B. The dispute should be resolved in favor of the customer.
   C. The dispute should be resolved in favor of senior management.
   D. The project manager should consult the project charter for guidance.

2. Which of the following statements is FALSE regarding a work breakdown structure?

   A. Activities should be listed in the sequence they will be performed.
   B. Every item should have a unique identifier.
   C. The work breakdown structure represents 100% of the work that will be done on the project.
   D. Each level of a work breakdown structure provides progressively greater detail.

3. The project charter is a document issued by:

   A. The stakeholders.
   B. The project manager.
   C. The customer initiating the project.
   D. Management.

4. The project has completed execution, and now it is time for the product of the project to be accepted. Who formally accepts the product?

   A. The project team and the customer.
   B. The quality assurance team, senior management, and the project manager.
   C. The sponsor, key stakeholders, and the customer.
   D. The project manager, the customer, and the change control board.

5.   Creating the work breakdown structure is an activity of which process?

   A. Scope initiation.
   B. Scope planning.
   C. Scope definition.
   D. Scope verification.

6.   The project charter should contain:

   A. The complete project scope.
   B. A list of the project team members.
   C. Milestones for major deliverables.
   D. The project objectives.

7.   The most important part of scope verification is:

   A. Gaining formal acceptance of the scope of the product from the customer.
   B. Checking the scope of the project against stakeholder expectations.
   C. Verifying that the project came in on time and on budget.
   D. Benefit/cost justification.

8.   The project charter is important because it:

   A. Identifies the stakeholders.
   B. Describes the product.
   C. Names the project manager.
   D. Defines the project sponsor's authority.

9.   Which of the following is NOT part of the Scope Management Plan?

   A. Senior management statement of fitness for use.
   B. The change management plan.
   C. Scope baseline.
   D. Constraints.

10. You have taken over as project manager for a data warehouse project that is completing the design phase; however, change requests are still pouring in from many sources, including your boss. Which of the following would have been MOST helpful in this situation:

    A. A project sponsor who is involved in the project.

    B. A well-defined scope management plan.

    C. A change control board.

    D. A change evaluation system.

11. What is the function of the project sponsor?

    A. To help manage senior management expectations.

    B. To be the primary interface with the customer.

    C. To fund the project and formally accept the product.

    D. To help exert control over the functional managers.

12. The project manager and the customer on a project are meeting together to review the product of the project against the documented scope. Which tool would be MOST appropriate to use during this meeting?

    A. User acceptance testing.

    B. Inspection.

    C. Gap analysis.

    D. Feature review.

13. You have just assumed responsibility for a project that is in progress. While researching the project archives, you discover that the project charter was never signed. Which of the following problems would this most likely cause?

    A. A lack of focus on the project.

    B. Inability to identify the project sponsor.

    C. Lack of customer buy-in to the project.

    D. A lesser degree of formal authority for the project manager.

14.   A team member makes a change to a software project without letting anyone else know. She assures you that it did not affect the schedule, and it significantly enhances the product. What should the project manager do FIRST?

A. Find out if the customer authorized this change.

B. Submit the change to the change control board.

C. Review the change to understand how it affects scope, cost, time, quality, risk, and customer satisfaction.

D. Make sure the change is reflected in the scope management plan.

15.   The product you have delivered has been reviewed carefully against the scope and is now being brought to the customer for formal acceptance. Which process is the project in?

A. Scope verification.

B. Scope auditing.

C. Scope closure.

D. Scope control.

16.   All of the following activities must be performed in scope initiation EXCEPT:

A. Select a project.

B. Apply expert judgment.

C. Identify the project manager.

D. Identify the project team.

17.   You are the project manager for a large construction project, and you identify two key areas where changing the scope of the product would deliver significantly higher value for the customer. Which of the following options is MOST correct?

A. Make the changes if they do not extend the cost and timeline.

B. Make the changes if they do not exceed the project charter.

C. Discuss the changes with the customer.

D. Complete the current project and submit the changes as a new project initiation.

18.   Which of the following activities is done FIRST?

    A. Identification of the project team.
    B. Creation of the work breakdown structure.
    C. Creation of the project charter.
    D. Creation of the statement of scope.

19.   Which of the following statements is TRUE concerning functionality that is over and above the documented scope?

    A. It should be channeled back through the change control board to ensure that it gets documented into the project scope.
    B. Additional functionality should be leveraged to exceed customer expectations.
    C. The final product should include all the functionality and only the functionality documented in the scope.
    D. Additional functionality should be reviewed by the project manager for conformity to the product description.

20.   **A project manager has been managing a project for six months, and everything has been going smoothly; however, now that the project is winding down, change requests are still pouring in. The project is ahead of schedule and on target for costs. Which of the following statements is true?**

    A. The project manager should influence the factors that cause change.
    B. The project manager should reject changes whenever possible.
    C. Changes introduced at any point in the project represent an unacceptable level of risk.
    D. Changes should be evaluated on the basis of how much value they deliver to the customer.

Answers to Scope Management Questions

1. B. In general, disagreements should be resolved in favor of the customer. In this case, the customer is the best choice of the four presented. 'A' is not a good choice because it is your job to keep the team focused on doing the work and out of meetings where they are arguing about the scope. Besides, the team brought you this problem, so their ability to resolve it is already in question. 'C' is incorrect because in most situations, project disputes should be resolved in favor of the customer and not in favor of senior management. 'D' is incorrect because the project charter is a very general and high-level document. As it is issued before either the scope statement or the work breakdown structure is defined, it would be of little use in resolving an issue of scope dispute.

2. A. You don't tackle activity sequencing as part of the work breakdown structure. That task comes later. Choice 'B' is incorrect since every WBS element does have a unique identifier. Choice 'C' is incorrect since the WBS is the definitive source for all of the work to be done. Remember – if it isn't in the WBS, it isn't part of the project. Choice 'D' is incorrect because the WBS is arranged as a pyramid with the top being the most general, and the bottom being the most specific.

3. D. Management (usually senior management) issues the project charter. Answer 'A' is incorrect since the stakeholders could be almost anyone on the project – even citizens. Answer 'B' is incorrect since the project manager is formally named in the charter. The charter gives the PM formal authority – not vice versa. Choice 'C' is incorrect since the customer is not required to issue a charter whenever they want something done. The charter is the performing organization's responsibility – not the customer's.

4. C. The project manager verifies the product with the key stakeholders, the sponsor, and in many cases, the customer.

5. C. The WBS is an output of scope definition.

6. D. The project charter needs to include the project's objectives. Choice 'A' is incorrect as the complete project scope is not a part of the charter, but rather a high-level project initiation document. 'B' is wrong since the team members are not identified at this point. 'C' is incorrect, because the deliverables and milestones would be a product of schedule development.

7.   A. It is important to understand the processes and their inputs and outputs! Whereas all of these choices may be important, the only one that is listed as a part of scope verification is to get customer acceptance of the product. The other activities may be done during the project, but they aren't part of the scope verification process.

8.   C. The project charter is important for several reasons, but the only correct choice in this list is that it names the project manager. 'A' is done as part of stakeholder management. 'B' is an input into initiation and is progressively elaborated throughout the planning processes. Choice 'D' is not correct because the sponsor typically comes from senior management and pays for the project. He does not derive his authority from a project document.

9.   A. is the only one that is not part of the scope management plan. It is a made up term. 'B', 'C', and 'D' all belong.

10.   B. This one is tricky. If you missed it, don't feel bad, but it is important to know that questions like this are on the exam. The reason 'B' is correct is that the scope management plan contains the scope and specifies how changes will be handled. If too many changes are pouring in, it is likely that the scope management plan was not well defined. 'A' is incorrect because it is not the sponsor's role to control change. 'C' is incorrect because if the change control board exists on your project, it only evaluates changes. The board is reactive, not proactive. 'D' is incorrect since the change evaluation system is a made up term, not found in PMI's processes.

11.   C. It is the sponsor's job to pay for the project and to accept the product. Choice 'A' is really the project manager's job. 'B' is the project manager's job as well. It is not a clearly defined job for the sponsor. 'D' is not a function of the sponsor.

12.   B. The project manager and customer are involved in the scope verification process, and the tool used here is inspection. The product is inspected to see if it matches the documented scope. 'A', 'C', and 'D' are not documented as part of the processes.

13.   D. is the best choice here. If the project charter is not signed by management, it may be very hard for the project manager to get the necessary attention in the organization. The project charter names the project manager and gives him authority to apply resources, so a lack of a signed charter might impede this.

14.   C. Notice the use of the word 'FIRST'. 'A' is wrong because the customer should never bypass the project manager to authorize changes directly. It is the project manager's job to authorize changes on the project. 'B' is incorrect since all changes might not go to the change control board. Even if a change control board exists on the project, the project manager doesn't automatically just send everything their way. The project manager should deal with it first. 'D' is incorrect because that would not be the FIRST thing to do in this case.

15.   A. The customer accepts the scope of the product in scope verification.

16.   D. The project team is identified later in the project, not in scope initiation.

17.   C. Choices 'A' and 'B' are no-nos on the PMP exam. You don't just make changes because they "add value." Does the customer want the change? Does the change increase the project risk or put the quality in jeopardy? Between 'C' and 'D', the best answer is 'C'. The reason is that just because the project manager thinks this is a good piece of functionality doesn't mean that he should automatically add it. The customer should have input into this decision as well. Choice 'D' might be correct in limited circumstances if you knew that you were at or near the end of the project, but changes on a project rarely require the automatic initiation of a new project.

18.   C. The charter happens as a part of initiation. 'A', 'B', and 'D' occur during planning. Although the processes on a project are not performed in the order they are listed in the PMBOK, initiation does need to happen before the other processes.

19.   C. Answers 'A', 'B', and 'D' are all incorrect, since they encourage adding or keeping the additional functionality. It is important not to add extras to the project for many reasons. The final product should be true to the scope. If you missed this, reread the section on scope management and gold plating.

20.   A. The project manager needs to be proactive and influence the root causes of change. 'B' is incorrect, because all change is not bad. Some changes can be quite beneficial to the project, and it is not the project manager's role to put a reject stamp on changes whenever possible. 'C' is incorrect because although some change may introduce an unacceptable level of risk, all change certainly does not. Some changes could dramatically reduce the project risk. 'D' is incorrect, because value is never the sole criterion for evaluating change. A change may deliver high value, but also introduce too much risk or cost.

Time Management

Difficulty	Memorization	Exam Importance	Corresponding PMBOK Chapter
High	High	High	Chapter 6

From the indicators at the top of the page, you can tell that this chapter will be slightly more difficult than the previous chapter on scope management. In order to help you prepare for this topic, this book has clearly broken down the practices and outlined the techniques and formulae you need to know in order to ace the questions on the exam. By the time you are through with this chapter, you may well have a higher level of confidence here than on any other section of the test.

Spending extra time in this chapter will yield direct dividends on the exam! Make sure that you learn both the processes and the techniques so that you may approach these questions with absolute confidence.

Philosophy

Project Time Management is concerned primarily with scheduling and schedule management. PMI's philosophy here, as elsewhere, is that the project manager should be in control of the schedule, and not vice versa. The schedule is built from the ground up, based on details such as the WBS, and rigorously managed throughout the life of the project.

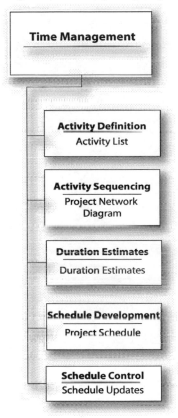

The processes of Project Time Management with their *primary* outputs

Time Management

Activity Definition
Activity List

Activity Sequencing
Project Network Diagram

Duration Estimates
Duration Estimates

Schedule Development
Project Schedule

Schedule Control
Schedule Updates

There are five processes related to time management that should be understood. They are:

1. Activity definition (list the project activities)
2. Activity sequencing (order the activities and create the project network diagram)
3. Activity duration estimating (determine time estimates for each activity)
4. Schedule development (create the schedule)
5. Schedule control (monitor schedule performance)

You will see from reading this chapter that the driving philosophy behind time management is mathematical; it is primarily cold, hard analysis. The project manager does not merely accept whatever schedule goals are handed down or suggested. Instead, he builds the schedule based on the work to be done and then seeks to make it conform to other calendar requirements, constraints, and strategic goals.

Additionally, while most of the topics within the PMBOK are related, the topics of scope, time, and cost (and to a slightly lesser degree, quality and risk) are particularly tightly linked. Changes made to one area will almost certainly have impacts elsewhere.

As in other areas, PMI prefers that project managers begin from the bottom up. The WBS, which was covered in the previous chapter, is a key input to time management processes. Using this comprehensive list of deliverables, you now define the work that must be done in order to produce these deliverables. Like the items in the WBS, the individual activities are then sequenced, and the duration estimates are applied to these activities.

This approach has many similarities to the practices in scope management. Most similar is that the list is comprehensive and complete.

Importance

Time management is of high importance, both in the application of PMI's methodology, and on the exam. There are a significant number of questions on the exam where you will need to apply formulae, calculate the critical path, and determine the effect of a change to the schedule.

The difficulties that many people encounter here fall into 3 categories:

1. Project managers are highly reliant on software to perform schedule and time calculations. While this is not a bad thing, being a PMP requires that you understand the theories and practices for time management that underlie the software.

2. Some people are intimidated by the mathematical and logical aspects of this section. Although the math is relatively simple, it does require memorization of a few key formulae.

3. Some project managers do not understand the diagramming techniques and processes. A reliance on intuition will not get you very far on these questions. You either know how to calculate them or you do not. It is far better to spend time learning the techniques than to try to fumble your way through them on the exam.

Preparation

A heavier reliance on memorization is necessary here. The memorization for time management falls into two categories:

1. There are several key terms that may be new to you, or they may have slightly different meanings than you are used to. Many of the questions on the exam will test your knowledge of specific terms and nuances, so it is important to be able to recognize and clearly understand them even if you do not memorize the definition word for word.

2. Second, there are formulae and techniques for diagramming that you will need to be able to apply on the exam. Memorization alone is not sufficient here. You must be able to calculate standard deviations, float, and critical path, among others.

Although the logic and math portions can be daunting to some people as they approach the exam, it should be pointed out that on the hard logic questions, the right answer is often much easier to determine than in the situational questions. Once you master the techniques presented in this chapter, you can work out the right answer on your own and simply match it to the list of choices. For many, these questions become favorites on the exam.

Creating the Activity List (Activity Definition)

Once the scope statement has been written and the WBS has been created, they are used to decompose the project into even greater detail. The result of this planning process (activity definition) is an activity list, a list of all the activities that need to take place for the project to be completed. The difference between work packages in a WBS and an activity list is that the activity list is more granular and is decomposed into individual activities. Work packages will often contain bundles of related activities that may involve multiple groups of people. It is these activities that comprise the activity list. The activity list is used as the basis for the next two planning processes, activity sequencing and activity duration estimating.

Network Logic Diagrams (Activity Sequencing)

There are usually several questions on the PMP that pertain directly to network logic diagrams. A network logic diagram is a picture in which each activity is drawn in the order it must be performed, and the amount of time each activity takes is represented with numbers. Activity sequencing is the planning process in which network diagrams are produced.

Network diagramming is the preferred method for representing activities, their dependencies, and sequences.

Two examples of network logic diagrams are displayed below. The first, in Figure 5-1, uses a convention known as activity on node to represent the activities. In this case, the nodes are shown as rectangles, and the activities are represented inside the node by letters of the alphabet. Duration units are shown above the nodes.

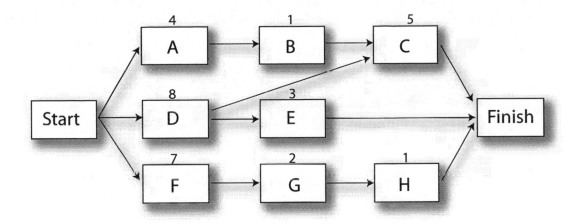

Figure 5-1: Network Diagram - Activity on Node

The second illustration of a network logic diagram in Figure 5-2 uses the activity on arrow convention. Instead of showing activities as the boxes, activities are represented on the arrows, with the duration shown above them. The nodes (circles) are junctions or points at which activities end and can be used to link them together or display sequence.

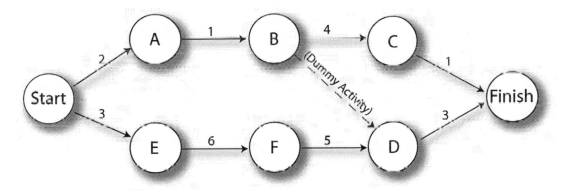

Figure 5-2: Network Diagram - Activity on Arrow

Both of these network diagramming techniques will be developed further in this chapter.

Activity Sequencing

Estimating Activities (Activity Duration Estimating)

Once the network diagram has been completed, each activity on it must be analyzed to determine how long it will take to complete. This process, another step in planning, is called activity duration estimating. In order to come up with these estimates, the project manager will need to have some idea of what resources are available to the project and what their capabilities are. Two of the tools used to create the estimates are expert judgment (the knowledge and background of the project manager and team members) and analogous estimating. Analogous estimating simply means basing the estimate on data from previously performed projects. This technique only works well if the projects were highly similar in nature. "Last time it took us two weeks to finish that activity, so we'll use 2 weeks as our estimate this time" would be an example of analogous estimating.

Quantitatively based duration and reserve time are two other methods of estimating the length of project activities. Quantitatively based durations are those in which the quantity of work to be performed (e.g., 100 miles of fiber-optic cable to be laid) is multiplied by a known unit rate (e.g., it takes 4 man-weeks to lay 1 mile of cable). Reserve time is simply a buffer built into estimates to allow for unanticipated delays.

Once activity duration estimates have been compiled and the network diagram is complete, the team has some other planning processes to complete from the other knowledge areas such as cost management and risk management. However, the next planning process that occurs within the time management knowledge area is schedule development.

Network Paths (Schedule Development)

One very important tool used in schedule development is a mathematical analysis technique called critical path method. You need to be very comfortable with this technique for the PMP exam, so a good portion of the rest of this chapter is dedicated to the subject.

The term "network path" refers to a sequence of events that affect each other on the project from start to finish. These activities would form a path through the project. Paths are important because they illustrate the different sets of sequences in which activities must be performed, and paths are used to identify areas of high risk on the project. In a real project plan, there will usually be numerous paths through the network diagram, and software is typically used to represent and calculate them.

To understand the paths, refer to the network diagram and corresponding tables below in Figure 5-3 and Tables 5-1 and 5-2.

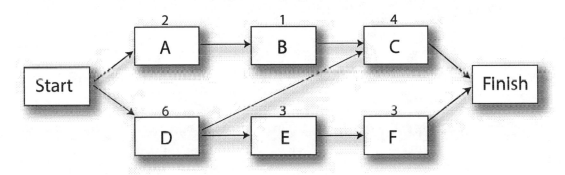

Figure 5-3: Network Logic Diagram – Activity on Node

Duration units shown in weeks

Activity	Duration (weeks)
A	2
B	1
C	4
D	6
E	3
F	3

Table 5-1: Individual activities

Path	Activities	Path Duration (weeks)
Start-A-B-C-Finish	2+1+4	7
Start-D-C-Finish	6+4	10
Start-D-E-F-Finish	6+3+3	12

Table 5-2: Network Paths

In the diagram and tables above, each node has a corresponding duration as listed in Table 5-1. Each possible path through the network is determined by following the arrows in the diagram in Figure 5-3. The arrows represent activity sequence, and in this example there are 3 paths through the system as illustrated in Table 5-2.

Critical Path (Schedule Development)

Determining the critical path through the network is a tool used heavily in creating the schedule. Critical path calculations show you where most of the schedule risk will occur.

The critical path is made up of activities that cannot be delayed without delaying the finish of the project. By following the steps taken in creating the network diagram, the critical path is determined simply by identifying the longest path through the system. In the previous example, it is Start-D-E-F-Finish, because activities D (6) + E (3) + F (3) will take 12 weeks, and this is the longest path through the system.

Keep in mind that it is not unusual to have more than one critical path on a project. This occurs when two or more paths tie for the longest path. In this event, schedule risk is increased because there is an increased number of ways the project could be delayed.

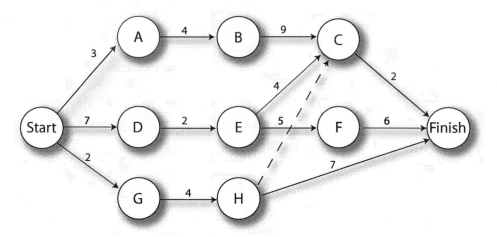

Figure 5-4: Network Logic Diagram - Activity on Arrow

Duration units shown in weeks

Consider the example in Figure 5-4. Because this is an activity on arrow network logic diagram, we calculate the activities and path slightly differently as illustrated in the following tables.

Activity	Duration (weeks)
Start-A	3
Start-D	7
Start-G	2
A-B	4
B-C	9
C-Finish	2
D-E	2
E-C	4
E-F	5
F-Finish	6
G-H	4
H-C	0
H-Finish	7

Table 5-3: Activity Durations

Path	Activities	Path Duration (weeks)
Start-A-B-C-Finish	3+4+9+2	18
Start D-E-C-Finish	7+2+4+2	15
Start-D-E-F-Finish	7+2+5+6	20
Start-G-H-C-Finish	2+4+0+2	8
Start-G-H-Finish	2+4+7	13

Table 5-4: Network paths

There are two key things to note about the previous example using activity on arrow.

1. The nodes in Table 5-3 are not listed individually, but in pairs. This is activity on arrow, so each arrow (activity) connects two nodes.

2. There is a "dummy activity," as indicated by the dotted line between nodes H and C. A dummy is technically not an activity, but is a way of representing a dependency between nodes; however, for the exam, it is easiest to think of a dummy activity as exactly the same as a normal activity, but with a duration of 0.

Float (Schedule Development)

After you have mastered the concepts for activity on node and activity on arrow, calculating float (sometimes referred to as "slack") is also easy. Before attempting any exercises, it is critical to understand the following:

1. Float is simply how much time an activity can slip before its path changes the critical path. Another way of thinking about float is that it is the maximum amount of time an activity can slip without pushing out the finish date of the project.

2. If an item is on the critical path, it has zero float. Although there are technical cases where this might not be true, you should not encounter any such examples on the exam.

Keeping the preceding two items in mind, let us revisit the activity on node network diagram in figure 5-3. Using this example:

Question: What is the float for activity D?

Answer: 0 weeks. Activity D cannot slip without affecting the finish date because it is on the critical path.

Question: What is the slack for activity C?

Answer: 2 weeks. If activity C slips by more than 2 weeks, then the path Start-D-C-Finish would delay the finish of the project.

There is a simple way to do this that will allow you to breeze through the questions on the PMP exam. The method is a brute force approach. If the exam asks you to calculate the slack for an activity, simply look at the project network diagram and find the duration you can substitute for that activity that will put it on the critical path. You should be able to zero in on the float right away. If you have created a path chart, such as the one in Table 5-5, this method is a snap.

Path	Activities	Path Duration (weeks)
Start-A-B-C-Finish	2+1+4	7
Start-D-C-Finish	6+4	10
Start-D-E-F-Finish	6+3+3	12

Table 5-5 – (corresponds to Figure 5-3)

In this example:

- Activity A has float of 5 weeks, because this activity may be delayed up to 5 weeks without delaying the finish of the project
- Activity B also has float of 5 weeks, because paths with activity B could slip up to 5 weeks without changing the project's finish date.
- Activity C is slightly trickier. It has a float of only 2 weeks. Even though it could slip 5 weeks in the first path listed in Table 5-5, if it slipped from 4 weeks to 6 weeks, then path Start-D-C-Finish would be on the critical path. Therefore, we take the smallest slippage possible and that becomes the float for this activity.

After a little practice, this will become the easiest and quickest way to calculate float. There are detailed exercises at the end of this chapter to help cement your understanding of this.

Note that on the exam you may see the terms *forward pass* or *backward pass* related to the critical path. These methods of determining early or late start or early or late finish are presented below.

Early Start

The early start date for an activity is simply the earliest date it can start when you factor in the other dependencies. This is the date the activity will start if everything takes as long as it was estimated. Consider the figure that follows (this diagram is the same as Figure 5-3, referenced earlier).

Question: Given the following diagram, what is the early start for activity B?

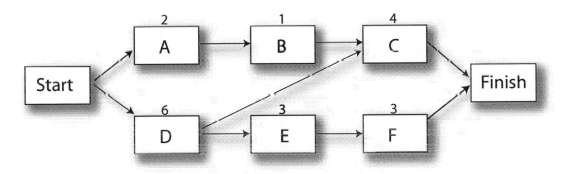

Units shown in weeks

The answer is week 3. The reason is that Activity A is scheduled to take 2 weeks. It begins on week 1, and finishes on week 2. Activity B could then begin on the first day of week 3.

This technique is called a "forward pass" because we have moved "forward" through the diagram, starting from the start date to perform our calculations.

Early Finish

The early finish date is the early start date plus the duration estimate minus 1 unit. In the example above, the early finish date for activity 'A' would be 2 weeks after the early start date. Since the early start date is week 1, the early finish would be week 2. This makes sense since the activity takes all of week 1 and all of week 2, finishing at the end of week 2.

Here we also performed a "forward pass," as again we based our calculations on the start date.

Late Start

The late start date for activity turns the problem around and looks at it from the other end of the network diagram. It asks, "What is the *latest* this activity could start and not delay the project's finish date?" Although there are many methods that may be used to calculate late start, the easiest way is to simply add the float to the early start. This will give us the absolute latest date that the activity can start and not impact the finish date, assuming that the activity takes as long as was estimated.

Given the example in the table above, what is the late start for activity 'B'?

Answer: Week 8. The reason is that this activity has 5 weeks of float, and if the early start is week 3, the late start would be week 3 + 5 weeks of float = week 8.

Remember that for activities with zero float or slack, the late start and the early start will be the same.

This technique is called a "backward pass". The reason is that you must begin at the end and work your way backward, evaluating how close activities may slide toward the finish without moving the finish.

Late Finish

An activity's late finish will be the late start plus the activity's duration estimate minus 1 unit.

In the example above, the late start week 8, and the duration is 1 week, so the late finish date would also be week 8. If the fact that both the start and finish are shown as week 8 confuses you, keep in mind that the start represents is the first day of week 8, and the finish represents the last day of week 8.

Remember that for activities with zero float or slack, the late finish and the early finish will be the same.

Calculating the late finish date by adding the activity's duration to the late start date is another example of a "backward pass".

Other Schedule Development Tools

PERT stands for Program Evaluation and Review Technique. It is a schedule development tool that is covered on the exam and you should memorize its formulae. In this method of estimating, 3 duration estimates are assigned for every activity. PERT is considered to be more accurate than CPM because it uses more estimates. The three duration estimates are:

- Pessimistic duration
- Optimistic duration
- Realistic duration

To get the PERT estimates, we apply the following formula:

$$\frac{\text{Pessimistic} + 4\text{X Realistic} + \text{Optimistic}}{6}$$

As you can see from the formula above, the PERT estimate factors in the best case, worst case, and most likely estimates to come up with a PERT estimate. This estimating process forces you to ask "What is the worst case?" and "What is the best possible scenario?" for planning purposes.

To demonstrate this formula, consider an activity that has a pessimistic estimate of 27 days, a realistic estimate of 10 days, and an optimistic estimate of 5 days. The application of the PERT estimate formula is as follows:

$$\frac{27 + (4 \text{ X } 10) + 5}{6}$$

Schedule Development

This reduces down to $72 \div 6 = 12$. The PERT estimate for this activity is 12 days. PERT estimates automatically factor in risk as well.

Another important formula to memorize for the exam is used to calculate the standard deviation for an estimate.

$$\sigma = \frac{Pessimistic - Optimistic}{6}$$

The value for standard deviation tells us how diverse our estimates are. If an activity has a pessimistic and optimistic estimate that are very far apart, the standard deviation (σ) will be very high, indicating a high degree of uncertainty and consequently a high degree of risk for this estimate.

Given these formulae, let us consider the following estimates for activities A, B, and C.

Activity	Optimistic	Pessimistic	Realistic
A	22	35	25
B	60	77	70
C	12	40	20

Table 5-6

Now, using the formulae above, we will calculate the PERT Estimate and Standard Deviation for each of these activities.

Activity	Optimistic	Pessimistic	Realistic	PERT Estimate	σ (Standard deviation)
A	22	35	25	26.17	2.17
B	60	77	70	69.5	2.83
C	12	40	20	22	4.67

Table 5-7

Monte Carlo Analysis

Monte Carlo Analysis is another schedule development tool used to predict likely schedule outcomes for a project and identify the areas of the schedule that are the highest risk.

This analysis is performed by computer and evaluates probability by considering a huge number of simulated scheduling possibilities. It is especially helpful for analyzing convergent paths, as illustrated in Figure 5-5. Where paths converge (common on most project plans), schedule risk increases. A computer employing Monte Carlo Analysis can perform what-if analysis and identify the highest risk activities that may not otherwise be apparent.

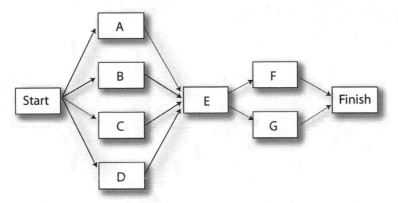

Figure 5-5: Convergent paths

Duration Compression (Schedule Development)

Two additional tools of schedule development that you will probably encounter on the exam involve shortening the schedule. They are crashing and fast tracking. Crashing involves adding resources to a project activity so that it will be completed more quickly. Crashing almost always increases costs. Fast tracking means that you re-order the sequence of activities so that some of the activities are performed in parallel, or at the same time. Fast tracking does not necessarily increase costs, but it almost always increases risk to the project since discretionary dependencies are being ignored and additional activities are happening simultaneously (more on discretionary dependencies shortly).

Original Estimate

Activity	Resources	Estimated days
200 yards of pipeline construction	1	12

"Crashed" Estimate

Activity	Resources	Estimated days
200 yards of pipeline construction	4	4

An example of crashing the schedule by adding more resources to an activity

Note that in the example above, as is often the case, increasing the number of resources does decrease the time but not by a linear amount. This is because activities will often encounter the law of diminishing returns when adding resources to an activity. The old saying "Too many cooks spoil the broth" applies to projects as well as cooking.

Schedule Development

Original Estimate

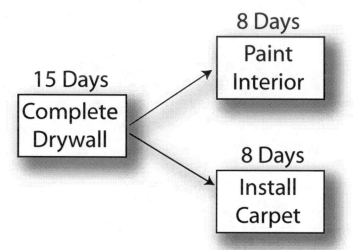

Original duration of 31 days

Fast Tracked Estimate

Fast tracked duration of 23 days

Note that fast tracking often results in some individual activities taking longer, and it increases the risk. In the example above, the workers may have a harder time moving around each other, thus increasing the time to paint and install carpet. Also, there is an increased risk associated with these activities. For example, the painters could damage the carpet, or the carpet installers could be hampered by the fresh paint.

Resource Leveling (Schedule Development)

Resource leveling is a tool used to even out the use of resources. Suppose your schedule calls for many resources for a few weeks and then just a few resources for the remaining weeks. This situation may not work well at all for the performing organization. Resource leveling involves modifying the schedule so that the use of resources is more consistent throughout the project.

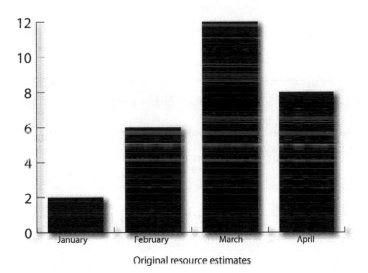

Original resource estimates

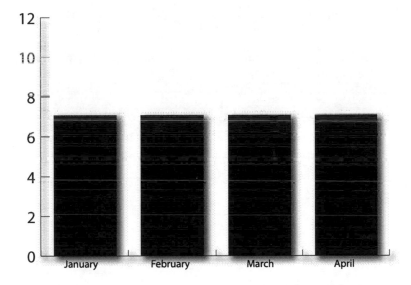

Leveled resource estimates, averaging out the resource usage

The Schedule (Schedule Development)

The most significant output of the schedule development process is the project's schedule. At a minimum, the schedule should contain every activity, the duration of each activity, and the planned start and finish dates for each activity.

The schedule is typically represented graphically, and there are different forms it may take. The most common forms are covered below:

Project Network Diagram

The project network diagram is a useful detail-driven tool that provides a powerful view of the dependencies and sequences of each activity. It is the best representation for calculating the critical path and showing dependencies on the project.

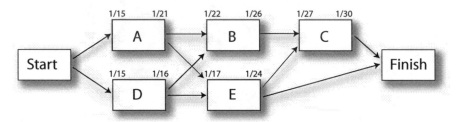

Gantt Charts (also called Bar Charts)

Gantt charts show activities represented as horizontal bars and typically have a calendar along the horizontal axis. The length of the bar corresponds to the length of the activity.

A bar chart, or Gantt chart, can be easily modified to show percentage complete (usually by shading all or part of the horizontal bar). It is considered to be a good tool to use to communicate with management, because unlike the project network diagram, it is easy to understand at a glance.

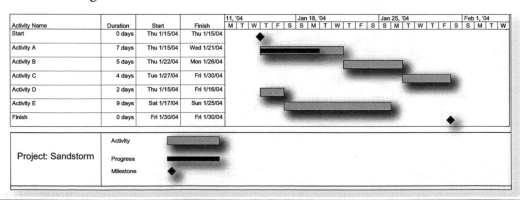

Schedule Development

Milestone Chart

A milestone chart, as the name implies, only represents key events (milestones) for the project. Milestones may be significant deliverables by you or external parties on the project.

Milestone charts, because of the general level of information they provide, should be reserved for brief, high level project presentations where a lot of schedule detail would be undesirable or even distracting.

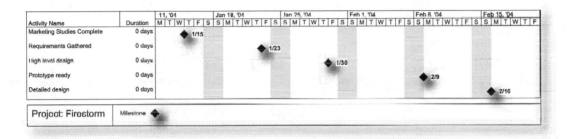

Schedule Control

As its name implies, schedule control is a controlling process. The idea behind controlling processes in general is to compare the work results to the plan and ensure that they line up. In this process, the schedule is controlled to make sure that time-related performance on the project is in line with the plan.

One of the more important concepts to master with schedule control (and most controlling processes in general) is that schedule changes are not only reacted to, but the schedule is controlled proactively. That is, the project manager should be out in front of the project, influencing changes before they affect the project. Of course, at times, changes to the schedule may occur, and the project manager will have to react to them, but the project manager should be proactive whenever possible.

Schedule Control Inputs

Schedule

The schedule provides the key input. As discussed previously, this process compares the plan to the results, and the schedule represents the planned activities over time.

Schedule Control

Performance Reports

The performance reports are a key part of schedule control. Performance reports are used as an input, and they provide the project manager with key information on how the project is actually progressing against the schedule. The project manager may then take appropriate action to ensure that the project results line up with the plan.

Change Requests

As change requests are made to the project, either changes to the schedule itself or changes that would affect the schedule, they become inputs to the controlling process to be evaluated.

Schedule Management Plan

The schedule management plan defines how the schedule will be managed and how changes to the schedule will be handled. It is where the schedule change control system is defined.

Schedule Control Tools and Techniques

Schedule Change Control System

The schedule change control system is the system that the project manager uses to receive, evaluate, and process schedule changes. It may involve forms, people, technologies, committees, or other means that provide structure for the project manager to handle changes to the schedule.

Variance Analysis

Variance analysis is of particular importance as a tool of the schedule control process. It is used to measure the difference between planned dates and actual dates, and may be used to forecast or provide information on where the plan and actual dates do not match.

Schedule Control Outputs

Schedule Updates

Updates to the schedule are a natural output of schedule control. Since it is always desirable for the actual dates to line up with the planned dates, change will often be made to the schedule in order to adjust it to reflect reality.

Corrective Action

One of the topics reinforced throughout this book is that corrective action is not about fixing past mistakes. It is all about making sure that the future results match the plan. This may be done by trying to influence the future results, or it could mean updating the plan, but the goal is for the plan and the results to line up.

Lessons Learned

Lessons learned, as they related to the schedule, should focus on documenting the variances between what was planned and what occurred. Specific attention should be paid to what would be done differently next time in order to prevent the variances.

Summary of Key Terms

You must understand each of the following key terms. You do not have to memorize every term word for word, but you should be able to recall the general definition and apply them on the exam.

Activity on Arrow Diagram - A type of network diagram where the activities are represented by the arrows. The nodes (usually circles) are used to connect or show dependencies. Activity on arrow diagrams are always shown "finish to start," where one activity is finished before the next one begins. This is the diagramming method that uses dummy activities (usually represented by dashed lines).

Activity Decomposition – Activity decomposition is similar to scope decomposition (remember the asteroids metaphor), except that the final result here is an activity list instead of the WBS.

Activity List – A list of every activity that will be performed on the project.

Activity Duration Estimates – Probable number of periods (weeks, hours, days, months, etc) this activity should take with the probable range of results. Example:

Activity Duration Estimate	Explanation
1 week +/- 3 days	The activity should take between 2 and 8 days, assuming a 5 day work week
1 month + 20% probability it will be accomplished later	There is an 80% likelihood that the activity will be completed within a month and a 20% chance that it will exceed a month.

Analogous Estimating – A form of expert judgment often used early on when there is little information available. Example: "This project is similar to one we did last year, and it took three months." It is performed from the top down, focusing on the big picture.

Backward Pass – The method for calculating late start and late finish dates for an activity (see explanation of float, early and late starts and finishes earlier in this chapter for a detailed explanation).

Critical Path – The paths through the network diagram that show which activities, if delayed, will affect the project finish date. For schedule, the critical path represents the highest risk path in the project.

Dependencies – Activities that must be completed before other activities are either started or completed.

Dependencies	Description	Example
Mandatory	Also called "hard logic," these activities must be followed in sequence.	Clearing the lot on a construction site before pouring the foundation.
Discretionary	Also called "soft logic." Expert judgment and best practices often dictate that particular activities are performed in a particular order. The dependencies are discretionary because they are based on expert opinion rather than mandatory or hard logic.	Painting the interior before putting down carpet.
External	Dependencies relying on factors outside of the project.	Zoning approval for a new building. Weather for a rocket launch.

Dummy Activity – An activity on a network diagram that does not have any time associated with it. It is only included to show a relationship, and is usually represented as a dotted or dashed line. Dummy activities only exist in activity on arrow diagrams.

Duration compression - Note that this topic is also discussed and illustrated earlier in this chapter.

Technique	Description	Example
Crashing	Applying more resources to reduce duration. Crashing the schedule usually increases cost.	If setting up a computer network takes one person 6 weeks, three resources may be able to do it in two weeks. Note – Crashing usually does not reduce the schedule by a linear amount.
Fast tracking	Performing activities in parallel that would normally be done in sequence. Fast tracking activities usually increases project risk, and these activities have a higher probability of rework.	Example: In XYX Corp, no coding on software modules is allowed until after the database design is complete, but when fast tracking, the activities could be done in parallel if it is not a mandatory dependency.

Delphi Technique - A means of gathering expert judgment where the participants do not know who the others are and therefore are not able to influence each other's opinion. The Delphi technique is designed to prevent groupthink and to find out a participant's real opinion.

Expert Judgment – A method of estimating in which experts are asked to provide input into the schedule. Combining expert judgment with other tools and methods can significantly improve the accuracy of time estimates and reduce risk.

Float – How much time an activity can be delayed without affecting the project's finish date. Also known as "slack."

Forward Pass – The method for calculating early start and early finish dates for an activity (see explanation of float and early and late starts and finishes earlier in this chapter).

Free float – Also known as "free slack." How much time an activity can be delayed without affecting the early start date of subsequent dependent activities. For example, consider the diagram below:

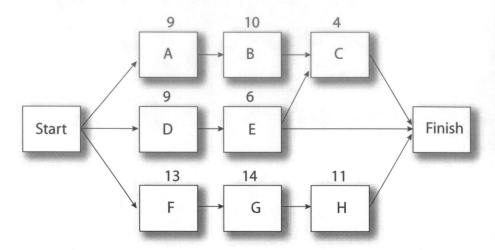

The free float of activity E would be determined by calculating how long it could slip before it impacted the early start of activity C. In this example, activity E has 4 units of free float. Note that this is different from its float, which is 19 units.

GERT – Graphical Evaluation and Review Technique. A diagramming method to show iterations and conditional branches.

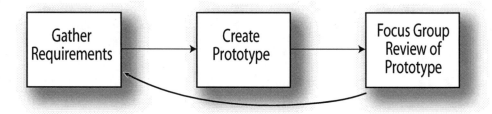

Heuristics – Rules for which no formula exists. Usually derived through trial and error.

Lag – The delay between the activity and the next one dependent upon it. For example, if you are pouring concrete, you may have a 3 day lag after you have poured the concrete before your subsequent activities of building upon it can begin.

Lead – Activities with finish to start relationships cannot start until their predecessors have been finished; however, if you have 5 days of lead time on an activity, it may begin 5 days before its predecessor activity has finished. Think of it as getting a head start, like runners in a relay race. Lead time lets the subsequent task begin before its predecessor has finished.

Mathematical analysis – A technique to show scheduling possibilities where early and late start and finish dates are calculated for every activity without looking at resource estimates.

Milestones – High level points in the schedule used to track and report progress. Milestones usually have no time associated with them.

Monte Carlo Analysis – Computer simulation that throws a high number of "what if" scenarios at the project schedule to determine probable results.

Network diagram – (also called network logic diagram or project network diagram). A method of diagramming project activities to show sequence and dependencies.

Negative Float – Negative float is a situation that occurs when an activity's start date occurs before a preceding activity's finish date. For instance, suppose that there is a constraint for an activity (Activity D) that involves a 1 day final inspection of a building that is to begin and be completed on July 15th; however, a preceding activity (Activity C) that encompasses testing the electrical components of the project does not finish until July 25th. If work is schedule 7 days per week, then it could be stated that Activity D has a negative float of 10 days.

Technically, negative float exists when an activity's finish date happens before its start date. In the example above, Activity D is supposed to finish at the end of the 15th; however, it cannot even begin until 10 days later. There Activity D has 10 days of negative float.

Negative float for an activity tells you that your schedule has problems. It most often occurs when immovable constraints or milestones are imposed by forces outside the project, causing an impossible situation. Negative float may be resolved by several methods, such as reworking the logic of the schedule, crashing, or fast-tracking.

Precedence Diagramming Method – (also called Activity on Node). A type of network diagram where the boxes are activities, and the arrows are used to show dependencies between the activities.

Reserve Time (Contingency) – A schedule buffer used to reduce schedule risk. The chart below represents the most common types of reserve for a project.

Contingency	Example
Project %	Add 15% to the entire project schedule
Project lump sum	Add 2 months calendar schedule to the project
Activity %	Add 10% to each activity (or to key, high-risk activities)
Activity lump sum	Add 1 week to each activity (or to key, high risk activities)

Schedule Baseline – The approved schedule that is used as a basis for measuring and reporting. It includes the originally approved project schedule plus approved updates.

Slack – See "Float."

Variance Analysis – Comparing planned versus actual schedule dates.

Key Terms

Exercises

In order to test yourself on time management, complete the following questions based on Figure 5-5 below.

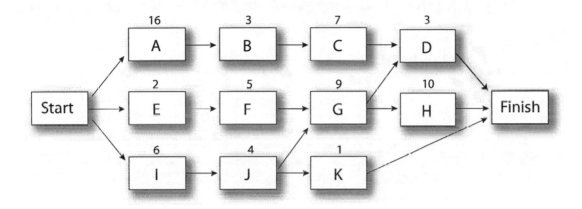

Figure 5-5: Project network diagram.
Durations shown in days

1. List all the paths through the network logic diagram as illustrated in Figure 5-5.

2. What is the critical path through the network diagram shown in Figure 5-5?

3. List the slack for each activity in the network.

4. Provided the table below, how many weeks long is the critical path?

Activity	Preceding Activity	Duration (in weeks)
Start		0
A	Start	6
B	A, E	2
C	B	2
D	C	3
E	Start	1
F	A, E	1
G	F, B	7
Finish	D, G	0

5. Given the table in question 4 above, describe the effect of activity D taking twice as long as planned.

6. An activity has 3 estimates, provided below:

   Optimistic   =   10 days
   Pessimistic   =   25 days
   Realistic   =   15 days

   What is the PERT estimate for this activity?

7. What is the standard deviation for the PERT activity in question 6?

Answers to Exercises

1. There are 6 possible paths through the system, listed in the table below:

Path
Start-A-B-C-D-Finish
Start-E-F-G-D-Finish
Start-E-F-G-H-Finish
Start-I-J-G-D-Finish
Start-I-J-G-H-Finish
Start-I-J-K-Finish

2. Because two paths tie for the longest duration, there are two critical paths:

*   Start-A-B-C-D-Finish – duration 29 days
*   Start-I-J-G-H-Finish – duration 29 days

Path	Durations	Total
Start-A-B-C-D-Finish	16+3+7+3	29 days
Start-E-F-G-D-Finish	2+5+9+3	19 days
Start-E-F-G-H-Finish	2+5+9+10	26 days
Start-I-J-G-D-Finish	6+4+9+3	22 days
Start-I-J-G-H-Finish	6+4+9+10	29 days
Start-I-J-K-Finish	6+4+1	11 days

3. This task is easier than it first appears since over 70% of the activities were on the critical path. Those activities automatically have zero slack; thus, no calculations are necessary for most of activities.

    The way to solve for these is to take each path listed above and go through them one at a time. If the path is a critical path, or if the activity is found on the critical path, simply skip it. If the path is not the critical path, then take the sum of the items on that path and subtract it from the total critical path. For activity E, it is found on 2 paths above. One of them totals 19, and the other 26. We always use the larger one and subtract it from the critical path total of 29. That leaves a slack of 29-26, or 3 for activity E.

Activity	On Critical Path?	Slack (Float) in days
A	Y	0
B	Y	0
C	Y	0
D	Y	0
E	N	3
F	N	3
G	Y	0
H	Y	0
I	Y	0
J	Y	0
K	N	18

4. Your first step in solving this problem is to draw out a network logic diagram. Your diagram should look similar to the one shown below:

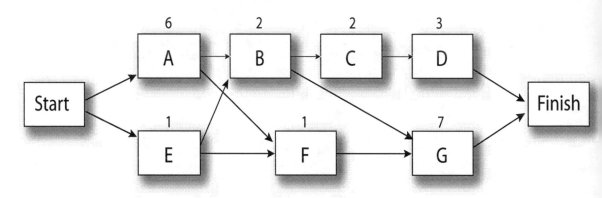

The next step is to list out all paths through the network:

Path	Durations	Total
Start-A-B-C-D-Finish	6+2+2+3	13
Start-A-B-G-Finish	6+2+7	15
Start-A-F-G-Finish	6+1+7	14
Start-E-B-C-D-Finish	1+2+2+3	8
Start-E-B-G-Finish	1+2+7	10
Start-E-F-G-Finish	1+1+7	9

The answer is 15 weeks, based on the fact that Start-A-B-G-Finish has a duration of 15 weeks, and that is the longest duration of any path.

5. If activity D were to take twice as long as planned, that would change its duration from 3 to 6 weeks. This would have two effects:

- The critical path would change. The new critical path would be Start-A-B-C-D-Finish.
- The project finish date would be extended by 1 additional week, meaning the overall project would take 16 weeks.

To arrive at this solution, reconstruct the table as follows:

Path	Durations	Total
Start-A-B-C-D-Finish	6+2+2+6	16
Start-A-B-G-Finish	6+2+7	15
Start-A-F-G-Finish	6+1+7	14
Start-E-B-C-D-Finish	1+2+2+6	11
Start-E-B-G-Finish	1+2+7	10
Start-E-F-G-Finish	1+1+7	9

Note how the longest path has changed to the first one in the table above.

6. The formula for PERT estimates is:

$$\frac{\text{Pessimistic} + \text{Optimistic} + 4 * \text{Realistic}}{6}$$

or...

$$\frac{25 + 10 + 4 * 15}{6}$$

This yields a PERT duration estimate of 15.83.

7. The formula for standard deviation is:
$$\frac{\text{Pessimistic - Optimistic}}{6}$$

or...

$$\frac{25\text{-}10}{6}$$

This yields a standard deviation of 2.5.

Time Exercises

Going Deeper

For further study in the area of Time Management, the following books and resources are suggested:

Kerzner, Harold. *Project Management: A Systems Approach to Planning, Scheduling, and Controlling.* New York: John Wiley & Sons, 2000.

Kliem, Ralph L.; Ludin, Irwin S. *Project Management Practitioner's Handbook.* New York: AMACOM Books, 1998.

Lewis, James P. *Project Planning, Scheduling & Control: A Hands-on Guide to Bringing Projects in On Time and On Budget.* Chicago, Il: McGraw-Hill Professional, 1995.

Lewis, James P. *The Project Manager's Desk Reference: A Comprehensive Guide to Project Planning, Scheduling, Evaluation, and Systems.* New York: McGraw-Hill Professional, 2000.

Williams, Paul B. *Getting a Project Done On Time : Managing People, Time, and Results.* New York: AMACOM Books, 1996.

Going Deeper

Time Management Questions

1. You are the project manager for the construction of a commercial office building that has very similar characteristics to a construction project performed by your company two years ago. As you enter activity definition, what is the BEST approach?

    A. Use the activity list from the previous project as your activity list.
    B. Generate your activities list without looking at the previous project's list and compare when your project's list is complete.
    C. Use the gap analysis technique to identify any differences between your project and the previous project.
    D. Use the previous activity list as a tool to help construct your list.

2. The customer has called a project team member to request a change in the project's schedule. The team member asks you what the procedure is for handling schedule changes. Where should you refer the team member to help him understand the procedure?

    A. The project office.
    B. The change control board.
    C. The schedule management plan.
    D. Inform the team member that the customer is always right.

3. Estimates should ideally be created:

    A. Always by more than one person.
    B. Always by only one person.
    C. From the bottom up.
    D. From the top down.

4. Senior management has called you in for a review to review the progress of your project. You have been allocated 15 minutes to report progress and discuss critical issues. Which of the following would be BEST to carry with you in this case?

    A. Milestone chart.
    B. The project network diagram.
    C. An expert from each functional area of the project so that all questions may be answered.
    D. Project status reports from your team members.

5. How does activity on node differ from activity on arrow?

    A. Activity on arrow is superior to activity on node.
    B. Activity on node is superior to activity on arrow.
    C. Activity on arrow may have dummy activities.
    D. Activity on node may have dummy activities.

6. The amount of time that an activity may be delayed without extending the critical path is:

    A. Lag.
    B. Grace period.
    C. Free factor.
    D. Slack.

7. Crashing differs from fast tracking because crashing:

    A. Usually increases value.
    B. Usually increases the cost.
    C. Usually saves more time.
    D. Usually saves more money.

8.   If senior management tells you "The last project we did like this cost us almost five million dollars," what estimating method is being used?

A. Delphi technique
B. Principle of equivalency of activities
C. Analogous estimating
D. Bottom-up estimating

9.   You are advising a project manager who is behind schedule on his project. The sponsor on the project is very unhappy with the way things have progressed and is threatening to cancel the project. The sponsor has accepted a revised due date from the project manager but did not allow any increased spending. Which of the following would represent the BEST advice for the project manager in this case?

A. Fast track the schedule.
B. Ask senior management for a new sponsor within the organization.
C. Crash the schedule.
D. Talk with the customer to see if budget may be increased without the sponsor's involvement.

10.   The project is nearly two months ahead of schedule, and things are going very well. Then a team member approaches the project manager with a problem. His deliverable on the project is running behind, and he needs an extra two weeks to complete his work. The project manager checks his project plan and finds that he has adequate reserves to do this without jeopardizing the project. Who should approve this request?

A. The customer.
B. The sponsor.
C. The project manager.
D. The project team.

11. What is the BEST tool to use to calculate the critical path on a project?

    A. Work breakdown structure.
    B. GERT diagram.
    C. Gantt chart.
    D. Project network diagram.

12. Consider the table at right:

    What is the critical path?

    A. Start-A-E-H-Finish.
    B. Start-C-E-H-Finish.
    C. Start-B-D-I-Finish.
    D. Start-B-D-G-Finish.

Activity	Duration	Dependent on
Start	0	
A	3	Start
B	4	Start
C	2	Start
D	2	B
E	5	A,C
F	1	B
G	6	D,F
H	11	E
I	8	D,F
Finish	0	G,H,I

13. Using the project network diagram you created for question 12, what is the float for activity D?

    A. 0
    B. 3
    C. 5
    D. 7

14. An activity has a duration estimate that is best case = 30 days, most likely = 44 days, and worst case = 62 days. What is the PERT estimate for this activity?

    A. 44.67 days
    B. 34.67 days
    C. 5.33 days
    D. 59.33 days

15. An activity has a duration estimate that is best case = 15 days, most likely = 20 days, and worst case = 25 days. What is the standard deviation for this estimate?

A. 3.33 days.
B. 20 days.
C. 0.83 days.
D. 1.67 days.

16. The purpose of a Graphical Evaluative Review Technique (GERT) chart is to:

A. Display resource usage in a graphical format.
B. Display schedule constraints in a graphical format.
C. Display cost as it relates to schedule in a graphical format.
D. Display schedule conditions and decisions in a graphical format.

17. Which of the following is the BEST description of the critical path?

A. The activities that represent critical functionality.
B. The activities that represent the largest portions of the work packages.
C. The activities that represent the highest schedule risk on the project.
D. The activities that represent the optimal path through the network.

18. Consider the table at right:

What is the length of the critical path?

A. 43
B. 45
C. 53
D. 54

Activity	Duration
Start-A	6
Start-E	11
A-B	7
B-C	8
C-D	14
D-Finish	8
E-F	21
F-C	0
F-H	6
E-G	8
G-H	7
H-D	7

19.   Consider the table in question 18. What is the slack for Activity H-D?

   A. 0
   B. 1
   C. 5
   D. 13

20.   Your project schedule has just been developed, approved, and
       distributed to the stakeholders and presented to senior management
       when one of the resources assigned to an activity approaches you and
       tells you that her activity cannot be performed within the allotted
       time due to several necessary pieces that were left out of planning. Her
       revised estimate would change the schedule but would not affect the
       critical path. What would be the BEST way for the project manager to
       handle this situation?

   A. Stick with the published schedule and allow for any deviation by
      using schedule reserve.
   B. Go back to activity duration estimating and update the schedule and
      other plans to reflect the new estimate.
   C. Hire an independent consultant to validate her claim.
   D. Replace the resource with someone who can meet the published
      schedule.

Answers to Time Management Questions

1.   D. The previous activity list would make an excellent tool to help you ensure that you are considering all activities. 'A' is incorrect because you cannot simply substitute something as intricate as a complete activity list. 'B' is incorrect because the other activity list would provide a good starting point and should be considered before you create your activity list. 'C' (gap analysis) is a tool that is used in the real world that is not defined by PMI, nor is it used in activity list definition.

2.   C. The schedule management plan, which becomes part of the project plan, would be the best source of information on how changes to the schedule are to be handled. 'A' is incorrect because the project office's job is to define standards – not to make decisions on tactical items such as this. 'B' is incorrect because the change control board may or may not even exist, and if it does exist, it usually approves or rejects scope changes. Answer 'D' would be the worst choice. The customer is not always right when it comes to requesting changes. Procedures should be defined and followed in order to improve the project's chances of success.

3.   C. Estimates should preferably be done from the bottom up, based on the details. 'A' is incorrect because you will not always have more than one person who is able to estimate an activity accurately. 'B' is incorrect because some estimates may require a team of experts. 'D' is incorrect because top-down (analogous) estimates are not generally as accurate as bottom-up estimates.

4.   A. Milestones show the high level status, which would be appropriate given the audience and time allocated for this update.

5.   C. Activity on arrow project network diagrams may have dummy activities, while activity on node diagrams cannot show dummy activities.

6.   D. The slack (or float) is the amount of time an activity may be delayed without affecting the critical path.

7.   B. Crashing adds more resources to an activity. This usually increases the cost due to the law of diminishing returns which predicts that 10 people usually cannot complete an activity in half the time that 5 people can. The savings from crashing are rarely linear. 'A' is incorrect because crashing does not directly affect the project's value. 'C' is incorrect because crashing may or may not save more time than fast tracking – depending on the situation. 'D' is incorrect because crashing usually costs more money than fast tracking.

8.	C. In this example management is providing you with analogous estimates.

9.	A. In this case, you must compress the schedule without increasing the costs. Fast tracking does not directly add cost to the project and is the best choice in this case. 'B' is incorrect. The sponsor is paying for the project. Do this, and your sponsor will probably be asking for a new project manager instead! 'C' is incorrect because crashing usually adds cost to the project, and that is not allowed in this scenario. 'D' is incorrect because the sponsor authorizes budget. Doing an end-run around the sponsor and going to the customer would be very inappropriate.

10.	C. This is what project managers do! They make decisions on the project. In this case, there is absolutely no reason for the project manager to escalate or defer this decision. It is clearly the responsibility of the project manager.

11.	D. The project network diagram shows duration and dependencies which would help you calculate the critical path. 'A' is incorrect because the WBS does not show durations or activity dependencies. 'B' is incorrect because GERT is most helpful for showing conditions and branches. 'C' is incorrect because a Gantt chart is very useful for showing percentage complete on activities but is not the best tool for showing activity dependencies or calculating the critical path.

12.	A. The critical path is determined in 3 steps. The first step is to draw out the project network diagram. Yours should look similar to the one depicted below (Note that activities B and C were moved to make the diagram neater – don't worry if your diagram does not look this neat):

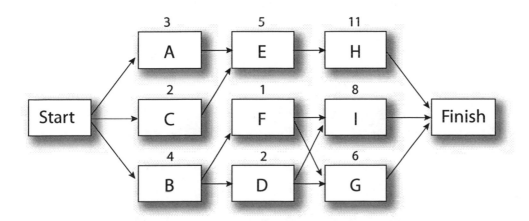

The next step is to list out all of the paths through the network. The six paths are:

Start-A-E-H-Finish

Start-C-E-H-Finish

Start-B-F-I-Finish

Start-B-F-G-Finish

Start-B-D-I-Finish

Start-B-D-G-Finish

The last step is to add up all of the values associated with each path as is done below:

Start-A-E-H-Finish = 0+3+5+11+0 = 19

Start-C-E-H-Finish = 0+2+5+11+0 = 18

Start-B-F-I-Finish = 0+4+1+8+0 = 13

Start-B-F-G-Finish = 0+4+1+6+0 = 11

Start-B-D-I-Finish = 0+4+2+8+0 = 14

Start-B-D-G-Finish = 0+4+2+6+0 = 12

The critical path emerges as Start-A-E-H-Finish because the path adds up to 19, which is longer than any of the other paths. If any of the activities in this path are delayed, the finish of the project will be delayed.

13. C. The float (or slack) of an activity is the amount of time it can slip without moving the critical path. In this case, we must calculate the float of activity 'D'. If activity 'D' was on the critical path, we would immediately know that the float was 0, but in this case it is not.

To solve this problem, we must first list out all of the paths. We will use the list from the previous question.

Start-A-E-H-Finish = 0+3+5+11+0 = 19

Start-C-E-H-Finish = 0+2+5+11+0 = 18

Start-B-F-I-Finish = 0+4+1+8+0 = 13

Start-B-F-G-Finish = 0+4+1+6+0 = 11

Start-B-D-I-Finish = 0+4+2+8+0 = 14

Start-B-D-G-Finish = 0+4+2+6+0 = 12

The next step is to identify the ones that have activity 'D' in them. They are:

Start-B-D-I-Finish = 0+4+2+8+0 = 14

Start-B-D-G-Finish = 0+4+2+6+0 = 12

Now the task is simple. We simply subtract the path sums from the length of the critical path for each (19-14 = 5, and 19-12 = 7), and finally we take the smaller of those two values which is 5. Therefore, the float for activity D is 5.

14.   A. The formula for a PERT estimate is (Pessimistic + Optimistic + 4x Realistic) ÷ 6. In this example, the terms were switched around slightly, but it equates to (62 + 30 + 4x44) ÷ 6 = 268 ÷ 6 = 44.67.

15.   D. The formula for standard deviation on the exam is: (Pessimistic – Optimistic) ÷ 6. Again, the terms are changed around slightly, but it equates to (25 – 15) ÷ 6 = 10 ÷ 6 = 1.67.

16.   D. GERT charts graphically depict branching, decisions, conditions, and similar scenarios.

17.   C. This one may have been difficult for you, because it is a non-traditional definition of the critical path. The critical path is the series of activities, which if delayed, will delay the project. This makes these activities the highest schedule risk on the project. 'A' is incorrect because the critical path has no relationship with functionality. 'B' is incorrect because the size of the work packages does not directly correlate to the

critical path. 'D' is incorrect because the critical path does not represent the optimal path through the network.

18. D. Another project network diagram; however, this is an activity on arrow diagram. It is solved in the same 3 steps. First, draw the project network diagram. Yours should look similar to the one depicted below:

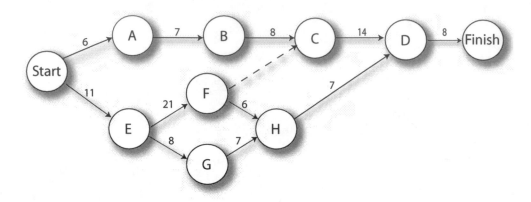

The second step in the process is to list all of the paths through the network. Don't forget that the "dummy activity" of F to C creates a relationship and thus another path through the network. The paths are:

Start-A-B-C-D-Finish

Start-E-F-C-D-Finish

Start-E-F-H-D-Finish

Start-E-G-H-D-Finish

Now add up all of the values associated with the activities on arrow as follows:

Start-A-B-C-D-Finish = 6+7+8+14+8 = 43

Start-E-F-C-D-Finish = 11+21+0+14+8 = 54

Start-E-F-H-D-Finish = 11+21+6+7+8 = 53

Start-E-G-H-D-Finish = 11+8+7+7+8 = 41

The length of the critical path emerges as 54.

19.   B. The slack, or float, for activity H-D is simple to calculate after the work we have already done on problem 18. The way to calculate this is to begin with the list we did for the critical path on the previous question.

Start-A-B-C-D-Finish = 6+7+8+14+8 = 43

Start-E-F-C-D-Finish = 11+21+0+14+8 = 54

Start-E-F-H-D-Finish = 11+21+6+7+8 = 53

Start-E-G-H-D-Finish = 11+8+7+7+8 = 41

Now, strike off every path that does not have activity H-D, as follows:

~~Start-A-B-C-D-Finish = 6+7+8+14+8 = 43~~

~~Start-E-F-C-D-Finish = 11+21+0+14+8 = 54~~

Start-E-F-H-D-Finish = 11+21+6+7+8 = 53

Start-E-G-H-D-Finish = 11+8+7+7+8 = 41

Finally, we take the critical path and subtract the sum from the remaining paths as follows:

54 – 53 = 1

54 – 41 = 13

The smaller of those two values (1) represents the slack, or float for activity H-D. It indicates how long activity H-D may slip before it moves the critical path. In this case, if it moves more than 1 unit, the critical path moves as well, and the project will be delayed.

20.   B. In this case, you would want to return to planning and update the plans. The project will not be delayed, and the resource has given a good reason why the dates need to be revisited (a common occurrence in the real world). 'A' is incorrect, because the plan should reflect reality – not an unrealistic estimate. 'C' is incorrect, because you cannot possibly get an outside opinion every time a resource needs to change a date. 'D' is incorrect, because the resource gave a good reason for the adjustment. It was not that she was lacking in training or ability, but that pieces were left out of planning. Therefore, 'B' is the all-around best answer.

Cost Management

The topic of cost management, like time management, has critical formulae that must be learned and understood. This chapter will explain these formulae clearly and provide methods and exercises for quick retention.

Most of the principles and techniques explained here, such as earned value, did not originate with PMI but were derived from long-standing practices in the fields of cost accounting, managerial accounting, and finance.

From the indicators at the top of the page, you can tell that most people find this chapter to be one of the more difficult ones. In order to help you prepare for this topic, this book has clearly broken down the practices and outlined the techniques and formulae needed to ace the questions on the exam.

Philosophy

While the actual tools and techniques behind cost management may be different from time management, the driving philosophy has several similarities. Costs should be planned, quantified, and measured. The project manager should tie costs to activities and resources and build the estimates from the bottom up.

In real-world practice, budgets are often determined prior to knowing costs. The reason for this is that many companies use fiscal year planning cycles that must be done far in advance of their project planning. Budget constraints are a fact of life, but instead of blindly accepting

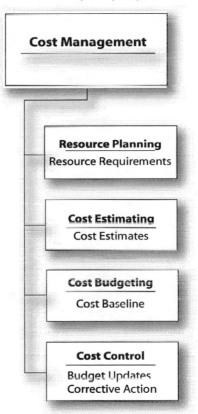

The processes of Project Cost Management with their *primary* outputs

Cost Management

Resource Planning
Resource Requirements

Cost Estimating
Cost Estimates

Cost Budgeting
Cost Baseline

Cost Control
Budget Updates
Corrective Action

whatever budget is specified by management, the project manager carefully reviews the scope of work and the duration estimates and then reconciles them to the projected costs. Adjustments to the project scope, the budget, or the schedule are much easier to justify by working up from a detailed level instead of from the top down. Although budgets are often the first thing created in the real world, PMI's approach is scope first, schedule second, and budget third.

Throughout this book, you will see that estimates should be built from the bottom up. At the point in the process where budgets are created, you should have a well-defined work breakdown structure and an activity list with duration estimates. Now budgeting becomes a task of applying resources and rates against those activities to create cost estimates, a baseline, and a cost management plan.

It is the project manager's job to constantly evaluate cost against time, scope, quality, and risk to ensure that all projections remain realistic and clearly defined.

Memorization of the formulae in this chapter is an absolute must, but you are also encouraged to take the time to thoroughly understand how each formula works. By the time you complete this chapter, the concepts should be intuitive to you.

Importance

The topic of cost management is of high importance for the exam, both in the understanding of PMI's processes, and the application of key formulae play a part here as well.

Preparation

Learning the 11 key formulae for cost management is a must. Learning to apply them is equally as important. The good news is that none of the formulae are overly difficult, and there are plenty of explanations and examples in this book to help cement the concepts.

As mentioned briefly above, memorization is important; however, *understanding the formulae is even more important.* Once you grasp the formulae and concepts, the memorization will be a snap. In fact, some people studying for the exam only memorize the concepts and reconstruct the formulae as needed. This is possible because each formula does make sense. Read and reread this chapter until they are clear to you.

Resource Planning

Each process defined by PMI has outputs, and the most important output of the resource planning process is that *resource requirements* are defined. Keep in mind that resources here refer not only to human resources but also to physical equipment and materials that the project will require.

You must determine how many resources will be needed and what their characteristics are before other processes, such as cost estimating, may be performed.

Two issues related to resource planning sometimes appear on the exam:

Life-cycle Costing

Instead of simply asking "How much will this product cost to develop?" life-cycle costing looks at the total cost of ownership from purchase or creation, through operations, and finally to disposal. It is a practice that encourages making decisions based on the bigger picture of ownership costs.

Value Engineering

Value engineering is the practice of trying to get more out of the project in every possible way. It tries to increase the bottom line, decrease costs, improve quality, shorten the schedule, and generally squeeze more benefit and value out of each aspect of the project. The key to value engineering is that the scope of work is not reduced by these other efforts.

Cost Estimating

Cost estimating is a planning process that takes many of the planning outputs produced up to this point, such as the WBS, the resource requirements, the activity duration estimates, etc., and uses them to create the team's best estimate as to how much the activities are going to cost.

Cost Estimating Tools

For cost estimating you should be familiar with the tools used to complete the process and the main outputs that are produced. The tools include:

Analogous Estimating (also known as top-down estimating)

This type of estimating bases estimates on the costs of previous projects that were similar in size, scope, and characteristics. The accuracy of this type of estimate depends on how similar the previous project is to the current one.

Parametric Modeling

Parametric models use industry numbers and apply them to the project's characteristics. The results may be highly accurate or inaccurate, depending on the quality of the estimates used and the accuracy of the inputs.

Bottom-up Estimating

If the previous planning activities were done properly, bottom-up estimating can be a very accurate technique for estimating costs. In this method, each work package is estimated individually. These estimates may involve experts, and preferably will include the person who will be doing the work. In any case, the person doing the work should be supportive of the final estimate for their work package.

Computerized Tools

Computerized tools may refer to any number of computer applications that help in scheduling and estimating, including spreadsheet programs. These tools may allow you to experiment with costing scenarios, see the impact of different decisions, and perform complex "what-if" analysis.

Cost Estimating Outputs

In addition to these tools, you should be aware that cost estimating has two main outputs. The first is cost estimates. There are five types of estimates you must learn for the exam. Contrary to what you may have practiced, each of these estimates is created in a planning process.

Estimates

There are five types of estimates identified by the Association for the Advancement of Cost Engineering International. These estimates typically are generated in order, from the most indefinite (order of magnitude estimate) to the most certain (control estimate).

Type of Estimate	Range of Estimate
Order of Magnitude Estimate	-50% to +100%
Conceptual Estimate	-30% to +50%
Preliminary Estimate	-20% to +30%
Definitive Estimate	-15% to +20%
Control Estimate	-10% to +15%

Cost Management Plan

The other important output of cost estimating is the cost management plan. Like the scope management plan and the schedule management plan, the cost management plan defines how changes to the plan (in this case, the cost baseline) will be identified, approved, and implemented. All such management plans are rolled up into the overall project plan, as discussed in Chapter 12 – Integration Management.

Cost Budgeting

There is not a great deal of content that must be learned for the planning process of cost budgeting. The main points to remember here are:

- Cost budgeting is a planning process.
- The document created by cost budgeting as an output is called the cost baseline.
- The schedule must be created before the cost baseline can be established. (If you see an exam question asking which comes first, your answer should be the schedule!)
- The same tools used in cost estimating (analogous estimating, bottom-up estimating, etc.) are used in creating the cost baseline.

Cost Control

Cost control is a controlling process that involves influencing and managing changes to the cost baseline created during project planning. While there are many tools and techniques listed in the PMBOK for cost control, by far the most essential for the PMP exam is the technique of earned value management.

The earned value analysis on the PMP is concerned with quantifying both cost and schedule. In a sense, the name "value" is a tricky bit of wording. It is based on the concept that as you perform work on the project, you are actually adding value back into the project. Earned value analysis measures how much value you have added to the project versus how much you had planned to add.

If you are wrestling with your understanding of earned value, think about the concept of debits and credits. In a double entry accounting system, for every debit to one account, there is a corresponding credit to another account. Earned value is similar in that if you spend a dollar on labor for your project, that dollar doesn't just evaporate into thin air. You are "earning" a dollar's value back into your project. If you buy bricks or computers, write code or documentation, or perform any work on the project, those activities earn value back into your project.

There are 11 key formulae associated with earned value management that often appear on the test, and they require both memorization and understanding. Following is a chart that presents a summary of the key terms used in earned value calculations.

Note that for Planned Value, Earned Value, and Actual Cost, there are older, equivalent terms that still show up on the exam. These older terms and their associated abbreviations are shown along with the current terms on the chart on the following page, and you must be able to recognize and apply either one on the exam.

Term	Abbreviation	Description	Formula
Budgeted At Completion	BAC	How much was originally planned for this project to cost.	No one formula exists. BAC is derived by looking at the total budgeted cost for the project.
Planned Value (also known as Budgeted Cost of Work Scheduled)	PV (or BCWS)	How much work should have been completed at a point in time based on the plan. (Derived by measuring where you had planned to be in terms of work completed at a point in the schedule).	Planned % Complete X BAC
Earned Value (also known as Budgeted Cost of Work Performed)	EV (or BCWP)	How much work was actually completed at a point in time. Derived by measuring where you actually are in terms of work completed at a point in the schedule.	Actual % Complete X BAC
Actual Cost (also known as Actual Cost of Work Performed)	AC (or ACWP)	The money spent at a point in time.	Sum of all costs for the given period of time.
Cost Variance	CV	The difference between what we expected to spend and what was actually spent at a point in time.	EV-AC
Schedule Variance	SV	The difference between where we planned to be in the schedule and where we are in the schedule.	EV-PV
Cost Performance Index	CPI	The rate at which the project performance is meeting cost expectations.	EV ÷ AC
Schedule Performance Index	SPI	The rate at which the project performance is meeting schedule expectations.	EV ÷ PV
Estimate At Completion	EAC	Projecting the total cost at completion based on project performance at a point in time.	BAC ÷ CPI
Estimate To Completion	ETC	Projecting how much will be spent on the project, based on past performance.	EAC - AC
Variance At Completion	VAC	The difference between what was budgeted and what will actually be spent.	BAC - EAC

Earned Value

Earned Value

EVM Example

Consider the following example:

You are the project manager for the construction of 20 miles of sidewalk. According to your plan, the cost of construction will be $15,000 per mile and will take 8 weeks to complete.

2 weeks into the project, you have spent $55,000 and completed 4 miles of sidewalk, and you want to report performance and determine how much time and cost remain.

Below, we will walk through each calculation to show how we arrive at the correct answers.

Budgeted at Completion

In the approach outlined by this book, we will always begin by calculating BAC. Budgeted at completion simply means, "how much we originally expected this project to cost". It is typically very easy to calculate. In our example, we take 20 miles of sidewalk * $15,000 / mile. That equates to a BAC of $300,000.

BAC = $300,000

Planned Value

The planned value is how much work was planned for this point in time. The value is expressed in dollars.

Planned Value = Planned % complete * BAC

We do this by taking the BAC ($300,000) and multiplying it by our % complete. In this case, we are 2 weeks complete on an 8 week schedule, which equates to 25%. $300,000 * .25 = $75,000. Therefore, we had planned to spend $75,000 after two weeks.

PV = $75,000

Earned Value

If you have been intimidated by the concept of earned value, relax. Earned value is based on the assumption that as you complete work on the project, you are adding value to the project. Therefore, it is simply a matter of calculating how much value you have "earned" on the project.

Planned value is what was planned, but earned value is what actually happened.

EV = Actual % Complete * BAC

In this case, we have completed 4 miles of the 20 mile project, which equates to 20%. We multiply that percentage by the BAC to get EV. It is $300,000 * 20% = $60,000. This tells us that we have completed $60,000 worth of work, or more accurately, we have earned $60,000 of value for the project.

EV = $60,000

Actual Cost

Building on the above illustration, we will calculate our actual costs. Actual cost is the amount of cost you have incurred at this point, and we are told in the example that we have spent $55,000 to date. In this example, no calculation is needed.

AC = Actual Cost

AC = $55,000

Cost Variance

Cost variance (CV) is how much actual costs differ from planned costs. We derive this by calculating the difference between EV and AC. In this example, it is EV of $60,000 – AC of $55,000. A positive variance (as in this case), reflects that the project is doing better on cost than expected.

For those who are curious, the reason we use EV in this formula instead of PV is that we are calculating how much the actual costs have varied. If we used PV, it would give us the variance from our plan, but the cost variance measures *actual* cost variance, and EV is based on actual performance, whereas PV is based on planned performance.

A positive CV is a good thing. It indicates that we are doing better on costs than we had planned. Conversely, a negative CV indicates that costs are running higher than planned.

CV = EV-AC

CV = $5,000

Schedule Variance

Schedule variance (SV) is how much our schedule differs from our plan. Where people often get confused here is that *this concept is expressed in dollars*. SV is derived by calculating the difference between EV and PV. In this example, the schedule variance is EV of $60,000 – PV of $75,000. A negative variance (as in this case) reflects that we are not performing as well as we had hoped in terms of schedule. A positive SV would indicate that the project is ahead of schedule.

SV = EV-PV

SV = -$15,000

Cost Performance Index

The cost performance index gives us an indicator as to how much we are getting for every dollar. It is derived by dividing Earned Value by the Actual Cost. In this example, Earned Value = $60,000, and our Actual Cost = $55,000. $60,000 ÷ $55,000 = 1.09.

This figure tells us that we are getting $1.09 worth of performance for every $1.00 we expected. A CPI of 1 indicates that the project is exactly on track. A closer look at the formula reveals that values of 1 or greater are good, and values less than 1 are undesirable.

CPI = EV ÷ AC

CPI = 1.09

Schedule Performance Index

A corollary to the cost performance index is the schedule performance index, or SPI. The schedule performance index tells us how fast the project is progressing compared to the project plan. It is derived by dividing earned value by the planned value. In this example, earned value = $60,000, and our planned value = $75,000. $60,000 ÷ $75,000 = 0.8. This tells us that the project is progressing at 80% of the pace that we expected it to, and when we look at the example, this conclusion makes sense. We had expected to lay 20 miles of sidewalk in 8 weeks. At that rate, after 2 weeks, we should have constructed 5 miles, but instead the example tells us that we had only constructed 4 miles. That equates to 4/5 performance, which is 80%. Like the cost performance index, values of 1 or greater are good, and values that are less than 1 are undesirable.

SPI = EV ÷ PV

SPI = 0.8

A common way for the cost performance and schedule performance index to be used is to track them over time. This is often displayed in the form of a graph, as illustrated below. This graph may be easily interpreted if you consider that a value of 1 indicates that the index is exactly on plan.

Schedule Performance Index Over Time
(same view with Cost Performance Index)

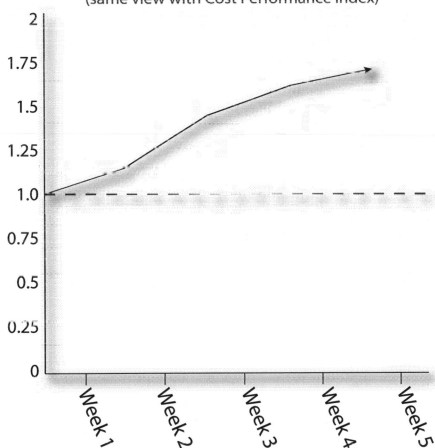

Earned Value

Estimate At Completion

Estimate at completion is the amount we expect the project to cost, based on where we are relative to cost and schedule. If that sounds confusing, think of it this way. If you know you are half way through the project, and you are currently 20% over budget, then the estimate at completion factors that variance out to the end of the project. There are many ways to calculate EAC; for the exam, the most straightforward way to calculate it is to take the BAC and divide it by our cost performance index. In this example, we expected to spend (BAC) $300,000 and our CPI is 1.09. $300,000 ÷ 1.09 = $275,229.36. This should make sense. We are doing better on costs than we had originally planned, and this value reflects that.

$$EAC = BAC \div CPI$$

$$EAC = \$275,229.36$$

Estimate To Completion

Estimate to completion is simply how much more we expect to spend from this point forward based on what we've done so far. It can be easily backed in to by taking our estimate at complete (what we expect to spend) and subtracting what we have spent so far (Actual Cost). Given the numbers above, it would be EAC of $275,229.36 - AC of $55,000 = $220,229.36. This tells us that we expect to spend $220,229.36 more, given our performance thus far.

$$ETC = EAC - AC$$

$$ETC = \$220,229.36$$

Variance at Completion

Variance at completion is the difference between what we originally budgeted and what we expect to spend. A positive variance indicates that we are doing better than projected, and a negative variance indicates that we expect the project to run over on costs.

In this example, our BAC was $300,000; however, our EAC is now $275,229.36. $300,000 - $275,229.36 = $24,770.64.

$$VAC = BAC - EAC$$

$$VAC = \$24,770.64$$

Types of Cost

Several types of questions regarding cost may appear on the exam. It is important to understand the difference between the different types of cost presented below:

Cost type	Explanation
Fixed	Costs that stay the same throughout the life of a project. An example is a piece of heavy equipment, such as a bulldozer.
Variable	Costs that vary on a project. Examples are hourly labor, and fuel for the bulldozer.
Direct	Expenses that are billed directly to the project. An example is the materials used to construct a building.
Indirect	Costs that are shared and allocated among several or all projects. An example could be a manager's salary. His people might be direct costs on a project, but his salary is overhead and would be considered an indirect cost.
Sunk	Costs that have been invested into or expended upon the project. Sunk costs are like spilt milk. If they are unrecoverable, they are to be treated as if they are irrelevant! This is difficult for many people to understand, but the statement "we've spent over 10 million dollars on this project, and we're not turning back now" is not good decision-making if the costs are unrecoverable, or "sunk".

Types of Costs

Exercises

Example 1

You are constructing 6 additional rooms on an office building. Each of the six rooms is identical, and the projected cost for the project is $100,000 and is expected to take 5 weeks.

At the end of the 2nd week, you have spent $17,500 per room and have finished 2 rooms; you are ready to begin on the 3rd.

1. Based on the information provided in the example above, fill in the values for the following table:

	Value
Budgeted At Completion	
Planned Value	
Earned Value	
Actual Cost	
Cost Variance	
Schedule Variance	
Cost Performance Index	
Schedule Performance Index	
Estimated At Completion	
Estimated To Completion	
Variance At Completion	

2. Is the project ahead of or behind schedule?

3. Is the project going to be completed over or under budget?

Example 2

Here is another example to test your understanding of these concepts.

You have planned for a project to write a software application to take 1 year. The costs to this project are budgeted at $12,500 per month.

Six months into the project, you find that the software application is 50% completed, and you have spent $70,000.

4. Based on the information provided, fill in the values for the following table:

	Value
Budgeted At Completion	
Planned Value	
Earned Value	
Actual Cost	
Cost Variance	
Schedule Variance	
Cost Performance Index	
Schedule Performance Index	
Estimated At Completion	
Estimated To Completion	
Variance At Completion	

5.   Is the project ahead of or behind schedule?

6. Is the project going to be completed over or under budget?

Cost Exercises

7. Mark one value in each column that shows the most desirable value given the information provided. (Note that some of these attributes are covered in Chapter 4 – Project Scope Management)

IRR	SPI	CPI	NPV	Payback Period	BCR	ROI
22%	1	.5	$25,000	16 mos	2	9%
0%	0	1	$95,000	2 yrs	1.5	12%
12%	.8	1.2	$50,000	16 wks	1	-2%
-3%	1.2	1.15	$71,000	25 mos	.2	3%

Answers to Exercises

1. Your answers should look like these:

	Value
Budgeted At Completion	$100,000
Planned Value	$40,000.00
Earned Value	$33,333.33
Actual Cost	$35,000.00
Cost Variance	-$1,666.67
Schedule Variance	-$6,666.67
Cost Performance Index	0.95
Schedule Performance Index	0.83
Estimated At Completion	$105,263.15
Estimated To Completion	$70,263.15
Variance At Completion	-$5,263.15

- BAC = $100,000.00
- PV = 2 weeks ÷ 5 weeks = 40% complete * 100,000 = $40,000
- EV = 2 rooms ÷ 6 rooms = 33.3% complete * 100,000 = $33,333.33
- AC = $17,500 per rooms * 2 rooms = $35,000
- CV = (EV) $33,333.33 – (AC) $35,000.00 = -$1,666.67
- SV = (EV) $33,333.33 – (PV) $40,000.00 = -$6,666.67
- CPI = (EV) $33,333.33 ÷ (AC) $35,000.00 = 0.95
- SPI = (EV) $33,333.33 ÷ (PV) $40,000.00 = 0.83
- EAC = (BAC) $100,000.00 ÷ (CPI) 0.95 = $105,263.15
- ETC = (EAC) $105,263.15 – (AC) $35,000.00 = $70,263.15
- VAC = (BAC) $100,000.00 – (EAC) $105,263.15 = -$5,263.15

2. Is the project ahead of or behind schedule?

   The project is behind schedule. The easiest way to determine this is by looking at the SPI. Since it is less than 1, we can determine that the project is not doing well in terms of the schedule.

3. Is the project going to be completed over or under budget?

   There are two ways to see that the project is going to run over budget. First, the CPI is less than 1. Second, the VAC is negative.

4. Check your answers against these:

	Value
Budgeted At Completion	$150,000.00
Planned Value	$75,000.00
Earned Value	$75,000.00
Actual Cost	$70,000.00
Cost Variance	$5,000.00
Schedule Variance	$0
Cost Performance Index	1.07
Schedule Performance Index	1
Estimated At Completion	$140,186.91
Estimated To Completion	$70,186.91
Variance At Completion	$9,813.09

- BAC = $150,000.00
- PV = 6 months ÷ 12 months = 50% complete * 150,000 = $75,000
- EV = Project is 50% complete * 150,000.00 = $75,000.00
- AC = $70,000 .00
- CV = (EV) $75,000.00 – (AC) $70,000.00 = $5,000.00

- SV = (EV) \$75,000.00 – (PV) \$75,000.00 = \$0
- CPI = (EV) \$75,000.00 ÷ (AC) \$70,000.00 = 1.07
- SPI = (EV) \$75,000.00 ÷ (PV) \$75,000.00 = 1
- EAC = (BAC) \$150,000.00 ÷ (CPI) 1.07 = \$140,186.91
- ETC = (EAC) \$140,186.91 – (AC) \$70,000.00 = \$70,186.91
- VAC = (BAC) \$150,000.00 – (EAC) \$140,186.91 = \$9,813.09

5. Is the project ahead of or behind schedule?

    This would be classified as a "trick" question, as neither answer is correct. Since the SPI is 1, we can see that the project is exactly on schedule.

6. Is the project going to be completed over or under budget?

    The project is projected to finish ahead of budget, due to the cost performance index being greater than 1.

7. The most desirable project attributes for each column are shaded in the chart below. Note that some of these formulae came from Chapter 4, Scope Management:

IRR	SPI	CPI	NPV	Payback Period	BCR	ROI
22%	1	.5	\$25,000	16 mos	2	9%
0%	0	1	\$95,000	2 yrs	1.5	12%
12%	.8	1.2	\$50,000	16 wks	1	-2%
-3%	1.2	1.15	\$71,000	25 mos	.2	3%

    Did you notice that for most of these measurements, the bigger value is the best one? That is true for all except for the payback period, where you want the shortest time to recoup project costs.

Going Deeper

The topic of cost management goes quite deep in the accounting field. In addition to the resources listed below, there are several excellent academic text books on the subject of cost accounting. For further study in the area of project cost management, the following books and resources are suggested:[1]

Cokins, Gary. *Activity-Based Cost Management - Making It Work: A Manager's Guide to Implementing and Sustaining an Effective ABC System.* McGraw-Hill Trade, 1996.

Horngren, Charles T. *Cost Accounting: A Managerial Emphasis.* Prentice Hall, 2002 .

Howes, Norman R. *Modern Project Management.* AMACOM, 2001.

Smith, Gaylord N. *Excel Applications for Cost Accounting.* South-Western College Pub., 1999.

Project Cost Management Questions

Note: Some of these questions are based on material covered in chapters 2, 3, and 4 as well as this chapter.

1. Your schedule projected that you would reach 50% completion today on a road construction project that is paving 32 miles of new highway. Every 4 miles is scheduled to cost $5,000,000. Today, in your status meeting, you announced that you had completed 20 miles of the highway at a cost of $18,000,000. What is your Planned Value?

    A. $12,800,000.
    B. $18,000,000.
    C. $20,000,000.
    D. $40,000,000.

2. If the CPI is 0.1, this indicates:

    A. The project is performing extremely poorly on cost.
    B. The project is costing 10% over what was expected.
    C. The project is only costing 90% of what was expected.
    D. The project is performing extremely well on cost.

3. Resource Requirements are used as an input into which process?

    A. Resource Planning.
    B. Cost Estimating.
    C. Cost Budgeting.
    D. Cost Control.

4. Based on the following Benefit Cost Ratios, which project would be the best one to select?

    A. BCR = -1.
    B. BCR = 0.
    C. BCR = 1.
    D. BCR = 2.

5. The difference between present value and net present value is:

    A. Present value is expressed as an interest rate, while net present value is expressed as a dollar figure.

    B. Present value is a measure of the actual present value, while net present value measures expected present value.

    C. Present value does not factor in costs.

    D. Present value is more accurate.

6. Your estimate for a task ranges from $150,000 to $350,000. These estimates represent:

    A. Cost estimate.

    B. Budgeted estimate.

    C. Order of magnitude estimate.

    D. Definitive estimate.

7. A project's cost reserves are best:

    A. Kept hidden from the team so they will not attempt to use the reserve.

    B. Added to the project tasks or the baseline as a buffer against overrun.

    C. Used to prevent actual costs from rising.

    D. Managed by the sponsor or the customer.

8. One of your team members makes a change to the budget with your approval. In what process is he engaged?

    A. Resource planning.

    B. Cost estimating.

    C. Cost management.

    D. Cost control.

9.   After measuring expected project benefits, management has four
      projects from which to choose. Project 1 has a net present value of
      $100,000 and will cost $50,000. Project 2 has a net present value of
      $200,000 and will cost $75,000. Project 3 has a net present value of
      $500,000 and will cost $400,000. Project 4 has a net present value of
      $125,000 and will cost $25,000. Which project would be BEST?

      A. Project 1.
      B. Project 2.
      C. Project 3.
      D. Project 4.

10.   Your project office has purchased a site license for a computerized tool
      that assists in the task of cost estimating on a very large construction
      project for a downtown skyscraper. This tool asks you for specific
      characteristics about the project and then provides estimating guidance
      based on materials, construction techniques, historical information, and
      industry practices. This tool is an example of:

      A. Bottom up estimating.
      B. Parametric modeling.
      C. Analogous estimating.
      D. Activity duration estimating.

11.   You are managing a project that is part of a large construction
      program. During the execution of your project you are alerted that the
      construction of a foundation is expected to experience a serious cost
      overrun. What would be your FIRST course of action?

      A. Evaluate the cause and size of the overrun.
      B. Stop execution until the problem is solved.
      C. Contact the program manager to see if additional funds may be
          released.
      D. Determine if you have sufficient budget reserves to cover the cost
          overrun.

12. If earned value = $10,000, planned value = 8,000, and actual cost = $3,000, what is the schedule variance?

   A. -$2,000
   B. $2,000
   C. $5,000
   D. $-5,000

13. Estimate to complete indicates:

   A. The total projected amount that will be spent, based on past performance.
   B. The projected remaining amount that will be spent, based on past performance.
   C. The difference between what was budgeted and what is expected to be spent.
   D. The original planned completion cost minus the costs incurred to date.

14. If a project has a CPI of .95 and an SPI of 1.01, this indicates:

   A. The project is progressing slower and costing more than planned.
   B. The project is progressing slower and costing less than planned.
   C. The project is progressing faster and costing more than planned.
   D. The project is progressing faster and costing less than planned.

15. Project A would yield $100,000 in benefit. Project B would yield $250,000 in benefit. Because of limited resources, your company can only perform one of these. They elect to perform Project B because of the higher benefit. What is the opportunity cost of performing Project B?

   A. -$150,000.
   B. $150,000.
   C. -$100,000.
   D. $100,000.

16. As a project manager, your BEST use of the project cost baseline would be to:

   A. Measure and monitor cost performance on the project.
   B. Track approved changes.

C. Calculate team performance bonuses.

D. Measure and report on variable project costs.

17. The value of all work that has been completed so far is:

A. Earned value.

B. Estimate at complete.

C. Actual cost.

D. Planned value.

18. If you have a schedule variance of $500, this would indicate:

A. Planned value is less than earned value.

B. Earned value is less than the estimate at complete.

C. Actual cost is less than earned value.

D. The ratio of earned value to planned value is 5:1.

19. If budgeted at complete = $500, estimate to complete = $400, earned value = $100, and actual cost = $100, what is the estimate at complete?

A. $0.

B. $150.

C. $350.

D. $500.

20. You have spent $322,168 on your project to date. The program manager wants to know why costs have been running so high. You explain that the resource cost has been greater than expected and should level out over the next six months. What does the $322,168 represent to the program manager?

A. Earned value

B. Actual cost

C. Planned value

D. Cost performance index

Answers to Cost Management Questions

1. C. Planned value is calculated by multiplying the Budgeted At Completion by planned % complete. Our cost per mile is planned at $1,250,000 ($5,000,000 ÷ 4 miles), and our Budgeted At Completion is 32 miles * 1,250,000/mile = $40,000,000. We planned to be 50% complete. Therefore, $40,000,000 * .50 = $20,000,000.

2. A. This terrible cost performance index indicates that we are getting ten cents of value for every dollar we spent; thus the project is doing very poorly on cost performance.

3. B. Resource requirements are used as an input for the cost estimating process. The resource requirements along with their rates are used to estimate cost. 'A' is incorrect, because the resource requirements are an output from resource planning.

4. D. With Benefit Cost Ratios, the bigger the better! BCR is calculated as benefit ÷ cost, so the more benefit, and the less cost, the higher the number.

5. C. There is a difference between present value and net present value. Present value tells the expected value of the project in today's dollars. Net present value is the same thing, but it subtracts the costs after calculating the present value.

6. C. This question is difficult. Order of magnitude estimates are -25% to +75%. In this example, $150,000 and $350,000 are -25% to +75% of $200,000.

7. B. Cost reserves are added to tasks or the baseline after they have been estimated. Cost reserves are used as a safety margin. If 'C' looked correct to you, consider that reserves do not affect the actual costs.

8. D. The main clue here is "change." If they are making approved changes, they are in a control process.

9. C. This one was very tricky! Net present value already has costs factored in, so they can be ignored here. The net present value is the only value you need to consider, and bigger is better!

10.   B. This is an example of parametric modeling. Parametric modeling is common in some industries, where you can describe the project in detail, and the modeling tool will help provide estimates based on historical information, industry standards, etc.

11.   A. This illustrates one of PMI's biggest biases on these questions. Your job as a project manager is almost always to evaluate and understand *first*. Know what you are dealing with before you take action, and don't just accept anyone's word for it - verify the information yourself!

12.   B. Schedule Variance is calculated as EV-PV. In this example, $10,000 - $8,000 = $2,000.

13.   B. The estimate to complete is what we expect to spend from this point forward, based on our performance thus far.

14.   C. Did the wording trip you up on this one? Make sure you read the questions and answers carefully since things were switched around on this one. A schedule performance index greater than 1 means that the project is progressing faster than planned. A cost performance index that is less than 1 means that the project is costing more than planned. Therefore choice 'C' is the only one that fits.

15.   D. Opportunity cost is simply how much cost you are passing up. In this case, by choosing project B, you are forgoing $100,000 in expected benefit from project A, and that $100,000 represents the opportunity cost.

16.   A. The cost baseline is used to track cost performance based on the original plan plus approved changes.

17.   A. Earned value is defined as the value of all work completed to this point.

18.   A. This is another tricky question because of the way it is worded. Schedule variance is calculated as earned value – planned value. In this case, schedule variance could only be positive if earned value is greater than planned value (or stated otherwise, if planned value is less than earned value). 'A' is the only choice that has to be true.

19.   D. The estimate at complete is what we expect to have spent at the end of the project. It is calculated by taking our budgeted at complete and dividing it by our cost performance index. Step 1 is to calculate our cost performance index. It is earned value ÷ actual cost, and in this case, it equals 1. Budgeted at complete is $500, and $500 ÷ 1 = $500. Therefore, 'D' is the correct answer, indicating that we are progressing exactly as planned.

20.   B. Look at the first sentence "You have spent $322,168…" Actual cost is what you have spent to date on the project.

Quality Management

Difficulty	Memorization	Exam Importance	Corresponding PMBOK Chapter
Medium	Medium	High	Chapter 8

The topics on the PMP borrow from numerous business disciplines such as psychology, math, accounting, and law. Previous formal study of these disciplines is beneficial but not necessary to pass the exam. This is especially true for the topic of quality management. The study of quality and its effect on business and projects has been the focus of considerable research, especially since the end of World War II, and volumes of research, usually focused on a few central theories, have been conducted and documented. Quality borrows heavily from the field of statistics, and a high-level explanation of some of the statistical tools and techniques is provided here.

There are numerous theories on quality, how it should be implemented, how it should be measured, and what levels of quality should be attained. You need to have a familiarity with the theories presented in this chapter before taking the exam.

Please note that the statistics and statistical examples here are greatly simplified, but they are adequate to get you through the exam. Topics on the PMP Exam, such as sampling, distribution, and deviations from the mean are built on underlying assumptions that you do not need to know in order to pass.

The processes of Project Quality Management with their *primary* outputs

Philosophy

PMI's philosophy of quality is derived from several leading quality theories, including TQM, ISO-9000, Six Sigma, and others. PMI looks at each of these theories in terms of the tools and techniques they provide.

PMI's philosophy of quality is also a very proactive approach. Whereas early theories on quality relied heavily on inspection, current thinking is focused on prevention over inspection. This evolution of thought is based on the fact that it costs more to fix an error than it does to prevent one.[1]

The responsibility of quality in PMI's philosophy falls heavily on the project manager. Everyone on the team has an important contribution to make to project quality; however, it is management's responsibility to provide the resources to make quality happen, and the project manager is ultimately responsible and accountable for the quality of the project.

The PMI process, as it relates to quality, is perhaps more important here than most other places. Quality planning, quality assurance, and quality control map closely to the Plan-Do-Check-Act cycle as described by Deming[2], and several questions on the exam rely heavily on your understanding of how quality activities flow and connect.

It is also important to understand that some of the investment in quality must be borne by the organization, since it would be far too expensive for each project to have its own quality program. An example might be a company investing in a site license for a software testing product that can be used across numerous projects.

Importance

Project quality management is one of the slimmer chapters both in this book and in the PMBOK, but it is of high importance on the exam. You should expect to see several exam questions that will relate directly to this chapter, so it will be necessary to become acquainted with the terms and theories as prescribed below, and then reread this chapter to ensure that you have mastered the topic.

In real world practice, quality formulae abound; however, the PMP does not currently require you to memorize or apply them. This chapter focuses, instead, on the concepts and terms.

Some parts of this topic will be revisited in later chapters in order to show how quality fits into the overall project management context.

Preparation

The quality processes, tools, techniques and outputs, found in this chapter must be learned and understood. You should expect to see questions on the PMP Exam that relate directly to these. Special attention will be paid to the key quality theories that show up on the exam, as well as terminology that you need to know.

Pay special attention to the differences between quality planning, quality assurance, and quality control. This is a tricky area for many people on the exam.

Quality Management Processes

Definition of Quality

The definition of quality you should know for the exam is "every characteristic that influences satisfaction."

Quality Processes

There are only three processes within project quality management, as listed in the table below. In the PMI framework, these processes touch three process groups: planning (quality planning), executing (quality assurance), and controlling (quality control).

Process	Key Inputs	Key Tools & Techniques	Key Outputs
Quality planning	• Quality policy • Standards and regulations	• Benefit/cost analysis • Benchmarking • Cost of quality • Design of experiments • Flowcharts	• Quality management plan
Quality assurance	• Quality management plan	• Quality audits • Same tools as quality planning	• Quality improvement
Quality control	• Work results • Quality management plan • Operational definitions • Checklists	• Inspection • Trend analysis • Sampling • Pareto charts	• Quality improvement • Rework • Process adjustments

Quality Terms and Philosophies

Total Quality Management (TQM)

A quality theory popularized after World War II that states that everyone in the company is responsible for quality and is able to make a difference in the ultimate quality of the product. TQM applies to improvements in processes and in results.[3]

Continuous Improvement

Also known as "Kaizen", from the Japanese Management term. A philosophy that stresses constant process improvement, in the form of small changes in products or services.

Kaizen

(See Continuous Improvement)

Just-In-Time (JIT)

A manufacturing method that brings inventory down to zero (or nearly zero) levels. It forces a focus on quality, since there is no excess inventory on hand to waste.

ISO 9000

Part of the International Standards Organization to ensure that companies document what they do and do what they document. ISO 9000 is not directly attributable to higher quality, but may be an important component of quality assurance, since it ensures that an organization follows their processes.

Standard Deviation

The concept of standard deviation is an important one to understand for the exam. Standard deviation is a statistical calculation used to measure and describe how data is organized. The following graphic of a standard bell curve illustrates standard deviation:

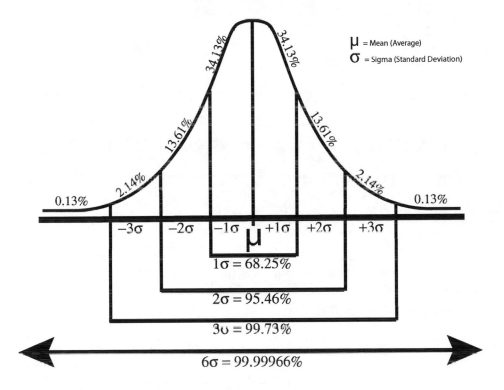

The standard deviation, represented by the Greek symbol σ (sigma), is calculated first by averaging all data points to get the mean, then calculating the difference between each data point and the mean, and finally averaging all of those differences.

If the data set is "normally distributed," as it is in the preceding chart, the following statistics will be true:

- 68.25% of the data points (or values) will fall ± 1 standard deviation from the mean.
- 95.46% of the values will fall ± 2 standard deviations from the mean.
- 99.73% of the values will fall ± 3 standard deviations from the mean.
- 99.99966% of the values will fall ± 6 standard deviations from the mean.

The standard deviation may be used in a few different ways in quality. For instance, the higher your standard deviation, the more diverse your data points are. It is also used to set quality levels (see the Six Sigma topic in this chapter), and to set control limits to determine if a process is in control (see the Control Charts topic in this chapter).

Six Sigma

Six sigma is a popular philosophy of quality management that focuses on achieving very high levels of quality by controlling the process and reducing defects (a defect is defined as anything that does not meet the customer's quality standards).

As you will remember from the section on the standard deviation, a σ (sigma) is defined as 1 standard deviation from the mean. At the level of 1 sigma quality, 68.25% of all outputs will meet quality standards. At the 3 sigma quality level, that number jumps to 99.73% of all outputs that meet quality standards. At the six sigma level, the number is 99.99966% of all outputs that meet quality standards. This means that when quality reaches six sigma standards, the results will be such that only 3.4 out of every 1,000,000 outputs do not meet quality standards. Six sigma quality strives to make the overwhelming majority of the bell curve fall within customer quality limits.

Six sigma puts a primary focus on quantifying, measuring, and controlling the quality of products, services, and results. It is based on the underlying theory that anything will vary if measured to a fine enough level.[4] The goal is to refine the process so that human error and outside influence no longer exist, and these variations are completely random. If done properly, the statistical outcome should follow the bell curve illustrated previously under the topic of standard deviation. The goal is to make six standard deviations (sigmas) of the outputs fall within customer's quality limits.

If this seems like a lot of information, the most important things to know for the exam are that six sigma is a quality management philosophy that sets very high standards for quality, and that one sigma quality is the lowest quality level, allowing 317,500 defects per 1,000,000 outputs, three sigma quality is higher, allowing 2,700 defects per 1,000,000, and six sigma quality is the highest of these, allowing only 3.4 defects per 1,000,000.

Also know that six sigma quality levels may not be high enough for all projects or all industries. For instance, the pharmaceutical industry, the airline industry, and power utilities typically strive for higher levels of quality than six sigma would specify.

Quality Planning

In quality planning, the project manager identifies which quality standards are relevant to the project and determines how to satisfy them. The driving factor here is that quality is a factor of planning – not inspection!

Quality planning is especially proactive. A key idea to memorize for the exam is that any time you are trying to prevent low quality *before* it has happened, you are in planning.

Quality Planning Inputs

Quality Policy

The organization's quality policy is a key input to the quality planning process. The quality policy is the performing organization's overall approach to quality. Issued by top management, it provides direction for other quality processes.

Standards and Regulations

Standards and regulations are inputs to quality planning. Standards are guidelines from a recognized body that are common practice to follow, while regulations are rules that must be followed.

Example: Standard: The size of copy paper (8.5" x 11")

                 Regulation: Fire codes for construction.

Quality Planning Tools and Techniques

Also important to learn are the tools of quality planning and quality assurance. These are described below. Note also that the same tools are used for both quality planning and quality assurance.

Benefit/cost analysis

There are both benefits and costs associated with quality, and it is important to understand these tradeoffs when planning.

Benchmarking

Previously completed projects may provide quality standards against which you can compare, or benchmark. For example, if you are on a pipeline construction project, and you have records showing that a similar project completed by your company averaged 1 defect per 10,000 feet of pipe, you may want to use this quality statistic as a benchmark for your project.

Flowcharting

Flowcharts show how various components relate in a system. Flowcharting can be used to predict where quality problems may happen. In addition to traditional flow charts, Cause and Effect Diagrams are another type of flowcharting.

Cause and Effect Diagram

Cause and effect diagrams are also known as Ishikawa diagrams or fishbone diagrams. In quality planning, these are used to show how different factors relate together and might be tied to potential problems.[5]

In quality planning, cause and effect diagrams are used as part of a proactive approach to improve quality by anticipating quality problems before they happen.

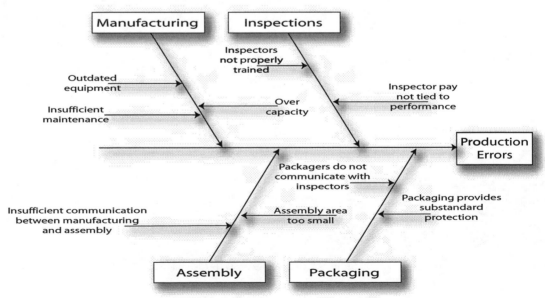

An example of an Cause and Effect (or Ishikawa or Fishbone) Diagram

Fishbone diagram

A common name for Cause and Effect Diagram, or Ishikawa Diagrams (see above) due to the way the chart appears like a fish's skeleton.

Cost of Quality

Cost of quality represents the cost of all efforts to deliver quality. Quality costs are typically categorized either as prevention, appraisal, or failure.

Quality Planning Output: Quality Management Plan

The quality management plan is the most important output of the quality control process and becomes a part of the Project Plan. The quality management plan describes how the quality policy will be implemented on this project. It addresses quality control, quality assurance, and quality improvement.

Quality Assurance

The quality assurance process assures that the process for this project is being followed. It is *not* about producing quality product. Quality assurance uses *audits* to make sure that the quality management plan is working and being adhered to exactly as planned.

Quality assurance (QA) is the sum of all of the quality activities performed in the project to meet quality standards. It is performed throughout the project, *but it is considered an executing process, not a planning process in the PMI framework.*

The key word to associate with quality assurance is audits. If you see a question on the exam that talks about auditing the quality process, your answer should reflect that audits are performed as part of the quality assurance process, not quality planning or quality control. Quality audits are periodic reviews of the project activities to ensure that they conform to the established quality process.

Don't forget that all the tools of quality planning - benefit/cost analysis, benchmarking, flowcharting, cause and effect diagrams, and cost of quality - are also used in quality assurance. The specific type of flowchart used for quality assurance is also a cause and effect chart, which is the same one covered as part of quality planning.

Quality Control

Quality control looks at specific results to determine if they conform to the quality standards. It involves both product and project deliverables, and is done *throughout the project* – not just at the end.

Quality control typically uses statistical sampling rather than looking at each and every output. Many volumes have been written about sampling techniques, and the practice is often very complex and is highly tailored to industry. For the purpose of the exam, you should memorize that statistical sampling, or random sampling, inspects a subset of the whole population.

Control uses the tool of inspection to make sure the results of the work are what they are supposed to be. Any time you find a part being inspected for quality, you can be sure that you are in the control process.

There are four tools associated with quality control: inspection, charts, statistical sampling, and trend analysis. Each of these is discussed below.

Inspection

Inspection involves looking at the results of a single activity or the overall process to evaluate conformance to quality.

Charts

Three types of charts associated with quality control that frequently appear on the PMP exam are control charts, flow charts (specifically cause and effect charts) and Pareto diagrams. Control and Pareto charts are discussed in this section, and cause and effect charts were covered earlier in this chapter as part of quality planning.

Control Charts

If a process is statistically "in control", it does not need to be corrected. If it is "out of control", then there are sufficient variations in results that must be brought back statistically in line. A control chart is one way of depicting variations and determining whether or not the process is in control

Control charts graph the results of a process to show whether or not they are in control. The mean of all of the data points is represented by a line drawn through the average of all data points on the chart. The upper and lower control limits are set at 3 standard deviations above and below mean.

If measurements fall outside of the control limits, then the process is said to be out of control. The assignable cause should then be determined.

An interesting rule that is used with control charts is known as the rule of 7. It states that if 7 or more consecutive data points fall on one side of the mean, they should be investigated. This is true even if the 7 data points are within the control limits.

Some control charts, especially those used in a manufacturing environment, represent the upper and lower limits of a customer's specification for quality as lines on the control chart. Everything between those lines would be considered within the customer's quality specification.

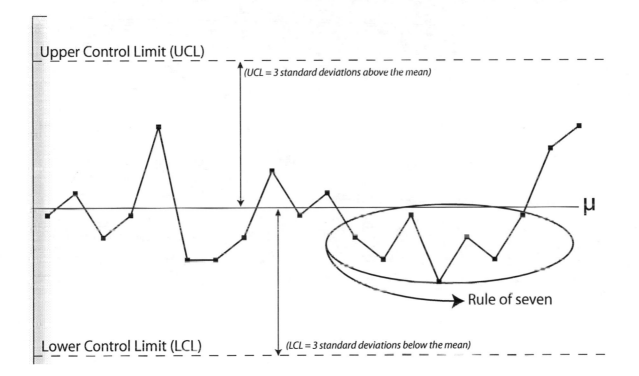

Pareto Diagram

Another type of chart used as a tool of quality control is the Pareto diagram. This is a histogram showing defects ranked from greatest to least. It is used to focus energy on the problems most likely to change results.

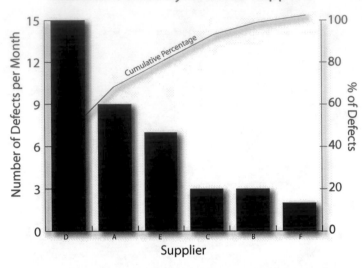

Sample Pareto Diagram showing a ranking of problems by supplier

Pareto's Law

Pareto diagrams are based on Pareto's Law, which is also known as the 80/20 rule. This rule states that 80% of the problems come from 20% of the causes, but there are variations on this theme. For the exam, know that Pareto's Law is also known as the 80/20 rule and that a Pareto chart is used to help determine the few root causes behind the majority of the problems on a project.

Statistical Sampling

Statistical sampling involves taking a sample (usually a random sample) of products or results from a population to evaluate their adherence to quality. A properly derived random sample in a normally distributed population will yield the same statistics as sampling the entire population, but with much less work.

Statistical Independence

When the outcome of two processes are not linked together or dependent upon each other, they are statistically independent. Rolling a six on a die the first time neither increases nor decreases the chance that you will roll a six the second time. Therefore, the two rolls would be statistically independent.

Standard Deviation

The standard deviation is a measurement of how diverse your sample is by measuring how far the sample varies from the average.

Mutually Exclusive

A statistical term that states that one choice excludes the others. For example, painting a house yellow and painting it blue or white are mutually exclusive events.

Trend Analysis

Trend analysis is a tool used in the quality control process that looks at previous quality performance to predict future results. This can be used to predict such things as number of defects or errors, rework, time and cost as it relates to quality, or similar indicators.[5]

Trend analysis is mathematical in nature and can be highly sophisticated in actual practice.

Going Deeper

Daniel, Wayne W; Terrel, James C. *Business Statistics.* Houghton Mifflin.

Kazmier, Leonard J. *Schaum's Outline of Theory and Problems of Business Statistics.* New York: McGraw-Hill Professional.

McLeary, Joseph Webb. *By the Numbers: Using Facts and Figures to Get Your Projects and Plans Approved.* New York: AMACOM.

Ryan, Thomas P. *Statistical Methods for Quality Improvement.* New York John Wiley & Sons, Inc. (US), 2000.

Quality Management Questions

1. You are a project manager, and your boss wants to meet with you to evaluate your project's performance in order to see how it is meeting the quality standards supplied by the company. In what process is your boss engaged?

    A. Total Quality Management.
    B. Quality control.
    C. Quality planning.
    D. Quality assurance.

2. If you were using a fishbone diagram to determine how factors might be linked to potential problems, you would you be involved in:

    A. Quality inspection.
    B. Quality prevention.
    C. Quality planning.
    D. Quality assurance.

3. Quality planning includes all of the following outputs EXCEPT:

    A. Quality management plan.
    B. Acceptance.
    C. Operational definitions.
    D. Checklists.

4. In a control chart, the mean is represented as a horizontal line on the control chart. This represents:

    A. The average of the control limits.
    B. The average of all data points.
    C. The average of all data points that are within specification.
    D. A means of identifying assignable cause.

5.   Quality audits are an important part of quality management because:

A. They allow for quantification of the risk.

B. They randomly audit product results to see if they are meeting quality standards.

C. They check to see if the quality process is being followed.

D. They are conducted without prior notice and do not allow team members time to cover up defects.

6.   If the results of activity A have no bearing on the results of activity B, the two activity would be considered:

A. Statistically unique.

B. Statistically independent.

C. Correlated, but not causal.

D. Mutually exclusive.

7.   The BEST tool to use to look for results that are out of control is:

A. Pareto chart.

B. Control chart.

C. Ishikawa diagram.

D. Statistical sampling.

8.   You are a project manager with limited resources on the project. Several quality defects have been discovered, causing the stakeholders concern. You wish to begin by attacking the causes that have the highest number of defects associated with them. Which tool shows defects by volume from greatest to least?

A. Pareto chart.

B. Control chart.

C. Ishikawa diagram.

D. Cause and effect diagram.

9.   In the process of managing a construction project, you discover a
        very serious defect in the way one particular section has been built.
        Your engineers analyze the section of the building and decide that the
        problem is actually relatively minor. In which process are you involved?

        A. Quality planning.
        B. Quality assurance.
        C. Quality control.
        D. Quality management.

10.   You are performing a project that has a lot in common with a project
        completed by your company two years ago. You want to use the
        previous project to help you determine quality standards for your
        project. Which of the following tools would be the BEST one to help
        you with this?

        A. Benchmarking.
        B. Control chart.
        C. ISO 9000.
        D. Total Quality Management.

11.   Which of the following is most representative of the Total Quality
        Management philosophy?

        A. Decreasing inventory to zero or near zero levels.
        B. Everyone can contribute to quality.
        C. Zero defects.
        D. Prevention is more important than inspection.

12.   Which of these quality standards is the highest?

        A. It is impossible to determine without further information.
        B. 99% quality.
        C. Three sigma quality.
        D. Six sigma quality.

13. Which quality process is performed first?

    A. Quality planning.

    B. Quality assurance.

    C. Quality control.

    D. Quality definition.

14. The standard deviation represents:

    A. The variance of all of the measurements.

    B. The average of deviations of individual values from the mean.

    C. The accuracy of the sample.

    D. The single best measure of quality.

15. On a control chart, the customer's acceptable quality limits are represented as:

    A. Control limits.

    B. Mean.

    C. Specification.

    D. Normal distribution.

16. A customer is concerned that the quality process is not being followed as laid out in the quality management plan. The best way to see if this claim is accurate is:

    A. Random sampling.

    B. Kaizen.

    C. Personally participate in the quality inspections.

    D. Audits.

17. Your organization practices just-in-time management. Which of the following would be the highest concern for a project manager operating in this company?

    A. Absenteeism.

    B. Lower quality of parts.

    C. Conflicting quality processes.

    D. Inventory arriving late.

18.   Reduced quality on a project would MOST likely lead to which of the following?

   A. Rework and increased cost risk.

   B. Absenteeism and decreased cost.

   C. Increased inspections and decreased cost.

   D. Reduced quality limits.

19.   Which of the following is NOT a part of the quality planning process?

   A. Benchmarking.

   B. Audits.

   C. Flowcharting.

   D. Design of experiments.

20.   A project manager wants to perform a code review, but to date over two million lines of code have been written for this project, and more are being produced every day. Rather than reviewing each line of code, the manager should consider:

   A. Automated testing tools.

   B. Trend analysis.

   C. Statistical sampling.

   D. Regression analysis.

Answers to Quality Management Questions

1. D. In this example your boss is auditing you to see if you are following the process. Remember that audits are a tool of quality assurance.

2. C. Quality planning is the correct answer here. Other than the big clue of "fishbone diagram", the words to key in on here were "might" and "potential". We aren't looking at actual problems, but ones that could happen. These are activities of quality planning, and the fishbone diagram is a tool used in the quality planning process.

3. B. Acceptance is not an output of quality planning. It is an output of quality control.

4. B. The mean represents the average of all of the data points shown on the chart, calculated simply by adding the values together and dividing by the number of values.

5. C. Audits are a tool of quality assurance that check to see if the process is being followed. Choices 'A' and 'D' are incorrect, and choice 'B' is referring to inspection, which is a tool of quality control.

6. B. If two events have no bearing on each other, they are statistically independent. Choice 'D' is when two events cannot both happen at the same time.

7. B. That is how a control chart is used. It visually depicts whether a process is in or out of control. Choice 'A' is used in quality control to rank problems by frequency. 'C', is used in quality planning to anticipate problems in advance. Choice 'D' is used in quality control to pick random samples to inspect.

8. A. Pareto charts rank defects from greatest to least, showing you what should get the most attention.

9. C. Quality control is the best choice here. Your clue here was the fact that your engineers had inspected something specific. This wasn't related to planning or process – it was a physical inspection of a work result, and that is what happens during the quality control process.

10. A. Benchmarking takes results from previous projects and uses them to help measure quality on your project. Benchmarks give you something against which you can measure.

11.   B. Total Quality Management stresses, among other things, that everyone contributes to the quality of the product and process.

12.   D. Six sigma represents 99.99966% of all work results that will be of acceptable quality in the manufacturing process. This is higher than 99% or 3 sigma, which represents a 99.73% quality rate.

13.   A. Quality planning should always happen first. Quality assurance and quality control would come after the quality management plan is in place. 'D' is not a PMI process. Keep in mind that the quality processes do run in a cycle, but planning should always happen first.

14.   B. The standard deviation measures how far each sample deviates from the average (mean), and then averages all of those deviations.

15.   C. The quality specification is the customer's quality requirements. 'A' represents the limits for what is in and out of statistical control, typically set at three standard deviations from the mean. 'B' is the average of all of the data points. 'D' is a statistical term relating to the way the data points are scattered.

16.   D. Audits, part of the quality assurance process, review the process and make sure that the process is being followed.

17.   D. The PMP Exam has several questions structured like this one. You could have any of the problems listed here, but the one you would be most concerned with is parts arriving late. An organization that practices just-in-time (JIT) does not keep spare inventory on hand.

18.   A. Rework and increased cost are likely outcomes of low quality. 'B' and 'C' are incorrect since decreased cost is not related to low quality. 'D' is incorrect, because you would not lower the quality limits or specifications just because the quality is bad.

19.   B. Audits are part of quality assurance. Choices 'A', 'C', and 'D' are all part of quality planning.

20.   C. Statistical sampling (may appear as random sampling) is the best choice. If the overall population is too large, accurate sampling can give you the same statistical results as measuring the entire population.

Human Resources

Difficulty	Memorization	Exam Importance	Corresponding PMBOK Chapter
Low	Medium	Medium	Chapter 9

Although the PMBOK treats the subject of human resources management lightly, you should expect several questions on the exam that cover a variety of theories, including leadership, motivation, conflict resolution, and roles within a project.

The content for this area of the test is drawn from basic management theory, organizational behavior, psychology, and of course, the field of human resources. If you have ever formally studied these subjects, you have probably been exposed to many of the theories in this chapter.

In managing a project, the project manager must also lead people. Some project managers may excel at organizing tasks and planning activities and be dismal at motivating other people.

This chapter covers the processes, inputs, tools, and outputs you will need to know in order to pass the exam.

Philosophy

PMI's approach to the area of human resource management is to define a role for everyone on the project and to define the responsibilities for each of these roles. Many people make the mistake of only understanding the role of the project manager, and never understanding the proper role of senior management, the sponsor, or the team. Instead of merely looking at their own role on the project, project managers must help define the roles and influence everyone who has a role on the project.

The processes of Project HR Management with their *primary* outputs

Human Resources Management

Organizational Planning

Roles and Responsibilities
Staffing
Management Plan

Staff Acquisition

Project Staff Assigned

Team Development

Performance
Improvement

PMI's philosophy of leadership and power are based on the realization that the project manager is rarely given complete and unquestioned authority on a project. Instead, he must be able to motivate and persuade people to act in the best interest of the project. He must be able to build a team and lead members to give their best effort to the project.

Importance

After professional responsibility, human resource management questions are considered by many people to be the easiest questions on the exam. This is because this is one of the few sections where many of the questions can be answered by using common sense. Unless you find these questions particularly difficult, it is a good idea to get comfortable with the information in this chapter and focus your attention on more challenging subject matter. A quick review of the theories and content prior to taking the exam should be adequate to help you through this section.

Preparation

The focus of this chapter will be on roles and responsibilities, motivational theories, forms of power, and leadership styles. In order to help you learn the critical material, several exercises have been added. While this knowledge area is considered to be one of the easiest ones, take the time to learn it. Questions from this section will appear on the exam.

This chapter, in particular, contains a significant amount of content that is not found in the PMBOK.

Project Manager's Responsibilities

The area of human resource management is one in which project managers exert much skill and effort. Among other project responsibilities, the project manager must:

- Negotiate with the functional managers to ensure that he gets a competent, committed staff
- Assign all project staff based on the needs of the project
- Create the project team directory
- Create the formal staffing management plan, which shows how everyone on the team will participate on the project
- Make sure the necessary staff training takes place
- Build the team, including rewards and training

These duties are divided into three processes: organizational planning, staff acquisition (both planning processes), and team development (an executing process).

Leading vs. Managing

There is a difference between leading and managing on a project. Managing has been defined as being about producing key results[1], while leading involves establishing direction, aligning people to that direction, and motivating and inspiring.[2]

There are several different styles of leading that are recognized throughout the field of project management. The following graphic may prove very helpful for the exam. In the early phases of the project, the project manager should take a very active role in the leadership of the project, usually directing the activities and providing significant leadership. As the project progresses, however, other styles of leading may be more appropriate. These styles of leading are less heavy-handed. Of course, the particular style of leading needed will vary from one project to the next.

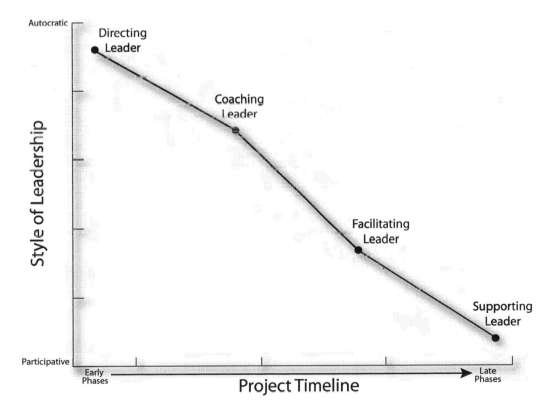

Organizational Planning

The process of organizational planning is primarily concerned with identifying and assigning roles and responsibilities for the project. Everyone on a project has a function, or role, and each role is accompanied by responsibilities. It is important for the project manager to understand those roles and responsibilities and help influence people in other roles in order to keep the project running smoothly.

The PMP exam typically has numerous questions that require an understanding of the roles on the following page:

Role	Explanation
Project manager	The project manager is ultimately responsible for the project. He is the person who uses company resources to accomplish the project goals. The project manager is empowered and responsible for delivering the best project that meets the business need. He is the one who communicates with the customer on performance and schedule issues.[3]
Functional Manager	The functional manager owns the resources. The functional manager will have more, less, or a shared amount of power with the project manager, depending on the organizational structure. The functional manager is responsible for any human resource activities, for their resources on a project, including reviews, disciplinary action, and issues of utilization. Since resources report to functional managers in most organizations, the functional manager is often involved in setting priorities.
Senior Management	For the exam, think of senior management as anyone who is above the project manager in the organization. Senior management prioritizes projects within the organization, helps define communication needs, resolves organization conflicts, and issues the project charter, which officially creates the project and gives the project manager formal authority. It is also senior management's role to create a productive environment for the project, including shielding the project from external influences.
Sponsor	The sponsor and the project manager are the owners of the project.[4] The sponsor usually comes from senior management,[5] but may be the customer in some cases. He communicates with the customer on cost and deliverables, and is responsible for funding the project. The sponsor formally accepts the product during scope verification and administrative closure and provides guidance to the project manager on objectives, planning, and key decisions. If the project manager is unable to resolve an issue with the customer on a project-related issue, the sponsor may get involved to work with the customer to reach resolution.
Stakeholder(s)	Anyone who has an interest (good or bad) in the project's outcome is a stakeholder. Stakeholders must be identified and prioritized, their needs must be understood, and they must be kept informed.
Team	The project team consists of everyone who is assigned work on the project. They participate in the creation of the project plan and need to be active in estimating and to buy into the estimates that are provided.

Organizational Planning

Outputs of Organizational Planning

When organizational planning is complete, two main documents will result: a responsibility assignment matrix (RAM), and a staffing management plan.

Responsibility Assignment Matrix

A responsibility assignment matrix is a means of assigning the project work to different project roles and specifying what responsibility each role has. It does not show when or how long these resources will be needed.

Role / Work Package	Project Manager	Business Analyst	Data Architect	Application Architect	Jr. Programmer	Sr. Programmer	Quality Control
Document scope	R	A					S
Review scope	A	P	R	R	R	R	R
Approve scope	A	S	S	S	S	S	S
Create database	R	R	A	P			
Design application	I	P	P	A	I	I	R
Code application	I	I	I	P	P	A	R
Application testing	P	P	P	P	P	P	A

A = Accountable, **I** = Input Required, **P** = Participant, **R** = Review, **S** = Signature Required

The roles on the RAM will usually be updated later in the project to include actual names or departments.

Staffing Management Plan

The staffing management plan is similar to other management plans discussed previously, but it focuses on how human resources will be managed, describing how individual team members will be included and then released from the project.

Resource Histogram

A resource histogram is a column chart that is frequently used in a staffing management plan. (See example following.) It simply shows the usage for resources for a given period of time. Typically resources increase from planning through executing, falling off in control and closure.

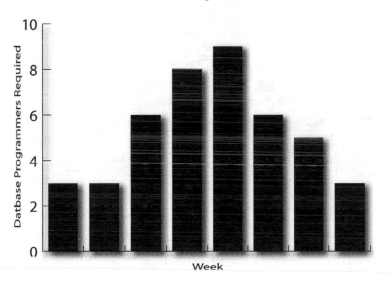

Database Programmers

Sample Resource Histogram

Staff Acquisition

Not much material from the staff acquisition process is essential for exam preparation. You do need to know that acquiring team members often requires negotiation (covered in Chapter 9 - Communications Management) and may also involve procurement (covered in Chapter 11 – Procurement Management) if you bring in staff outside of your organization.

One thing many people find confusing is that staff acquisition is a planning process and not an executing process. At this point, resources are being assigned, but the actual work of the project is not being executed.

Team Development

Team Development

The bulk of material on the exam relating to human resource management comes from the process of team development, which is an executing process. Team development requires a basic understanding of general leadership theory and skills, conflict management theory, and reward/recognition systems. An explanation of each of these theories and terms are described below.

Management by Objectives (MBO)

The principle behind MBO is to ensure that an organization's teams and team members have a clear understanding of the company's objectives, as well as an awareness of their roles and responsibilities in achieving those objectives. MBO is a technique used to encourage self-leadership within an organization, letting the objective motivate the person instead of the manager or the task doing so.

In order for MBO to work properly the objectives must be clearly defined and visible, the project work should be aligned to those objectives, and team members should understand how their roles and activites on a project directly support their organizational objectives.

In an organization that uses MBO, objectives and performance are reviewed periodically to evaluate how managers and teams are performing.

General Leadership Theory/Skills

The most important subject within the area of general management skills is the topic of power. Power is the ability to influence the behavior of others. It may be positive, as in the example of providing a reward for a job well done, or negative, as in the example of firing someone for making a mistake.

There are a variety of forms of power recognized in organizational theory. You should know the following forms of power for the exam:

Reward Power

Reward power is the ability to give rewards and recognition. Examples include a pay raise, time off, or any other type of reward that would motivate the person.

Expert Power

Expert power exists when the manager is an expert on the subject. For instance, the person who architected a part of a software system would probably have significant expert power on a project that used that system. People would listen to the architect because he had credibility. A subject matter expert usually has significant power to influence and control behavior.

Legitimate

Also known as formal power, legitimate power is the power that the manager has because of his position. This type of power comes from being formally in charge of the project and the people and has the backing of the organization.

Strong, broad-based, formal authority for a project manager is unusual[6] and would usually indicate a projectized organizational structure.

Referent

Referent power is a form of power that is based on respect or the charismatic personality of the manager. It is ultimately rooted in a persuasive ability with people. Another usage of referent power is when a less powerful person allies with a more powerful person and leverages some of the superior's power. For instance, if the project manager is very close to the CEO of the company, his power will probably be higher because of that alliance.

Punishment

Also known as coercive power, this type of influence is the ability to punish an employee or withhold a reward from them if a goal is not met. "If this module does not pass quality control by the end of next week, you are all fired" would be an example of a manager using punishment power.

Best Forms of Power

In addition to being able to identify the different types of power a project manager can use, you should also know that PMI considers reward and expert the most effective forms of power and punishment the least effective.

Conflict Management

Consider for a moment the problem of a door that is stuck shut. There are several ways to approach this problem:

- You may want to throw your weight against the door, pounding it with your shoulder.
- You might elect to try to go in the room from another point of entry.
- You could try to take the hinges off the door to make it come apart.
- You might choose to ignore the problem of the stuck door, avoiding it altogether, or hope someone else will take care of it.
- You could attempt to find out why the door was stuck in the first place and deal with that problem.

In the same way there are several ways to approach conflict resolution. Because conflict is inevitable, you should be aware of the common ways of handling it:

Problem-Solving

Problem-solving involves confrontation, but it is confrontation of the problem and not the person! It means dealing with the problem head on. Using this technique, the project manager gets to the bottom of the problem and resolves the root causes of the conflict.

Although the word "confrontation" may have negative connotations, this type of conflict resolution is highly favored, as it is proactive, direct, and deals with the root of the problem. Consequently, it is most often the correct answer on the exam when questions of conflict resolution arise.

Compromise

Compromise takes place when both parties sacrifice something for the sake of reaching an agreement. On the test, compromise may be presented as "lose – lose" since both parties give up something.

Forcing

Forcing is exactly what the name implies. It is bringing to bear whatever force or power is necessary to get the door open. Although forcing may work well in the case of a stuck door, this is considered to be the worst way to resolve project conflict. Forcing doesn't help resolve the underlying problems, it reduces team morale, and it is almost never a good long-term solution.

Smoothing

Using smoothing, the project manager plays down the problem and turns attention to what is going well. The statement "We shouldn't be arguing with each other. Look at how well we've done so far, and we're ahead of schedule," would be an example of smoothing.

Smoothing downplays conflict instead of dealing with it head on and does not produce a solution to the conflict. Instead, smoothing merely tries to diminish the problem.

Withdrawal

Withdrawal is technically not a conflict resolution technique but a means of avoidance. A project manager practicing withdrawal is merely hoping the problem will go away by itself. Needless to say, PMI does not favor this method of conflict resolution because the conflict is never resolved.

Constructive and Destructive Team Roles

Related to the area of conflict management is the project manager's ability to recognize and deal with constructive and destructive roles on his or her team.

Constructive Team Roles	
• Initiators	• Clarifiers
• Information seekers	• Harmonizers
• Information givers	• Summarizers
• Encouragers	• Gate Keepers

Destructive Team Roles	
• Aggressors	• Topic Jumper
• Blockers	• Dominator
• Withdrawers	• Devil's Advocate
• Recognition Seekers	

Constructive Team Roles

Initiators

An initiator is someone who actively initiates ideas and activities on a project. This role is considered positive because it is proactive and can be highly productive.

Team Development

Information seekers

Information seekers are people on the team who actively seek to gain more knowledge and understanding related to the project. This is a positive role because fostering an understanding among the team is important, and open communication should be valued.

Information givers

An information giver, as its name implies, is someone who openly shares information with the team. Although not all information may be shared (for instance Classified, or Secret information must be kept confidential), the overarching principal is to foster good communication and a good flow of information on the project.

Encouragers

Encouragers maintain a positive and realistic attitude. On the project, they focus on what can be accomplished, not on what is impossible. This is a positive role because it contributes to team morale.

Clarifiers

A clarifier, as the name suggests, is someone who works to make certain that everyone's understanding of the project is the same. This is a positive role because it ensures that everyone has a common understanding of the project goals and details.

Harmonizers

In music, harmony is not the same as the melody, but it compliments and enhances the melody. Similarly, a harmonizer on the project will enhance information in such a way that understanding is increased. This is a positive role because the overall understanding of the project and the project context, or the details surrounding it, is enhanced.

Summarizers

Summarizers take the details and restate them succinctly or relate them back to the big picture. This is a positive role because details on the project may become overwhelming, but the summarizer can keep things simple enough for everyone to understand the higher purpose of the tasks.

Gate Keepers

The term *gate keeper* has two possible uses in project management literature. The first definition is used differently in project management than it is in other business disciplines. A gate keeper is someone who draws others in. Someone who says, "We haven't heard from the other end of the table today," would be an example of a gate-keeper.[7] This is a very positive role because it encourages the entire team to participate on the project.

The other usage comes from someone who judges whether the project should continue at different stages (known as the stage-gate approach). This gate-keeper makes decisions about whether the project is still achieving the business need and if it is justified in continuing to a subsequent phase.[8]

Both of these usages of gate-keeper are considered to be constructive roles on the project.

Destructive Team Roles

The effective project manager will be able to identify destructive roles within the team and diminish or eliminate them.[9]

Aggressors

An aggressor is someone who is openly hostile and opposed to the project. This is a negative role because it serves no productive purpose on the project.

Blockers

A blocker is someone who blocks access to information and tries to interrupt the flow of communication. This is a negative role because of the disruptive effect poor communication can have on a project.

Withdrawers

A withdrawer does not participate in discussion, resolution, or even the fleshing out of ideas. Instead, he is more likely to sit quietly or not participate at all. This is a negative role because it usually produces a team member that does not buy in to the project and can have a negative effect on the overall team morale.

Recognition Seekers

A recognition seeker looks at the project to see what is in it for him. He is more interested in his own benefit rather than the project's success. This is a negative role because of the damaging effect on team morale and because a recognition seeker may ultimately jeopardize the project if doing so somehow personally benefits him.

Team Development

Topic Jumper

A topic jumper disrupts effective communication by constantly changing the subject and bringing up irrelevant facts. This is a negative role[10] because it prevents topics from being fully discussed and brought to closure.

Dominator

The dominator is someone who disrupts team participation and communication by presenting their opinion forcefully and without considering the merit of others' contributions. He will likely talk more than the rest of the group and will bully his way through the project. This is a negative role[11] because valid opinions are often quashed, and the project may take on a one-dimensional quality.

Devil's Advocate

A devil's advocate is someone who will automatically take a contrary view to most statements or suggestions that are made. This may be a positive or negative role on the project, but it is most often associated with a negative role since it often disrupts and frustrates communication and discourages people from participating.

Sources of Conflict

One last area of conflict management you should understand is based on research that suggests that the greatest project conflict occurs between project managers and functional managers. Most conflict on a project is the result of disagreements over schedules, priorities, and resources. This finding runs contrary to a commonly held belief that most conflicts are the result of personality differences. If you see a question asking you the cause of most conflict on a project, the best answer will be one related to project schedules and priorities.[12]

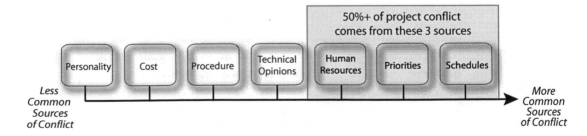

Reward and Recognition Systems

Maslow's Hierarchy of Needs

Maslow's Hierarchy of Needs is a basic theory of human motivation that project managers should understand. Abraham Maslow grouped human needs into five basic categories as illustrated in the following diagram.

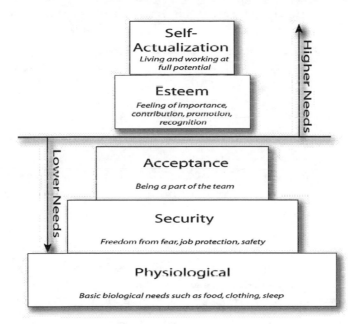

Maslow's theory states that these needs form a hierarchy, since the needs at the bottom must be satisfied before the upper needs will be present.[13] As an example, people cannot reach their full potential if they do not have sufficient food or safety.

Every project manager should understand the needs of the team members and how they interrelate so that he can help them to perform at their full potential.

McGregor's Theory X and Theory Y

McGregor's organizational theory states that there are two ways to categorize and understand people in the workplace.

Managers who ascribe to Theory X presume that people are only interested in their own selfish goals. They are unmotivated, they dislike work, and they must be forced to do productive work. Theory X managers believe that constant supervision is necessary to achieve desired results on a project.

Those who practice Theory Y assume that people are naturally motivated to do good work. "Y managers" believe that their team members need very little external motivation and can be trusted to work toward the organization's or project's goals.[14]

An assembly line organization may treat everyone as an "X Person," monitoring and measuring every move, whereas an organization that encourages telecommuting might be more prone to treat employees as "Y People." However, it should be understood that it is the manager, not the organization, that ascribes to Theory X or Theory Y, and the style of management is not determined by the type of work being performed.

Contingency Theory

The Contingency Theory, developed by Fred E. Fiedler in the 1960s and 1970s, states that a leader's effectiveness is contingent upon two sets of factors. The first set of factors measures whether the leader is task-oriented or relationship-oriented. The second set evaluates situational factors in the workplace, such as how stressful the environment is.[15]

The practical application of this theory suggests that in stressful times, a task-oriented leader will be more effective, while in relatively calm times, a relationship-oriented leader will function more effectively. The inverse is also true. What makes a leader effective in one setting may actually work against him in another.

Herzberg's Motivation-Hygiene Theory

This theory has nothing to do with personal hygiene as the name might incorrectly cause you to conclude. Instead, Herzberg conducted studies to quantify what factors influence satisfaction at work.

Similar to Maslow's theory, Herzberg's Motivational-Hygiene theory states that the presence of certain factors does not make someone satisfied, but their absence will make someone unsatisfied. In this case, hygiene factors must be present, but they do not motivate by themselves. Motivation factors will motivate, but they will not work without the hygiene factors in place.[16]

Hygiene Factors	Motivation Factors
Company Policy	Achievement
Supervision	Recognition
Good relationship with boss	Work
Working conditions	Responsibility
Paycheck	Advancement
Personal life	Growth
Status	
Security	
Relationship with co-workers	

Herzberg's theory is based on the assumption that workers want and expect to find meaning through their work.[17]

Expectancy Theory

The expectancy theory states that the anticipation of a reward or good outcome is a motivation. This theory is often employed in training animals, and it relies on providing a reward for a job well done.[18]

For instance, if you promise your team a day off if a certain milestone is achieved, that would possibly motivate them to work harder to reach that goal, but expectancy theory only works if the person or team believes the outcome is achievable. If a sales team is promised a $10,000 bonus if they reach a goal but none of them believe the goal is remotely possible, they will probably not be motivated by the reward and will not work harder to reach the goal.

Achievement Theory

Achievement theory states that people need three things: achievement, power, and affiliation.

Achievement is the desire to accomplish something significant. Power is the desire to influence the behavior of others. Affiliation is the desire to belong to a group, or to fit in with your coworkers.

Achievement theory focuses on using these three human desires as the means to motivate employees.

Collocation

Collocation is a term that refers to building team unity by locating all team members in the same physical work space, with adjoining cubicles or offices. A "war room" is a type of collocation in which one room or area within the project office is set aside for the exclusive use of the

Team Development

project team for meetings, information centers, or other types of team collaboration.

Collocation can be with the team or even with the customer. It can be a powerful tool for team building and resolving communication problems.

Gaining Commitment

Except in a very few organizations, the project manager must share power with functional managers and others. In these situations, it can be very challenging to gain project team member commitment, since these team members typically report to the project manager with a "dotted line."

As such, one of the key leadership challenges for the project manager is to gain commitment from team members and functional managers so that everyone is working toward the common goals of the project.[19]

Two tools for gaining commitment are presented below:

Organizational alignment

Make sure the team knows how the project is aligned with the company's vision. This will ensure that they feel "relevant." If the project is not aligned with the organization, make sure the team knows how this will help the organization to branch out or grow. Fostering a feeling of significance and relevance is key here.

Personal alignment

Sometimes more challenging than organizational alignment is to align the goals of the individuals with the goals of the team. Challenging work and opportunities for growth and advancement will motivate many people to work harder on the project. A manager can create a supportive environment for team members by providing such things as training, rewards, and opportunities for people to participate in leadership.

Team Development

Going Deeper

Kerr, Steven. *Ultimate Rewards: What Really Motivates People to Achieve.* Harvard Business Review Book Series, Boston, MA: Harvard Business School Press, 1997.

Meyer, John P., Allen, Natalie Jean. *Commitment in the Workplace: Theory, Research, and Application; Advanced Topics in Organizational Behavior.* Thousand Oaks, CA: Sage Publications, Inc. 1997.

Tracey, William R. *Human Resources Management & Development Handbook.* New York: AMACOM

Going Deeper

Human Resource Management Questions

(Note that some of the following human resources questions, especially those covering project roles and organizational structures, relate to material found in chapters 2 and 3 as well as this chapter).

1. If you hear a project manager saying to a customer "We all agree that this project is important. Let's not fight over a few thousand dollars," what conflict resolution technique is the project manager trying to use?

    A. Smoothing.

    B. Problem Solving.

    C. Forcing.

    D. Compromising.

2. Who manages the resources in a matrix organization?

    A. Senior management.

    B. Functional managers.

    C. Project manager.

    D. Human resources.

3. What is considered the LEAST desirable form of power for a project manager to exercise?

    A. Formal.

    B. Referent.

    C. Punishment.

    D. Forcing.

4. Which statement below BEST matches a Theory X manager's beliefs:

    A. People want to be rewarded for their work.

    B. People have higher needs that will not emerge until the lower needs have been satisfied.

    C. People will contribute to work if left alone.

    D. People can not be trusted.

5.   The staffing management plan:

   A. Must be created by human resources.
   B. Is a part of the resource management plan.
   C. Is a tool of team development.
   D. Is an output of the organizational planning process.

6.   Which problem solving technique produces the most lasting results?

   A. Confrontation.
   B. Smoothing.
   C. Compromising.
   D. Withdrawing.

7.   The most important role of the project sponsor is to:

   A. Manage and resolve conflicts between the team and upper management.
   B. Provide and protect the project's financial resources.
   C. Provide and protect the project's human resources.
   D. Balance the project's constraints regarding time, scope, and cost.

8.   Human resource management encompasses:

   A. Organizational planning, staff acquisition, and performance reporting.
   B. Resource planning, staff acquisition, and performance reporting.
   C. Resource planning, staff acquisition, and team development.
   D. Organizational planning, staff acquisition, and team development.

9.   Which of the following is NOT an input into organizational planning?

   A. Project interfaces.
   B. Role and responsibility assignments.
   C. Staffing requirements.
   D. Constraints.

10.   Which of the following is a constructive team role?

   A. Information seeker.
   B. Recognition seeker.
   C. Blocker.
   D. Devil's advocate.

11. Maslow's Hierarchy of Needs theory concludes that:

   A. The strongest motivation for work is to provide for physiological needs.
   B. Hygiene factors are those that provide physical safety and emotional security.
   C. Psychological needs for growth and fulfillment can be met only when lower-level physical or security needs have been fulfilled.
   D. The greater the financial reward, the more motivated the workers will be.

12. Which of the following is NOT true of team building?

   A. Team agreement should be obtained on all major actions.
   B. Team building requires role modeling on the part of the project manager.
   C. Team building becomes less important as the project progresses.
   D. Teamwork cannot be forced.

13. Team building is primarily the responsibility of:

   A. The project team.
   B. The project manager.
   C. Senior management.
   D. The project sponsor.

14. A war room is an example of:

   A. Contract negotiation tactics.
   B. Resource planning tools.
   C. A functional organization.
   D. Collocation.

15. Which of the following is NOT a process of human resources management?

   A. Staff acquisition.
   B. Organizational planning.
   C. Resource planning.
   D. Team development.

16. A project coordinator is distinguished from a project manager in that:

    A. A project coordinator has no decision-making power.

    B. A project coordinator has less decision-making power.

    C. A project coordinator has no authority to assign work.

    D. A project coordinator takes on larger projects than a project manager.

17. Which of the following is not a tool used in team development?

    A. Reward and recognition systems.

    B. General management skills.

    C. Collocation.

    D. Interviewing.

18. One potential disadvantage of a matrix organization is:

    A. Highly visible project objectives.

    B. Rapid responses to contingencies.

    C. Team members must report to more than one boss.

    D. The matrix organization creates morale problems.

19. A project manager in Detroit is having difficulty getting the engineers in his company's Cleveland office to complete design documents for his project. He has sent numerous requests to the VP of Engineering (also in Cleveland) for assistance in getting the design documents, but so far his efforts have been unsuccessful. What kind of organization does this project manager work in?

    A. Functional.

    B. Hierarchical.

    C. Strong matrix.

    D. Projectized.

20. A responsibility assignment matrix is the output of:

    A. Resource planning

    B. Organizational planning

    C. Staff acquisition

    D. Team development

Answers to Human Resource Management Questions

1. A. Smoothing occurs when the person trying to resolve the conflict asks everyone to focus on what they agree upon and diminishes the items on which there is disagreement.

2. B. The functional manager has resource responsibilities in a matrix organization. In this type of organizational structure, the project manager must work with the functional managers to secure resources for a project.

3. C. Punishment. 'D' is a problem solving technique – not a form of power.

4. D. Theory X managers believe that people cannot be trusted and must be watched and managed constantly.

5. D. The staffing management plan is created during the organizational planning process.

6. A. Confrontation is getting to the root of the problem and is the best way to produce a lasting result and a real solution.

7. B. The project sponsor provides the funds for the project. He may or may not take on other roles, but this is his defining role on the project.

8. D. Resource planning is a cost management process and performance reporting is a communications management process.

9. B. Role and responsibility assignments are the result, or output, of organizational planning.

10. A. Information seeker. Recognition seekers are more concerned with getting in the spotlight than with facilitating communication. Blockers reject others' viewpoints and shut down discussion. Devil's advocate – bringing up alternative viewpoints - can be either positive or negative, but it is listed in most project management literature as a destructive team role because when it is negative it is very negative! Information seekers are constructive because they ask questions to gain information.

11. C. This question might have been difficult for you. 'A' is not necessarily true, because Maslow stated that any level of his "pyramid," provides the greatest level of motivation when the needs of the levels below have

already been met. Thus physiological needs such as food and shelter will be the greatest motivator for workers to do a good job when those needs are unmet. But once the lower level needs are met, the needs of the next level become the greatest motivators.

12.   C. Successful team building *begins* early in project development, but it is a continuous process throughout the life of the project.

13.   B. Team building must be carried out under the direction of a strong leader. The project manager has the only project role that allows for regular, direct interaction with the team.

14.   D. Collocation is the practice of locating all team members in a central location, or collocation. Another variation of a war room is a conference room devoted exclusively to use by a particular project team. It is a tool of team development used in human resource management.

15.   C. Resource planning is a planning process that takes place as a part of cost management - not human resources management.

16.   B. A project coordinator has some authority and some decision making power, but less than a project manager.

17.   D. Interviewing is not a tool of team development! The process of team development occurs during project execution and involves motivating and supporting the existing team, not adding staff to the team.

18.   C. In a matrix organization, team members report to both the project manager and the functional manager. This can sometimes cause confusion and can lead to conflict on a project and within the organization.

19.   A. The clue in the question that indicates a functional organization is the project manager's low authority; he must appeal to the head of the engineering department rather than making his request directly to the team members.

20.   B. Resource planning is not a human resources management process. Organizational planning is the human resources process in which roles and responsibilities are assigned, often presented in a responsibility assignment matrix.

Communications Management

Difficulty	Memorization	Exam Importance	Corresponding PMBOK Chapter
Medium	Medium	Medium	Chapter 10

9

Communications management is considered to be one of the easier knowledge areas to study for the PMP. Although project communications management can be very political and tricky in an organization, the volume of material for the test and the difficulty is relatively low.

Many people who study this material are surprised that it is not related to the skill of communication through verbal and written media, in areas such as project writing styles, persuasion, and presentation methods, but that is not the focus of this chapter. Rather, communications management covers all tasks related to producing, compiling, sending, storing, distributing, and managing project records. This knowledge area is made up of processes to determine what to communicate, to whom, and how often. It involves understanding who your stakeholders are and what they need to know.

Communications management also requires that you accurately report on the project status, performance, change, and earned value, and that you pay close attention to the administrative project closure where permanent records are generated, updated and archived. Overall, it includes formal and proactive methods.

The processes of Project Communications Management with their *primary* outputs

Communications Management

Communications Planning
Communications Management Plan

Information Distribution
Project Records, Reports

Performance Reporting
Performance Reports
Change Requests

Administrative Closure
Project Closure
Archives
Lessons Learned

Philosophy

There is an old joke in project management circles about "mushroom project management," in which you manage projects the same way you grow mushrooms – by keeping everyone buried in manure, keeping them in the dark, and checking back periodically to see what has popped up.

PMI's philosophy is, as you may have guessed, quite different. It focuses on identifying who the stakeholders are and keeping them properly informed throughout the project. Communication under PMI's philosophy may be a mixture of formal and informal, written and verbal, but it is always proactive and thorough. It is essential that the project manager distribute accurate project information in a timely manner and to the right audience.

Importance

Communications management is of medium importance on the exam, bordering on high. You may see several questions that relate directly to this chapter, so it will be necessary to become acquainted with the terms and theories presented below.

Preparation

Although the volume of material in communications management is smaller than most of the other areas, there are key concepts that must be learned. Be prepared for several questions on the test specifically related to the process of administrative closure, as well as the inputs, tools and techniques, and outputs for each process. The reason the focus is on these areas is that they are formally defined, and most test takers do not find them intuitive.

Two other areas of key importance are the communications model and understanding channels of communication. You can expect to see questions about these on the exam.

There are not as many exam questions related to this section as there are to some of the others, and by carefully reviewing this chapter, and the exercises, you should be in good shape for the exam.

Communications Planning

In communications planning you determine the "who, what, when, and where" of communications. It involves a careful analysis of the stakeholders and a determination of what information they need, how it will be distributed, how often, and using what media. This is typically done very early on in a project. The outputs of this process are the communications requirements and the communications management plan.

Communications Management Plan

A simple, but accurate definition of the communications management plan is a document providing the details on the "who, what, when, and where" of communications. This plan provides all of the information necessary to explain how all project communications will be produced and distributed, as well as to whom, when, and how often. It also details how stakeholders can access information between status meetings or published reports.

Information Distribution

Information distribution is an executing process in which information is made available to project stakeholders; it is the execution of the communications management plan.

There are several key concepts related to information distribution that you should be familiar with for the exam: the communications model, communications methods, rules for meetings, and the project manager's role in communications. Also important are the model of communication channels and an understanding of communication blockers.

Communications Model

The communications model is a formal way of understanding how messages are sent and received. This model defines the responsibilities between the sender and the receiver.

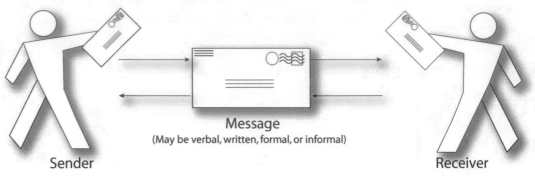

Message
(May be verbal, written, formal, or informal)

Sender   Receiver

The Communications Model

The sender's responsibilities are to:

- Encode the message clearly
- Select a communication method
- Send the message
- Confirm that the message was understood by the receiver

The receiver's responsibilities are to:

- Decode the message
- Confirm that the message was understood

Messages can be conveyed in verbal and nonverbal ways. Below are some terms related to different ways of communicating:

Active Listening

Active listening requires that the receiver takes active steps to ensure that the sender was understood. It is similar to effective listening (below).

Effective Listening

Effective listening requires the listener's full thought and attention. To be effective as a listener means to monitor non-verbal and physical communication and to provide feedback indicating whether the message has been clearly understood.

Feedback

Feedback refers to the verbal and nonverbal cues a speaker must monitor to see whether the listener fully comprehends the message. Nodding and smiling might be considered positive feedback and indicate that the message is understood and received, whereas nodding and a blank stare might indicate that the message needs to be re-coded for better communication. Asking questions or repeating the speaker's words are also ways to give feedback.

Non-Verbal

Nonverbal communication takes place through body language, such as facial expressions, posture, hand motions, etc. A good listener must attend to non-verbal communication.

Paralingual

Paralingual communication is vocal but not verbal – for example, tone of voice, volume, or pitch. A high-pitched squeal does not employ words but certainly communicates!

Methods of Communication

There are four methods of communication covered on the exam, and it is very important to understand what they are and how and when they are used. Many people find the difference between formal and informal to be non-intuitive the first time they encounter it. The methods of communication are covered in the following table.

Method	Examples	When used
Informal written	E-mail messages, memorandums	Used frequently on the project to convey information and communicate.
Formal written	Contracts, legal notices, project documents (e.g. the Charter), important project communications	Used infrequently, but essential for prominent documents that go into the project record. The project plan is a formal written document.
Informal verbal	Meetings, discussions, phone calls, conversations	Used to communicate information quickly and efficiently.
Formal verbal	Speeches, mass communications, presentations	Used for public relations, special events, company-wide announcements, sales.

Information Distribution

Be aware that not just the message but the medium determines whether a form of communication is formal or informal.

Effective Meetings

While meetings are an important part of good communication, effective and productive meetings are rare in the real world. Meetings should be held for a clear purpose and should involve only the people necessary.[1] Their main purpose is to make decisions and communicate decisions. Meetings with no clear purpose simply should not be held.

Following are ingredients to an effective meeting. Most of these should be intuitive, and test takers should focus on understanding the list rather than memorizing it:

- Clearly define the reason, issues, and processes for the meeting
- Establish clear objectives for the meeting
- Publish and follow a written agenda
- Have a structure for conducting the meeting
- Foster creative thinking
- Drive toward making decisions and not only toward discussion
- Listen and communicate collaboratively
- Control communication during the meeting. This does not mean that you micro-manage every detail of every discussion, but rather that you keep the discussion relevant and aligned with the topics
- Include all of the necessary people and only the necessary people. Meetings are important, but can be a tremendous waste of time
- Document the meeting through written minutes

Kickoff Meeting

The kickoff meeting is an opportunity to bring the team together, along with key stakeholders, the sponsor, the customer, and senior management and discuss the project plan. Additionally it is considered a good practice to share lessons learned from previous projects during the kickoff meeting.[2]

Project Manager's Role in Communications

The project manager's most important skill set is that of communication. It is integral to everything the project manager does. You may see questions on your exam asking you what the project manager's most important job or most important skills are, or how most of the project manager's time is spent. The answer is usually related to communications. It is estimated that an effective project manager spends about 90% of his time communicating[3], and fully 50% of that time is spent communciating with the project team.

Also note that while communications take up a majority of the project manager's working day, one individual cannot control everything communicated on a project, nor should he try. Project managers who ask that every single e-mail or conversation be filtered through them first are generally demonstrating that they are *not* in control on the project. Instead, the project manager should be in control of the communications *process*. This is done by creating a strong communications management plan and adhering to it.

Communication Channels

The topic of communication channels refers to how many paths of communication can exist on a project. *Expect at least one to two questions on the exam to relate directly to this topic.* Because the project manager needs to manage and be in control of project communications, it is important to understand that adding a single person on a project can have a significant impact on the number of paths or channels of communication that exist between people.

$$\text{Channels} = n(n-1)/2$$

(Where n – the number of people on the project)

The formula above for calculating communications channels looks complicated, but is actually a simple geometric expansion. Before memorizing the formula, refer to the two illustrations below. You can see from the drawing that 4 people produce 6 communication channels, as is confirmed by the formulae:

$4 * (4-1) \div 2 = 6.$

If there were 5 people, the formula would be applied as:

5 * (5-1) ÷ 2 = 10

By understanding the drawings that follow and the way people interrelate to form communication channels, the concept should be easy to comprehend.

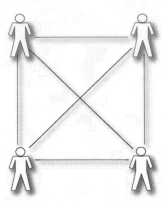

4 people create 6 communication channels as illustrated above.

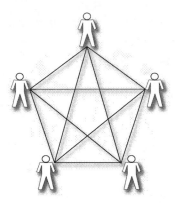

5 people create 10 communication channels, or paths, as depicted in this illustration

Communications Blockers

A communication blocker is anything that interferes with the sender encoding the message or the receiver decoding it. It can include anything that disrupts the communication channels.

Information Distribution

Performance Reporting

Performance reporting is a controlling process that involves reporting to the stakeholders on how resources are being used, including status reports, progress reports, and forecasts.

Trend Analysis

Trend analysis is a tool of performance reporting. It involves looking at the project's previous performance and predicting future trends. If the project's cost performance index is deteriorating, action is required. If the schedule variance is shrinking, the project manager would want to understand why.

Earned Value Management

Also note that earned value management is identified as a tool for performance reporting. Remember that earned value analysis involves calculating the variances to schedule and budget and estimating future project performance on the basis of those calculations. It belongs here in communications management because the project's progress must be communicated out to the stakeholders.

The outputs of performance reporting include performance reports and change requests. Note that performance reports may be presented as bar charts, histograms, S-curves, or tables. Change requests are handled as specified in the appropriate management plan; e.g., budget change requests will be handled as described in the cost management plan, or schedule change requests would be handled as described in the schedule management plan.

Administrative Closure

There are a significant number of questions on the exam related to contract and administrative closure, so it is important to understand what it is and when it is done. *Administrative Closure is the most important topic in this section.* It is heavily stressed in PMI's process, partially because it is often overlooked in actual practice. Several key things must happen in this process, including:

- Documenting performance
- Assembling all project documentation, memos, communications, etc.
- Finalizing all payments
- Collecting and documenting lessons learned
- Releasing resources

It is also important to understand that administrative closure must be done *any time a project or phase ends*. For example, if a project is canceled prior to completion, the project needs to enter administrative closure. This is often a good test as to how committed an organization is to the disciplines of project management. Administrative closure includes:

Project Archives – Creating a complete set of indexed project records for the project.

Project Closure – Verifying that the project has met all of the customer's requirements.

Lessons Learned – Documenting what variances occurred on the project, and what the underlying causes were. Documentation should also include what was done to correct the project, and what was learned by the performing organization to avoid the problems that were encountered. Over time, lessons learned are often incorporated into best practices.

Finally, note that administrative closure is one of only two processes assigned to the closing process group. The other closing process is contract closeout, a function of procurement management. You may encounter an exam question asking which of these two closing processes occurs first. The answer is that contract closeout happens first, and administrative closure is always the final process for any phase of the project or of the entire project.

Administrative Closure

Exercises

1. Calculate the number of communication channels that would exist between 8 people.

2. Draw a line connecting the specific form communication on the left to the corresponding type of communication on the right.

E-mail

                                            Informal Written

Testimony before congress

                                            Formal Written

Speech at a trade show

                                            Informal Verbal

Contract addendum

                                            Formal Verbal

Hallway conversation with a coworker

Communication Exercises

Answers to Exercises

1. Calculate the number of communication channels for 8 people.

    With 8 individuals, there are 28 communication channels as proven by the formula $8 * (8-1) \div 2 = 28$

    A graphical depiction of the 28 communication channels between the 8 people

2. **The forms of communication are illustrated below:**

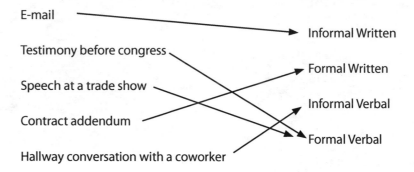

E-mail

Testimony before congress

Speech at a trade show

Contract addendum

Hallway conversation with a coworker

Informal Written

Formal Written

Informal Verbal

Formal Verbal

Communication Exercises

Going Deeper

Arthur, Diane. *The Complete Human Resources Writing Guide.* New York: AMACOM Books, 1997.

McLeary, Joseph Webb. *By the Numbers: Using Facts and Figures to Get Your Projects and Plans Approved.* New York: AMACOM Books, 2000.

Pinto, Jeffrey K. *The Project Management Institute: Project Management Handbook.* Jossey-Bass Business & Management Series, 1998.

Communication Management Questions

1. If there were 4 people on the project team and 9 more are added, how many additional channels of communication does this create?

   A. 6.
   B. 30.
   C. 36.
   D. 72.

2. The process to create a plan showing how all project communication will be conducted is known as:

   A. Communications modeling.
   B. Communications management planning.
   C. Information method.
   D. Communication distribution planning.

3. The responsibility of decoding the message rests with:

   A. The sender
   B. The receiver
   C. The communications management plan
   D. The communications model

4. Which of the following is NOT an output of information distribution?

   A. Project records
   B. Project reports
   C. Project presentations
   D. Performance reports

5. Your latest review of the project status shows it to be more than 3 weeks behind schedule. You are required to communicate this to the customer. This message should be:

   A. Formal and written.
   B. Informal and written.
   C. Formal and verbal.
   D. Informal and verbal.

6.   Which of the following would be an activity of administrative closure?

A. Verifying that the scope of work was completed.

B. Contract closure.

C. Updating team members' records.

D. Taking the customer out to dinner.

7.   The majority of a person's communication is:

A. Verbal.

B. Non verbal.

C. Documented.

D. Unnecessary.

8.   Meetings should do all of the following EXCEPT:

A. Publish an agenda.

B. Produce written meeting minutes.

C. Foster creative thinking.

D. Include short, frequent breaks.

9.   The kickoff meeting should involve:

A. The team, key stakeholders, customer, sponsor, and management.

B. The customer and the team.

C. The customer and the sponsor.

D. The team, customer, and sponsor.

10.   Stakeholders are identified in which process?

A. Communications planning.

B. Information distribution.

C. Performance reporting.

D. Administrative closure.

11. You are about to attend a bi-weekly status meeting with your program manager when she calls and asks you to be certain to include earned value analysis in this and future meetings. Why is earned value analysis important to the communications process?

    A. It communicates the project's long term success.
    B. It communicates how the project is doing against the plan.
    C. It communicates the date the project deviated from the plan.
    D. It communicates the value to cost ratio.

12. You receive a last minute status report from a senior member of the project team that you believe is incorrect. It shows tasks as complete that you are almost certain are no more than 60% complete, and it documents deliverables as having being turned over to the customer that you do not believe are even finished yet. You are walking into a communication meeting with key stakeholders. What is the BEST way to handle this problem?

    A. Ask the team member who wrote the report to sign the bottom of it.
    B. Ask the stakeholders to wait a few minutes while you try to verify the information.
    C. Summon the project team to the meeting and get to the bottom of the discrepancy.
    D. Do nothing with this status and provide an amended report at the next meeting with the stakeholders.

13. The MOST important skill for a project manager to have is:

    A. Good administrative skills.
    B. Good planning skills.
    C. Good client facing skills.
    D. Good communication skills.

14. What is the final task that needs to be performed on a project?

    A. Update all plans.
    B. Release the team.
    C. Deliver the completed product.
    D. Obtain signoff.

15.   A project manager is holding a meeting with stakeholders related to the status of a large project for constructing a new runway at a major airport. The runway project has a CPI of 1.2 and an SPI of 1.25, and the manager is going to have to deliver the message to the stakeholders that a crucial quality test has failed. What kind of communication does this meeting represent?

   A. Formal verbal.
   B. Informal verbal.
   C. Para lingual.
   D. Nonverbal.

16.   You have just taken over as the project manager for a new runway for a major airport. The project is already in progress, and there are over 200 identified stakeholders on the project. You want to know how to communicate with these stakeholders. Where should you be able to find this information?

   A. It depends on the type of project.
   B. The stakeholder management plan.
   C. The communications management plan.
   D. Communication requirements.

17.   Trend analysis is:

   A. Analyzing trends from similar projects to determine probable effects.
   B. Looking at emerging industry trends and planning accordingly.
   C. Evaluating past results to predict future performance.
   D. An output of information distribution.

18.   Marie is a project manager who is involved in a meeting with the customer. After the customer makes a statement, Marie carefully reformulates and restates the message back to them. What is Marie practicing in this case?

   A. Listening skills.
   B. Project communications management.
   C. Professional courtesy.
   D. Passive listening.

19. Lessons learned should contain:

    A. The collective wisdom of the team.

    B. Feedback from the customer as to what you could have done better.

    C. Information to be used as an input into administrative closure.

    D. Analysis of the variances that occurred from the project's baseline.

20. In which process would earned value analysis be used?

    A. Communications planning.

    B. Information distribution.

    C. Performance reporting.

    D. Administrative closure.

Answers to Communication Questions

1. D. If there were 4 people, there would have been 6 communication channels. 9 more would create 13, which equals 78 communications channels. The question is asking how many *additional* channels were created, so the answer is 78-6 = 72.

2. B. Communications management planning is determining how the overall communication process will be carried out. It is the general plan for communications.

3. B. In the communications model, it is the sender that encodes, and the receiver decodes the message.

4. D. Did you get tricked by this one? Performance reports are an output of the performance reporting process.

5. A. Communication on schedule slippage, cost overruns, and other major project statuses should be formal and in writing. That doesn't mean you can't pick up the phone to soften the blow, but the formal communication is what counts here.

6. C. Choice 'A' is incorrect since it is an output of scope verification. 'B' is incorrect since it is an output of contract closure (a separate process). 'D' would be a fine thing to do, but it is not a defined activity of administrative closure.

7. B. Most of a person's communication takes place non-verbally. It is body language that carries much of the message. 'A' is the opposite of the correct answer. 'C' is incorrect since most of the communication is non-verbal, but not written (documented). 'D' may well be true for some people, but it is not the right answer here.

8. D. Short and frequent breaks are not formally prescribed. That is not to say that meetings should be long and breaks should never be taken. Only that short, regular breaks are not a good choice for all meetings, and the other choices are. Short, frequent meetings may well break the continuity and interrupt the flow of a productive meeting. 'A', 'B', and 'C' are all characteristics of a good meeting.

9.   A. The kickoff meeting should get everyone together. Choices 'B', 'C', and 'D' are all subsets of the right answer.

10.   A. Stakeholder analysis is an important activity that takes place in communications planning. In it, the stakeholders and their needs are identified.

11.   B. Earned value analysis is a communication tool, and it's all about how the project is doing against the plan.

12.   B. This is a hard question, but be prepared for questions like this on the PMP! The reasoning behind it is this: a project manager should always communicate good information and should always report the truth. 'A' is wrong because it isn't about getting your team member to sign off. Accurate information is more important than accountability. 'C' is incorrect because it is not the team's job to go to these meeting. They should be doing the work on the project. 'D' is incorrect because waiting only postpones the situation and delays getting accurate information to the stakeholders. Choice 'B' is best in this case, because it is the only one that gets accurate information to the stakeholders as quickly as possible.

13.   D. Good communication skills are the most important skills a project manager can have! Project managers spend more time communicating than anything else.

14.   B. Releasing the team, which is part of administrative closure, is the last activity. Most of the other choices require that the team be around to perform them!

15.   B. Many people incorrectly guess 'A' for this question, but meetings are classified as informal verbal. Even when the subject matter is important!

16.   C. The stakeholders and their communication needs are all contained in the communications management plan.

17.   C. Trend analysis uses past results from this project to show trends and predict future results.

18.   A. Marie is practicing good listening skills to make sure she communicates well with her customer.

19.   D. This is important! Lessons learned focus on things that went wrong and things that went right during the project (i.e. variances from your plan) and what was learned from that.

20.   C. Earned value analysis is a tool of performance reporting, since earned value analysis factors in the difference between what was planned and the work that was actually accomplished. This information can then be distributed out to the appropriate stakeholders.

Risk Management

Difficulty	Memorization	Exam Importance	Corresponding PMBOK Chapter
High	Medium	Medium	Chapter 11

10

Risk management is a very rich field, full of information and tools for statistical analysis. In the real world, actuaries anticipate risk and calculate the probability of risk events and their associated cost, and entire volumes are written on risk analysis and mitigation. In this section, you do not need to know every tool and technique associated with risk. Instead, this chapter focuses on the high level interactions within the different risk processes.

Philosophy

By this time, you should have picked up on the fact that very little in PMI's methodology is reactive. The overriding philosophy is that the project manager is in control and proactively managing events. The project manager must understand how to anticipate and identify areas of risk, how to quantify and qualify them, and how to plan for them.

Importance

Risk is one of the areas many people find difficult on the exam. The material may be new or unfamiliar, and the techniques may take some work in order to master.

Preparation

In order to pass this section of the exam, you need to understand the risk management plan and the terms related to risk. The PMBOK contains 40 inputs, 23 tools and techniques, and 25 outputs for the risk management processes. All of these processes are valid, but the secret

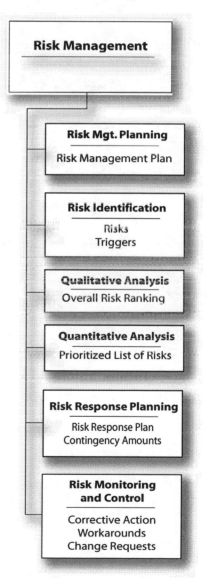

The processes of Project Risk Management with their *primary* outputs

Risk Management

Risk Mgt. Planning
Risk Management Plan

Risk Identification
Risks
Triggers

Qualitative Analysis
Overall Risk Ranking

Quantitative Analysis
Prioritized List of Risks

Risk Response Planning
Risk Response Plan
Contingency Amounts

Risk Monitoring and Control
Corrective Action
Workarounds
Change Requests

is that most of them are either common sense or they rarely show up on the exam. This chapter focuses on the essential few that you need to know. Material is organized around these six processes, building upon the different components that go with each one.

Risk

PMI's usage of the word "risk" is different than many project managers and organizations may have encountered before. Risk has two characteristics that must be understood for the exam:

1. Risk is related to an uncertain event.
2. A risk may affect the project for good or for bad. Although risk usually has negative connotations, it may well have an upside.

The topic of risk management is composed of six processes. These are shown in the diagram on the first page of this chapter, with the major outputs listed below each process.

Risk Management Planning

A project performed in a field where your company has no history is inherently more risky than a type project you have done time and again. If you are a construction company, then writing your own software may be very risky. A construction project on the beach in the Gulf of Mexico during hurricane season will inherently carry more risk than the same project constructed farther inland.

The project itself is one major factor that is considered during the risk management planning process. The other is the organization's tolerance for risk. Is this project going to make or break the company? Does the organization have a high tolerance for risk, or is it highly risk-averse? All of these factors contribute to the risk management planning process.

Risk Management Plan

The only output of risk planning is the risk management plan. This is the plan that shows how all of the information related to risk will be structured. It is general, not specific, in that it describes the approach to risk and does not detail or evaluate every risk on the project. The risk management plan does, however, describe who will be involved in risk management and how often risk management activities will be performed. Methods for evaluating, reporting on, and tracking risks will also be defined.

Risk Identification

Risk identification is the process that moves from a general plan to specific details. It assembles a group that could include the project team, risk management team, stakeholders, users, and both internal and external experts. The Delphi Technique, described in Chapter 5 – Time Management, is a tool that is often used in risk identification, along with brainstorming and other information-gathering techniques.

Risks

The job of the aforementioned group is to identify and document potential risks to the project. A second pass is often made by just the project team and key stakeholders to narrow this large list down to a smaller list of actual risks.[1] One output of this process is a list of risks that will be considered for this project.

Triggers

Another important output of the risk identification process is identification of the risk triggers. Triggers alert you to the fact that a risk event is about to happen (or is happening). For instance, suppose the financial health of a subcontractor is considered a risk, since if the contractors go out of business, your project will probably not make its delivery date. As a result, you want to monitor their monthly financial statements. Financial statements that show a serious problem could be a risk trigger since they warn of a development problem.

Qualitative Risk Analysis

What are the chances that a risk event will occur? What would the impact be if the event does occur? These are the questions you will be evaluating in qualitative risk analysis.

There is a general misunderstanding about qualitative analysis in that people believe it should be subjective. This is not the case. As the PMBOK states, qualitative analysis should be unbiased and accurate.[2] It is not based on guesses or a gut feeling. Qualitative analysis is basing your analysis on the characteristics of the risk event rather than hard numbers, but it is still objective analysis.

Two important outputs should be learned for qualitative risk analysis:

Prioritized list of risks

The way you prioritize them is flexible (high, medium, low, or 1-10, etc), but the output of qualitative risk analysis should be a list of risks that reflects the overall risk on the project.

Overall risk ranking for the project

A risk ranking can be used for a number of purposes, including supporting the decision of whether or not the project should be continued. If a project is determined to be high risk, it may be unacceptable to an organization.

Quantitative Risk Analysis

As you might have guessed from the name, the process of quantitative analysis is all about assigning hard numbers to the risk.

Quantitative Risk Analysis Tools

The following tools and techniques are a part of quantitative risk analysis:

Interviewing

Interviews with experts, including the people who will be doing the work, are a primary tool used to quantify the risk on a project. The information you gather from these individuals varies, depending on how you will quantify the risk, but for the exam you should assume that you will be using PERT estimates, which include estimates for the a best case, the worst case, and the most likely time for the task.

Sensitivity Analysis

Sensitivity analysis evaluates how sensitive the project is to risk. For the exam, simply understand that it is a technique to determine which risk events have the biggest impact on the project. Even if uncertainty is high for one particular event, it may have only a small impact on the overall project.

Decision Tree Analysis

Decision trees are tools used to depict the likelihood of an event occurring and cost associated with that event. The estimated cost is multiplied by the probability of the risk occurring, and that number is added to the original cost estimate. The decision tree below compares the costs and associated risk factors of purchasing a commercial software package with writing a custom application. In this example, the cost of the commercial package is higher when risk is left out of consideration. However, when the risk of implementation is considered, the equation shifts.

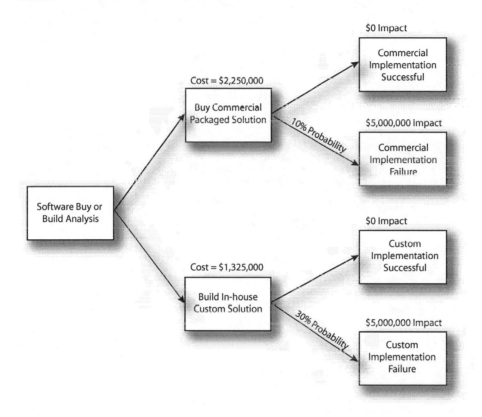

The numbers for this decision tree work out as follows:

	Initial Cost	Risk cost	Probability	Total
Commercial Package	$2,250,000	$5,000,000	10%	$2,750,000
Custom Software	$1,325,000	$5,000,000	30%	$2,825,000

*The totals above were calculated by first multiplying the risk cost by the probability and then adding it to the initial cost. E.g. $5,000,000 * 10% = $500,000. $2,250,000 + $500,000 = $2,750,000.*

In the preceding example, the analysis shows that the custom software has a higher overall cost due to the higher risk. Decision trees can get very complex as they grow larger, but this method is a good overall tool to quantify the outcome of various options.

Simulation

This is a favorite topic on the exam. Monte Carlo analysis, also discussed in Chapter 5 – Time Management, is a tool that takes details and assembles a big picture. Performed by computer, Monte Carlo analysis throws large numbers of scenarios at the schedule to see what the impact of certain risk events is. This technique will show you what is not always evident by simply looking at the schedule. It will often identify tasks that may not appear inherently high risk, but in the event they are delayed, the whole project may be adversely affected.

Outputs of Quantitative Risk Analysis

The outputs of quantitative risk analysis are important. They are the numerical basis by which you will evaluate risk.

Do not forget that risk may be beneficial! As an example, when you purchase a lottery ticket, you are running the risk that you will win money, and that risk can be quantified. If you are constructing a building, you would plan for a certain amount of bad weather to impact the construction schedule; however, you run the risk that the weather will be worse than anticipated as well as the risk that the weather will be better than anticipated. This usage of the word risk is counter-intuitive to many people but it is correct within the domain of project management, because *the risk is in the uncertainty, not just in the outcome.*

Prioritized list of quantified risks

Lists of risk should be prioritized by the numbers in this process. For instance, based on the expected value (probability x $ impact), the following 4 risks are ranked in the table. The rankings would show you how to manage these risks.

Risk	Probability	Impact	Expected Value
Risk B	25%	$1,750,000.00	$ 437,500.00
Risk C	50%	$ 600,000.00	$ 300,000.00
Risk D	80%	$ 200,000.00	$ 160,000.00
Risk A	13%	$ 152,200.00	$ 19,786.00

Risk Response Planning

Risk Response Planning Tools and Techniques

You will almost certainly see exam questions related to the risk responses. Be sure you can identify different responses based on behaviors described in the test questions.

Avoidance

Risk avoidance occurs when you change your plan to eliminate the risk. For instance, referring back to a previous example, suppose you determined that constructing a building on the coast of the Gulf of Mexico was too high a risk event. Moving the building to a location that had never had a building destroyed by weather would be an example of risk avoidance.

Transference

Risk transference happens when you seek to shift the risk from your organization or project to another party. In the example above, taking out an insurance policy would be risk transference.

Information technology projects, especially software project, are infamous for high cost risk. If you contracted with a software company to develop the software at a fixed price, that would be an example of transferring the risk. (You'll see in Chapter 11 – Procurement Management that the type of contract you use with vendors can also affect your project's risk management).

Mitigation

Mitigation is a way to lessen the risk. It may be focused on lessening the probability that the risk will occur or on lessening the impact if it does occur. Using the construction example above, planning to accomplish the majority of the construction outside of hurricane season would be an example of risk mitigation. Using construction methods and materials that would be less affected by disastrous weather would be mitigation as well.

Acceptance

Acceptance occurs when you take on the risk. If none of the options listed above are rational, the risk may simply have to be accepted by the team. Acceptance falls into two broad categories:

Active Acceptance - Active acceptance is when the project manager accepts the risk, but develops contingency and fallback plans in case it does occur.

Passive Acceptance - In contrast to active acceptance, passive acceptance is simply doing nothing and hoping that the risk does not occur. No risk response plans are created. If the risk does occur, the project team will deal with it then.

Outputs of Risk Response Planning

Risk Response Plan

Whereas the risk management plan is general, the risk response plan is very specific. It is the major output of risk response planning. It describes the risks, tells who owns them, how they will be dealt with, and what any contingency and fallback plans are.

Reserves/Contingencies

After performing risk response planning the team may decide to build a buffer into the schedule and/or the budget as a hedge against risks. Such reserves are an output of risk response planning.

Residual and Secondary Risks

Risk response planning also results in the identification of two other types of risks. Residual risks are those risks that remain and were not avoided, mitigated, or transferred. Secondary risks are those risks that come about as a result of a planned risk response. Secondary risks must be identified and a response should be planned for each one.

Risk Monitoring and Control

Risk monitoring and control looks at the risks that have been found and makes sure all of the risk plans are being executed as planned. This process involves careful monitoring and regular audits to make sure that the risk management plan and the risk response plan are being followed and that they are working.

Once again, it is the tools and outputs of this process that most often appear on the exam. Listed below are the critical tools and outputs to know.

Tools of Risk Monitoring and Control

Risk Audits

Risk audits are used to examine how well the risk responses are working. The response is evaluated (usually by someone above or outside the project) to see if:

1. The risk management plan was followed.
2. The response was appropriately executed.
3. The response properly addressed the risk.

Earned Value Analysis

Are you surprised to see this topic reappear here? Earned value analysis appears as a tool for time, communications, and risk monitoring. A low CPI or CV would alert risk auditors that the project is at budget risk, while a low SPI or SV would provide a warning that the project is at risk for missing the schedule. Remember that risk can take on several forms. A risk event may damage the success of the project, it may delay the project, or it may send costs soaring.

Because risk may also be beneficial, a high CPI (greater than 1), indicating that you are beating your cost plan, would be the realization of a risk event.

Outputs of Risk Monitoring and Control

There are only a handful of outputs of risk monitoring and control that regularly show up on the exam, and if you understand the process so far, most of them will make sense. They are listed below.

Workarounds and Corrective Action

If a risk has been accepted and it happens, then the team will have to work around it. Those workarounds must be documented back into the project plan. Workarounds are also implemented for unanticipated risk events for which no response was planned.

Corrective action is simply the action taken as a result of carrying out the workaround plan (if the risk was accepted or unplanned) or the planned response (if the risk was anticipated).

Changes

When risk events occur, it stands to reason that they will create changes to the project plan as well. This may create a sort of ripple effect on the project, triggering changes to many facets of the project.

Risk Database

A risk database is where all the lessons learned in risk management on the project are collected and stored. The word "database" does not dictate that this has to be a computerized tool. The database could be as simple as a paper-based file.

Risk Monitoring/Control

Going Deeper

This is a very condensed list of the many excellent volumes on risk management. Because much of the literature on risk management is highly customized to industry, it would be impractical to try and list all recommended reading for this subject here. Therefore only broadly applicable titles are included.

Borge, Dan. *The Book of Risk*. New York: John Wiley & Sons, Inc. (US), 2001.

Crouhy, Michel, Galai, Dan, Mark, Robert. *Risk Management*. New York: McGraw-Hill Professional, 2000.

Culp, Christopher L. *The Risk Management Process: Business Strategy and Tactics*. New York: John Wiley & Sons, Inc. (US), 2001.

Wang, John X., Roush, Marvin L. *What Every Engineer Should Know About Risk Engineering and Management, Vol. 36*. New York: Marcel Dekker, Inc., 2000.

Young, Peter C., Tippins, Steven C. *Managing Business Risk: An Organization-wide Approach to Risk Management*. New York: AMACOM Books, 2000.

Going Deeper

Risk Management Questions

1. You are managing the construction of a data center, but the location is in an area highly prone to earthquakes. In order to deal with this risk, you have chosen a type of building and foundation that is particularly earthquake resistant. This is an example of:

    A. Risk transfer.
    B. Risk avoidance.
    C. Risk mitigation.
    D. Risk acceptance.

2. You are evaluating the risk by assigning numbers to the risk. This is an example of:

    A. Monte Carlo analysis.
    B. Quantification analysis.
    C. Qualification analysis.
    D. Simulation.

3. As part of your project, you have identified a significant risk of cost overrun on a software component that is integral to the product. Which represents the BEST strategy in dealing with this risk?

    A. Outsource the software development.
    B. Insure the cost.
    C. Double the estimate.
    D. Eliminate the need for this component.

4. How is earned value analysis used in project risk management?

    A. As part of risk identification.
    B. As part of quantitative risk analysis.
    C. As part of risk response planning.
    D. As part of risk monitoring and control.

5.   Refer to the diagram below. What is the expected value of Result A?

   A. $200,000.
   B. $100,000.
   C. $50,000.
   D. $25,000.

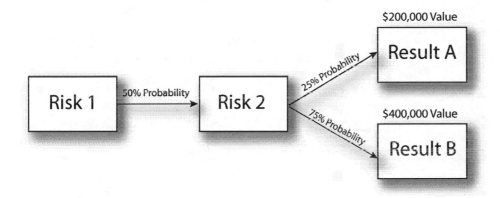

6.   Refer to the diagram from the previous question. What risk
     management tool is employed in this diagram?

   A. Earned value management.
   B. Sensitivity analysis.
   C. Decision tree analysis.
   D. Flowcharting.

7.   An overall risk ranking for the project is an output of which process?

   A. Qualitative risk analysis.
   B. Risk management planning.
   C. Risk identification.
   D. Risk monitoring and control.

8.   If a project manager is taking corrective action, which process is he
     involved in?

   A. Qualitative risk analysis.
   B. Risk management planning.
   C. Risk identification.
   D. Risk monitoring and control.

9. What is the BEST source of information about potential risk on your project?

   A. Computer risk analysis.
   B. Interviews with team members from other projects.
   C. Historical records from similar projects.
   D. Your own experience in this industry.

10. You have just finished a thorough Monte Carlo analysis for your project. Which of the following would the analysis MOST likely identify?

   A. Divergent paths causing risk.
   B. Points of schedule risk.
   C. Points of schedule conflict that lead to risk.
   D. Gaps in the project path that could create risk.

11. Your company is beginning a new building project and has assigned you the role of project manager. During the first few meetings with stakeholders you become aware of several risks that are of concern to the project sponsor. The topic of risk management, however, has yet to be addressed. What is the first thing you should do to address the project risks?

   A. Develop a risk management plan.
   B. Identify project risks.
   C. Plan responses to project risks.
   D. Determine how risks will be controlled.

12. Risk management planning is:

   A. A process of identifying potential risks for a project.
   B. Deciding how risk management activities will be structured and performed.
   C. Assessing the impact and likelihood of project risks.
   D. Numerical analysis of the probability of project risks.

13. All of the following are outputs from risk identification EXCEPT:

    A. Probability of achieving cost/time objectives.

    B. Risks.

    C. Triggers.

    D. Inputs to other processes.

14. **Residual risks are:**

    A. Secondary risks.

    B. Risks that have been transferred.

    C. Risks that have been accepted and addressed.

    D. Risks that have been mitigated.

15. **A risk rating matrix is useful for:**

    A. Risk identification.

    B. Qualitative risk analysis.

    C. Quantitative risk analysis.

    D. Risk response planning.

16. **The BEST definition of risk management is:**

    A. The process of identifying, analyzing, and responding to risk.

    B. The process of reducing risk to the minimum level possible for the project.

    C. The process of proactively ensuring that all project risk is documented and controlled.

    D. Creation of the risk response plan.

17. **Which of the following is NOT a tool or technique for gaining expert opinion as it relates to risk?**

    A. Brainstorming.

    B. Delphi technique.

    C. Monte Carlo Analysis.

    D. Expert interviews.

18. Which of the following is NOT a valid risk response?

A. Risk mitigation.

B. Risk avoidance.

C. Risk transference.

D. Risk redirection.

19. Which of the following statements is TRUE regarding risk?

A. All risk events must have a planned workaround.

B. All risk events are uncertain.

C. All risk events are negative.

D. All risk events should be covered by a contingency budget amount.

20. Which of the following is NOT a valid way to reduce risk?

A. Select a contract type that reduces risk.

B. Insure against the risk.

C. Create a workaround for the risk.

D. Plan to mitigate the risk.

Answers to Risk Management Questions

1. C. The best answer here is risk mitigation since you are taking steps to lessen the risk. 'A' is incorrect because you are not transferring the risk to anyone else. 'B' is incorrect because you would need to relocate in order to completely avoid the risk of earthquake. 'D' is incorrect because you are not merely accepting the risk – you are taking steps to make it less severe.

2. B. When you are assigning a number, such as a dollar amount, to the risk, you are quantifying the risk. 'A' is a tool used to analyze risk, and 'C' is when you use characteristics of the project instead of numbers to analyze risk. 'D' is incorrect because simulation helps you understand risk, but it is a tool of the quantitative analysis process.

3. A. Outsourcing the software development could allow you to cap the cost. 'B' is not a good choice because costs for development such as this cannot be insured in a cost-effective manner. 'C' is not correct because doubling the estimate does not deal with the root of the problem. It only arbitrarily changes the estimate. 'D' is incorrect because you cannot simply eliminate every high risk component in the real world.

4. D. Earned value analysis is a tool of risk monitoring and control.

5. D. The way this problem is solved is by multiplying out the probabilities times the value. In this case, it the 50% probability of Risk 1 X the 25% probability of Risk 2 X the $200,000 value of result A. .5 X .25 * 200,000 = $25,000.

6. C. This is an example of decision tree analysis.

7. A. Qualitative analysis produces an overall risk ranking for the project.

8. D. Corrective action is always the result of a controlling process. The controlling process for risk is risk monitoring and control.

9. C. Historical records from similar projects would provide you with the best source of information on potential risks. 'A', 'B', and 'D' are all good inputs or tools, but they would not be as pertinent or helpful as the records from other similar projects.

10.   B. One of the things Monte Carlo analysis would show you is where schedule risk exists on the project. 'A' is incorrect, because it is typically convergent and not divergent tasks that create schedule risk. 'C' is incorrect because it is not looking for schedule conflicts – those would be corrected in your schedule development. 'D' is incorrect because gaps in the project path do not, by themselves, cause risk.

11.   A. You should develop the risk management plan. A risk management plan will outline how all risk planning activities and decisions will be approached. Methods of risk identification, qualification, quantification, response planning, and control will all follow the development of the risk management plan.

12.   B. Risk management planning is not planning for actual risks (which include choices 'A', 'C', and 'D'); it is the PROCESS of deciding how all risk planning activities and decisions will be approached. It is the plan for how to plan.

13.   A. Determining the probability of a risk is a quantifiable statistical analysis and is an output of risk quantification.

14.   C. Residual risks are those that could not be avoided, transferred, or mitigated. They may also include minor risks that have been accepted after changing the project plan. Choice 'A' is incorrect because secondary risks are risks that arise from taking action on a primary risk. 'B' and 'D' do not conform to the definition of a residual risk.

15.   B. A risk rating matrix assigns relative values to a risk's impact on project objectives and is a tool used in qualitative risk analysis. 'A' is incorrect because risk rating takes place after risk identification. 'C' is incorrect because quantitative analysis applies numerical analysis to the risks, but the risk rating matrix uses non-numerical characteristics. 'D' is incorrect because risk response planning uses other tools, such as earned value analysis.

16.   A. The process of identifying, analyzing, and responding to risk is the definition of risk management.

17.   C. Monte Carlo Analysis, which is a computer-based analysis, might be useful for revealing schedule risk, but it would not be useful for gaining expert opinion. Choices 'A', 'B', and 'D' are all tools used as part of project risk management.

18.   D. Risk redirection is a fabricated term. 'A', 'B', and 'C' are all risk responses determined in risk response planning.

19.   B. Risk events are, by definition, uncertainties. These could either be positive or negative. 'A' is incorrect because some risks are simply accepted and have no workaround. 'C' is incorrect because a risk may be positive or negative. 'D' is incorrect because not all risks are budgeted. Some are transferred to other parties or are too small or unlikely to consider.

20.   C. Read these questions carefully! The workaround is what you do if the risk occurs, but it does not reduce the risk as the question specified. 'A', 'B', and 'D' all focus on reducing risk by transferring or mitigating it.

Procurement Management

Difficulty	Memorization	Exam Importance	Corresponding PMBOK Chapter
High	Medium	Medium	Chapter 12

11

Procurement management is the set of processes performed to obtain goods, services, or scope from outside the organization.[1]

Procurement management is one of the most difficult knowledge areas on the exam. One reason it is so difficult is that very few people have formal procurement training in their background.

Much of procurement management is based on Article II of the Uniform Commercial Code (UCC), a mammoth document that has been adopted as a platform for commerce law in the United States. Article II of the UCC deals specifically with contract law relating to commerce, and it is on this foundation that most of the legal framework for procurement management is built.

Philosophy

PMI's procurement management approach was steeped in the practices of formal government procurement processes. In fact many of the processes, tools, techniques, and outputs found here are near duplicates of those used by many government and military institutions in the United States.

The overarching philosophy of procurement management is that it should be formal. Many people's practical experience may differ from this rigid approach, but it is necessary to understand it and to be able to apply PMI's philosophy on the exam.

The processes of Project Procurement Management with their *primary* outputs

Procurement Management

Procurement Planning
Procurement Management Plan

Solicitation Planning
Procurement Documents
Evaluation Criteria

Solicitation
Proposals

Source Selection
Contract

Contract Administration
Correspondence
Payments
Payment Requests

Contract Closeout
Formal Acceptance

Importance

Several questions on the exam will be drawn from procurement management. If formal procurement is new to you, this material is especially important.

There are not any formulae to learn or complex techniques to apply; however, there is a significant amount of material.

Preparation

In order to make this section manageable, the material has been pared down to the bare minimum. In general, it would be wise to take special care in this section if you do not have a background in formal procurement activities.

There are test preparation resources that will insist that you must memorize every input, output, tool, and technique for procurement management as listed in the PMBOK. That practice is not advocated here, although if you are particularly talented at memorization you may still elect to do that. The PMBOK was not written to be memorized. It was written to be practiced and applied. Although there is plenty of material in this book that you are required to memorize in order to pass the PMP Exam, the *many* parts of the procurement management process are not among them.

As a more targeted approach, you are provided herein with key terms, concepts, and the essential components of the procurement management process that you must understand for the purposes of the PMP exam. Therefore, this chapter is *not* a full dissertation on the procurement process. Those who would like a more in-depth treatment on the subject are encouraged to read one of the many fine volumes referenced at the end of this chapter.

PMI's core procurement management process is quite involved. Test takers would do well to read this chapter carefully and then read Chapter 12, Project Procurement Management of the PMBOK 2000.

Procurement Processes

There are six processes in procurement management, tying with risk management for the most processes of any knowledge area on the exam. These processes are displayed in the figure at the beginning of the chapter. Note that only the essential tools, techniques, and outputs are listed, although this is only a fraction of the ones described by PMI.[2]

Procurement Roles

In procurement management, there are two primary roles defined, and the project manager could play either of these roles. In fact, it is not uncommon for project managers to play both roles on the same project. The roles are:

Buyer

The organization or party purchasing (procuring) the goods or services from the seller.

Seller

The organization or party providing or delivering the goods or services to the buyer.

Procurement Planning

The first process performed as part of procurement is procurement planning. This process involves looking at the project and determining which components or services of the project will be made or performed internally and which will be "procured" from an external source. After that decision is made, the project manager must determine the appropriate type of contracts to be used on the project.

The primary tools and outputs are described below:

Make or Buy Analysis

The first step in procurement planning is to perform "make or buy" or "build or buy" analysis. This technique is an evaluation of the benefits and drawbacks of doing the work within your organization or using an external person or group.

There are nearly unlimited factors that can influence the decision to make or buy, but among the most important ones are:

Expertise – Are we able to do the work ourselves?

Capacity – Do we have the time and resources to do the work internally?

Cost – Is it cheaper for us to do the work ourselves?

Core Competency – Is this central to our business, or do we do this type of work particularly well?

Opportunity Cost – Will we be missing out on other opportunities if we take on this work?

Trade Secrets – Will we be divulging too much proprietary information by outsourcing this work?

The final result of make or buy analysis is a decision either to perform the work or service internally or to go outside the organization for it. Both the organization's broader goals and the project's immediate needs should be considered in this decision.

Contract Type Selection

When procuring goods or services, the type of contract that governs the deal can make a significant difference in who bears the risk. There are three categories of contracts you must know for the test. They are listed below with information on each one:

Fixed Price Contracts

Fixed price contracts are the easiest ones to understand. There is generally a single fee, although payment terms may be specified so that the cost is not necessarily a lump sum payable at the end.

This type of contract is very popular when the scope of work is thoroughly defined and completely known. Two types of fixed price contracts are:

Fixed Price Incentive Fee

The price is fixed, with an incentive fee for meeting a target specified in the contract, such as finishing the work ahead of schedule.

Fixed Price Economic Price Adjustment

This type of contract is popular in cases where fluctuations in the exchange rate or interest rate may impact the project. In this case, an economic stipulation may be included to protect the seller or the buyer. The economic stipulation may be based on the interest rate, the consumer price index, cost of living adjustments, currency exchange rates, or other indices.

Cost Reimbursable Contracts

There are two common types of cost reimbursable contracts:

Cost Plus Fixed Fee

The seller passes the cost back to the buyer and receives an additional fixed fee upon completion of the project.

Cost Plus Incentive Fee

The seller passes the cost back to the buyer and gets an incentive fee for meeting a target (usually tied back to keeping costs low) specified in the contract.

Time and Materials Contracts

In a time and materials contract, the seller charges for time, plus the cost of any materials needed to complete the work.

Contract Risk

The buyer, the seller, or more frequently, some combination of the two bears the risk for the contract. The type of contract, along with the terms and conditions, is the primary factor that determines who bears the project risk.

The chart below shows general rules related to project risk; however, it should be noted that the rules listed are not always the case. Although most of risk in the contracts listed below appears to be squarely on the buyer's shoulders, in reality, most contracts use terms and conditions to shift some, if not a majority of the risk back to the seller.

Type of Contract	Who Bears the Risk	Explanation
Fixed Price	Seller	Since the price is fixed, cost overruns may not be passed on to the buyer, but must be borne by the seller.
Cost Plus Fixed Fee	Buyer	Since all costs must be reimbursed to the seller, the buyer bears the risk.
Cost Plus Incentive Fee	Buyer and Seller	The buyer bears most of the risk here, but the incentive fee for the seller, motivates that seller to keep costs down.
Time and Materials	Buyer	The buyer pays the seller for all time and materials the seller applies to the project.

Statement of Work (SOW)

The statement of work, or SOW, is an output of the procurement planning process. The SOW is the document summarizing the work to be performed, and it may be written by either the buyer or the seller to determine what services will be performed or what goods will be delivered on the project.

When written by the buyer, it should provide sufficient detail for sellers to determine whether or not they are qualified to bid on this project.[3]

When the statement of work is written by the seller, it often includes an explanation as to how the seller plans to approach the work or solve the problems.[4]

Because the statement of work is often generated before all details are known or understood on a project, it may be revised considerably as the project progresses. Regardless of whether the buyer or seller creates the SOW, it should be as detailed as possible at that point in the project.

Procurement Management Plan

The procurement management plan is usually a high-level document that describes how the other procurement processes (solicitation planning, solicitation, source selection, and contract closeout) will be approached and managed. The plan may be formal or informal, depending on the need.

Solicitation Planning

Now that the procurement management plan has been written, and the contract types have been selected, solicitation planning is the next logical step.

Solicitation planning is the process that prepares the documents for solicitation. Why a separate process related to documents? Because procurement is often highly formal and the terms of the work and contract should be thoroughly documented.

For the purposes of the exam, we will focus on two outputs from solicitation planning. They are:

Procurement Documents

Procurement documents are used to get proposals from prospective sellers. These documents should provide enough detail and structure to make sure that the prospective sellers are responding to the same scope of work, but they should also be flexible enough to encourage sellers to be creative in their approach to the problem. Many times, procurement documents specify the "what" of the project or product in great detail, but leave the "how" to the prospective seller.

The buyer prepares documents to describe the work and the general terms of the work being procured. Contrary to popular belief, the descriptions may be general or specific, depending on the goal of the buyer. For instance, if the buyer only knows that a storage facility is needed, and that is all that is important for this project, then the procurement documents do not necessarily need to be highly detailed. On the other hand, if a complex software application with exacting requirements is being procured, then the documentation produced by the buyer should be very specific.

Typically, if the buyer's procurement documents are general, then the seller's response should be very specific. Likewise, if the buyer's procurement documents are specific, then the seller's response may well provide less detail. The response could even be as simple as providing a price and a date.

The procurement documents can take on many forms, such as a request for quotation (RFQ), an invitation for bid (IFB), and a request for proposal (RFP), to name a few.

Evaluation Criteria

An output of solicitation planning, the evaluation criteria specify how the different sellers will be evaluated and judged. Criteria may include such things as the seller's experience, certification, how long the seller has been in business, its financial stability, etc. Note that evaluation criteria do not have to be completely objective.[5] If the buyer has a good reason to slant the bidding process and that slanting is openly disclosed and legal, then it may be appropriate.

Solicitation

Solicitation is the executing process of getting responses from prospective sellers as to how the project scope of work can be delivered and for what prices. The procurement process is designed to encourage proper competition for the project among sellers. There may, however, be times when you are not able to open the bidding up to more than one seller. For instance, if the seller had a patent on the item you needed, or if the seller was the sole source for that item, an open bidding process would be precluded. There also may be scenarios in which you do not have the luxury of time to go through the process of source selection, or the piece may so small as not to warrant formal solicitation. In such cases, it may be acceptable to bypass the solicitation process and negotiate directly with one seller.

Solicitation Tools

Bidder's conference

A bidder's conference, or pre-bid conference, is a meeting with prospective sellers prior to bidding. This practice allows sellers to clarify questions on the project and help ensure that they all have the same understanding about the project.

Advertising

Many projects, especially projects undertaken as part of a government initiative, advertise their bids using newspapers, journals, or the Internet. Often companies and government entities keep approved sellers lists and use them to advertise their solicitations.

Solicitation Outputs

Proposals

Proposals are prepared and submitted by the prospective sellers and describe their abilities to satisfy the solicitation. As discussed previously, the proposals need to provide the proper amount of detail as a response to the buyer.

Source Selection

Source selection is an executing process in which the bids are measured against the evaluation criteria, and a supplier is chosen. The final output of this process is the contract.

Contract Negotiation

Not all contracts must be negotiated, but those that require negotiation should involve the project manager. The ultimate goal of contract negotiation is that the results be mutually agreeable to all parties. Mutual agreement is often difficult to achieve, partially because most people are not as skilled at negotiation as they believe themselves to be. Additionally, there is an unrecognized mentality among many people that they do not feel like they won unless they feel like the other party lost. Many otherwise solid deals have been ruined because of such expectations. Remember for the exam that one goal of contract negotiation is a good working relationship between the seller and the buyer.

Negotiation tactics

You do not need to memorize this list, but you should become familiar with the negotiation tactics listed here:

- Impose a deadline (limit the time available for negotiating)
- Spring a surprise (withhold information for a tactical purpose)
- Claim limited authority ("I'm not authorized to decide")
- Claim the missing man ("I have to check with my boss back at the office")

- Claim fair and reasonable demands (appeal to a desire for equity)
- Impose delays (ask for a recess, create a diversion)
- Reasoning (working together toward a common goal)
- Confuse the opponent (distort information to create confusion)
- Withdraw (make a false attack and then withdraw it)
- Point out concessions (make the other party feel he is being unreasonable)
- Go to Arbitration (involve a neutral third party in the decision)
- Fait Accompli (claim that a demand has already been met and cannot be changed)

Contract

The single most essential concept in this section is that of the contract. A contract is defined as "a set of promises constituting an agreement between parties giving each a legal duty to the other."[6]

Although you do not need to be a lawyer to pass the PMP Exam, project managers must understand the elements of a contract for their projects! It is not sufficient for a project manager to rely solely on others to comprehend the contract and all of its pieces. However, because a contract is often a highly technical legal document, the project manager should use appropriate legal resources such as the organization's legal department, corporate counsel, or the contract administrator to assist him in this. A project manager who attempts to decipher all of the legal language and the subtle nuances and implications that accompany many legal phrases without any outside expertise is exposing the project, the organization, and himself to an unacceptable level of risk.

A contract is official and legal, and should be highly specific. Not just any agreement is a contract. The following elements must be present for a contract to exist:

Legal purpose

Explanation: Legal purpose simply means that you cannot have a legal contract if the purpose or activity is not legal.

Example: You cannot setup a legally binding contract in the United States to buy or sell heroine, since the drug is illegal in the U.S.A.

Consideration

Explanation: There must be something performed or given in exchange by all parties.

Example: You cannot have a legally binding contract where one party agrees to build a house for another party for free since nothing is given in "consideration" or exchange.

Mutuality

Explanation: All parties must agree on the contract for the contract to be binding. There must be an offer and an acceptance.

Example: Company A makes an offer to buy Company B's pipeline for $25,000,000.00. Company B does not accept. In this case, there is no contract.

Obligation

Explanation: A contract must oblige the parties to some duty.

Example: You enter a contract that has no real obligation attached. A contract that does not require anyone to do anything is not a valid contract.

Competent parties

Explanation: All parties must be legal and competent.

Example: You cannot establish a contract with yourself. In most cases, you cannot establish a contract with a minor. You cannot establish a contract with a corporation that does not legally exist. Additionally, you cannot hold a gun to someone's head and ask them to sign a contract, or exert any other form of duress or undue influence. In those cases, the "contract" would be invalid.

Terms and Conditions and Special Provisions

The terms, conditions, and special provisions are parts of the contract that represent specific elements of the agreement. They will provide the *details* on what things will be covered in the contract and how they will be handled. For instance:

- Payment details
- Ownership of results
- Damages and Penalties
- Scope of Work

For the PMP exam, you do not need to understand everything that could potentially be in the terms and conditions of a contract. You do need to know that terms and conditions contain details that are vitally important to the contract and that the project manager needs to understand all of them.

Verbal and Written Contracts

In United States contract law, a handshake or a verbal agreement is generally every bit as binding as a formally written agreement (provided you can prove the other part really agreed). While this may be technically true, good project management practice requires that contracts be formal, and a written contract is highly favored over a verbal one. If it is important enough to constitute an agreement, it is important that it be put in writing.

Contract Administration

Contract administration is the process of verifying that the seller meets the contract specifications. Since the contract is a legal document, the project team needs to be aware of the legal ramifications of everything they do in this regard.

Contract administration may be especially challenging on large project with numerous contract components and teams.

Contract Change Control System

The contract change control system is a tool of contract administration. It is the set of procedures used to modify the contract. This may include the correspondence, signoffs, and procurement methods that must be used in order to affect change to the contract.

Contract Correspondence

Because the contract is a legal document, the terms and conditions often require that correspondence related to the contract performance be formal and in writing. As an example, the project manager should not assume that they may simply declare a seller to be in material breach on a contract. Such action may require one or several prior written notices.

Contract Closeout

Questions about contract closeout appear regularly on the exam. In the contract closeout process the terms of the contract are formally accepted, including the deliverables, and the contract is closed. Take the time to memorize the previous statement and to understand that contract closeout is a process of procurement management. You will probably have questions on the exam that will ask you the difference between contract closeout and administrative closure (covered in Chapter 9 – Communications Management). Here are the most important facts to know:

- Contract closeout happens *before* administrative closure.
- In contract closeout, both parties verify that everything specified in the contract has been satisfied. Only then is the contract considered complete.
- The contract is formally completed during the contract closeout process.
- Project records are updated and files are created related to the contract and contract performance.
- Procurement audits are a tool of the contract closeout process. Like the audits used in quality, they are conducted by management to ensure that the entire procurement process is being followed.

Going Deeper

Formal procurement is a subject few dare to read for pleasure; however, the subject is rich with information and good practices. The following volumes contain a more thorough treatment of the subject along with excellent resources on purchasing and procurement:

Burt, David N.; Pinkerton, Richard L. *A Purchasing Manager's Guide to Strategic Proactive Procurement.* New York: AMACOM Books, 1996.

Cavinato, Joseph L.; Kauffman, Ralph G. *The Purchasing Handbook: A Guide for the Purchasing and Supply Professional.* New York: McGraw-Hill Professional, 2000.

Procurement of Goods. Washington, D.C. World Bank, 2000. ISBN 0821347136

Procurement of Works. Washington, D.C. World Bank, 2000. ISBN: 0821347144

Going Deeper

Procurement Management Questions

1. The contract type that represents the highest risk to the seller is:

   A. Fixed price plus incentive.
   B. Cost reimbursable.
   C. Fixed price.
   D. Cost reimbursable plus incentive.

2. You have been tasked with managing the seller responses to a request for proposal issued by your company. The seller responses were numerous, and now you have been asked to rank the proposals from highest to lowest in terms of their response. What are you going to use as a means to rank the sellers?

   A. Evaluation criteria.
   B. Request for quotation.
   C. Seller response guidelines.
   D. Expert opinion.

3. Make or buy analysis takes place during:

   A. Procurement planning.
   B. Solicitation planning.
   C. Solicitation.
   D. Source selection.

4. Which of the following is NOT a requirement for a legal contract?

   A. Must be between legal parties.
   B. Must be for a legal purpose.
   C. Must have consideration.
   D. Must specify legal recourse.

5. You are managing a large software project when the need for a new series of database tables is discovered. The need was previously unplanned, and your organization's staff is 100% utilized. You decide to go outside the company and procure this piece of work. When you meet with prospective sellers, you realize that the scope of work is not completely defined, but everyone agrees that the project is relatively small, and your need is urgent. Which type of contract makes the MOST sense?

    A. Fixed price.
    B. Time and materials.
    C. Open ended.
    D. Cost plus incentive fee.

6. Your project plan calls for you to go through procurement in order to buy a specialty motor for an industrial robot. Because of patent issues, this motor is only available from one supplier that is across the country. After investigation, you believe that you could procure the motor from this company for a price that is within your budget. What is your BEST course of action?

    A. Revisit the design and alter the specification to allow for a comparable motor.
    B. Procure the motor from this source even though they are the sole source.
    C. See if the component may be produced in another country, dodging your country's patent issues.
    D. Take the product out of the procurement management process.

7. You have a supplier that is supplying parts to you under contract. The terms and conditions give you the right to change the contract at any time, and you need to significantly lower the quantities due to a change in project scope. How should you notify the supplier?

    A. Take them to lunch and explain the situation gently to preserve the relationship.
    B. Have your attorney call their attorney.
    C. Communicate with the supplier via e-mail.
    D. Send them a formal, written notice that the contract has been changed.

8. Your project has been terminated immediately due to a cancellation by the customer. What action should you take FIRST?

   A. Call a meeting with the customer.
   B. Enter contract closeout.
   C. Ask your team leads for a final status report.
   D. Verify this change against the procurement management plan.

9. You are evaluating proposals from prospective sellers. What process are you involved in?

   A. Source selection.
   B. Procurement management.
   C. Solicitation planning.
   D. Contract administration.

10. Your project scope calls for a piece of software that will control a valve in a pressurized pipeline. Your company has some experience with this type of software, but resources are tight, and it is not part of your company's core competency. You are considering involving other sellers but want to decide whether it is a better decision to produce this within your company or source it externally. What activity are you performing?

    A. Source selection.
    B. Make or buy analysis.
    C. Rational project procurement.
    D. Evaluation criteria.

11. Your organization is holding a bidders conference to discuss the project with prospective sellers, and a trusted seller you have worked with many times in the past has asked if they can meet with the project manager the day before the conference to cover some questions they do not wish to ask in front of other sellers. Should your organization meet with the seller?

   A. Yes, the more that prospective sellers know about the project, the better.
   B. Yes, they are your primary seller, and past history should be factored in.
   C. No, prospective suppliers should be kept on equal footing.
   D. No, that would represent an illegal activity.

12. The most important thing to focus on in contract negotiations is:

   A. To negotiate the best price possible for your project.
   B. To maintain the integrity of the scope.
   C. To negotiate a deal that both parties are comfortable with.
   D. To make sure legal counsel or the contract administrator has approved your negotiating points.

13. If a project manager was performing contract administration, which of the following duties might he be performing?

   A. Sending out invoices.
   B. Negotiating the contract.
   C. Closing the contract.
   D. Performing make or buy analysis.

14. Who generally bears the risk in a time and materials contract?

   A. The buyer.
   B. The seller.
   C. The buyer early in the project and the seller later on.
   D. It depends on the materials used.

15. Your company is outsourcing a project in an area where it has little experience. The procurement documents should be:

    A. Completely rigid to ensure no deviation from sellers.
    B. Flexible enough to encourage creativity in seller responses.
    C. Informal.
    D. Based on industry standards.

16. The statement of work on a project should provide:

    A. Enough detail for the prospective seller to complete the project.
    B. Enough detail to describe the product, but no so much as to divulge trade secrets.
    C. Enough detail to perform make or buy analysis.
    D. Enough detail for the prospective seller to know if they are qualified to perform the work.

17. You are the project manager for a seller who has been selected to construct an industrial kitchen for a large food services company. Before the contract negotiations, the buyer confides in you that design is not finalized, and they want you to begin work with incomplete specifications. What type of contract should you ask for in the negotiations?

    A. Fixed price.
    B. Cost plus incentive fee.
    C. Time and materials.
    D. Cost plus fixed fee.

18. The product or result of the project is created during which process group?

    A. Project lifecycle.
    B. Contract administration.
    C. Project executing.
    D. Work package processing.

19.   Your program manager has asked to meet with you and review your documentation from a recent seller selection. What is your program manager engaged in?

   A. Seller verification.
   B. Seller efficiency evaluating.
   C. Procurement planning.
   D. Procurement auditing.

20.   You have completed a project and delivered the full scope of the contract. The buyer agrees that you have technically satisfied the terms of the contract but is not satisfied with the end results. In this case, the contract is:

   A. Contested.
   B. Complete.
   C. Poorly written.
   D. Lacking terms and conditions.

Answers to Procurement Management Questions

1. C. Fixed price is the highest risk to the seller since the seller must bear the risk of any cost overruns. Choice 'B' would provide the highest risk to the buyer.

2. A. The evaluation criteria will provide the guidelines by which you can evaluate and rank responses.

3. A. Make or buy analysis is a tool used during the procurement planning process.

4. D. All of the others are requirements for a legally binding contract. Legal recourse is something that is usually provided by the law and not the contract.

5. B. Time and Materials. Choice 'A' is incorrect because the scope is not defined enough to establish a fair fixed price. Choice 'C' is a made up type of contract. Choice 'D' would not make sense in this case since the seller's costs are not abundantly clear, and this type of contract would create too much risk.

6. B. This one may trick some who think that it is wrong to use a sole source. In many cases it is the only choice. 'A' would not be good since the design has nothing to do with this. 'C' is not necessary in this case, since the issue is not a legal issue. Choice 'D' would be completely invalid since the item is still being procured outside of your organization.

7. D. Choices 'A', 'B', and 'C' are all verbal. Contract changes should always be made in writing!

8. B. The question asks for your FIRST action, and the most appropriate action is to enter contract closeout. Choices 'A' and 'C' may be appropriate at some point, but if a project is terminated, contract closure needs to be performed.

9. A. If you are evaluating proposals, you are involved in source selection.

10. B. Make or buy analysis is the process where an organization decides whether it should produce the product internally or outsource it.

11.   C. If you are involved in formal procurement, you should make every effort to keep sellers on equal footing. If one seller is provided with an advantage, it negates much of the value of the procurement process.

12.   C. The most important point is to create a deal that everyone feels good about. 'A' sounds like a good choice, but it is incorrect, since the best possible price might not be fair to your seller, and that could create a bad scenario for the project in the future. 'B' is important, but that is not the primary focus of negotiations. 'D' may or may not be necessary, depending on the situation.

13.   A. One of the activities in contract administration is to send out invoices or requests for payment. Make sure to learn the primary process inputs, tools, techniques, and outputs for procurement planning.

14.   A. In a time and materials contract, the buyer has to pay the seller for all time and materials, and often times it involves an incomplete scope definition. Therefore, the buyer is the one most at risk.

15.   B. In this scenario, you want sellers to respond with their own ideas. Procurement documents should be rigid enough to get responses to the same scope of work, and flexible enough to allow sellers to interject their own good ideas and creativity.

16.   D. A statement of work should be as complete as possible, and at least complete enough for the seller to determine if they are qualified to do the work.

17.   C. The major clue here is that the scope of work is not completely defined and they want you to begin work anyway. In that case, the project is at a higher risk, and a time and materials contract shifts much of that risk back to the buyer.

18.   C. The actual work packages are performed during the executing process group.

19.   D. Procurement audits are a tool of contract closeout and are used to confirm that the contract was adhered to.

20.   B. If the scope of the contract is complete and no other terms were breached, then the contract is complete.

Integration Management

Difficulty	Memorization	Exam Importance	Corresponding PMBOK Chapter
Medium	Low	High	Chapter 4

12

Integration management is the practice of making certain that every part of the project is coordinated. In the PMBOK, this knowledge area is presented early on (Chapter 4 of the PMBOK); however, in this book it is placed near the end, primarily because the content in integration management builds upon the other processes. A thorough understanding of the other knowledge areas of project management makes this topic easier to grasp.

In integration management, the project manager assembles the project plan, executes the plan, and verifies the results of the work. At the same time, the project manager must prioritize different objectives that are competing for time and resources and also keep the team focused on completing the work.

Philosophy

The philosophy behind integration management is twofold:

1. During the executing processes of the project, decision-making can be a chaotic and messy event, and the team should be buffered from as much of this clamor as possible. This is in contrast to the planning processes where you want the team involved. You do not want to call a team meeting during execution every time a problem arises. Instead, the project manager should make decisions and keep the team focused on executing the work packages.

The processes of Project Integration Management with their *primary* outputs

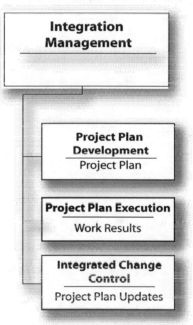

Integration Management

Project Plan Development
Project Plan

Project Plan Execution
Work Results

Integrated Change Control
Project Plan Updates

2. The processes that make up project management are not discrete. That is, they do not always proceed from start to finish and then move on to the next process. It would be wonderful if design always finished and went to production without ever needing to be revisited; however, that is not the way these things typically go, and PMI's process recognizes that.

Integration management focuses on these processes and how they fit together and interact with each other.

Importance

The importance of this section is high! You should expect several questions on the exam that relate directly to this chapter.

Preparation

The difficulty factor on this material is considered medium. If you have heard the rumor that it is the most difficult section on the test, you can relax. Integration management is not the hardest section. However, while it may not be as difficult in a technical sense as the chapters on time or cost, the material may be new to many project managers and thus present a challenge. The best preparation for this section is to learn the integration management processes and their main inputs, tools, and outputs, and most importantly, the interaction among these processes. Then focus on the essential definitions.

Project Integration Management

Integration management is all about the project plan and managing changes to it. The reason that the word "integration" is used is that changes made in any one area of the project must be integrated into the rest of the project. Changes are not made in a vacuum, and while that is true for most of the processes in this book, it is especially true among project plan development, project plan execution, and integrated change control.

Project Plan Development

Project plan development is one of the three processes that make up integration management. It involves taking the planning outputs from the other planning processes and producing the project plan.

All of the work on the project must be planned, scheduled, and budgeted, and the sum of all of this effort makes up the project's scope. All the planning processes that are covered in the other knowledge areas flow into project plan development. For example, activity sequencing (producing the network diagram) and cost budgeting (creating the cost baseline) are all connected to project plan development. Project plan development is the umbrella term that encompasses all the planning processes.

Project Plan Development Inputs

The project plan is a formal document that is used to guide the execution and control of the project. It contains the following elements:

- Scope Statement
- Work Breakdown Structure
- Network Diagram
- Schedule
- Budget
- Constraints
- Assumptions
- Historical Inputs
- Organizational Policies
- Scope Management Plan
- Cost Management Plan
- Schedule Management Plan
- Communications Management Plan
- Quality Management Plan
- Risk Management Plan
- Risk Response Plan
- Procurement Management Plan
- Staffing Management Plan

Rather than memorize the previous list, be able to recognize the elements of the project plan. Each of the planning outputs covered in the other knowledge areas becomes part of the project plan, in addition to the constraints, assumptions, and historical records. Any policies that your company has also need to be reflected in the project plan, as they may need to be considered by others.

Project Plan Development

Project Plan Development Tools and Techniques:

Project Plan Methodology

Every organization has its own method or approach to project planning. Some have a formal methodology with specific steps that are always followed; others may approach planning in a less rigid way. The methodology that a company uses may include specific project phases, standard forms to fill in, templates provided by the project office, or software tools used specifically for project plan creation.

Stakeholder Input

Stakeholders have experience and expertise that should be considered when pulling together a project plan. Bear in mind for the exam that whenever possible, the people who will be doing the work on the project should be involved in planning the project. The project manager will want to involve the team in planning those areas where they are most affected.

Project Management Information System

The project management information system (PMIS) is a broad term that covers the whole system for gathering and communicating outputs throughout the entire project. In project plan development, the PMIS is the tool that the project manager uses to gather and store all the information related to the project. Note that this tool is associated with ALL of the integration management processes – project plan development, project plan execution, and integrated change control.

Earned Value Management

Earned value management, covered in depth in Chapter 6 – Cost Management, is a part of project plan development as well. The reason EVM belongs here is that it integrates scope, time, and cost together. It is part of the planning process because you are determining what your planned value will be.

An important part of earned value management is the Control Account Plan (CAP), sometimes referred to as a Cost Account Plan.

The CAP is associated with a node on the work breakdown structure, and is used to measure performance on cost and performance on schedule. The CAP is especially applicable for project integration management, because it integrates scope, time, and cost.

Project Plan Development Outputs

The Project Plan

> The project plan is used as a plan for execution and control, and as a baseline against which progress may be measured.

Supporting Detail

> The project plan does not rest completely on its own. The details that explain and support the decisions and estimates should be included with the project plan.

Project Plan Execution

> The execution of the project plan is where the work packages are completed by the team. Project plan execution is the primary process in the executing process group. There are several inputs to this process, but it is the tools, techniques, and outputs that are most important, so we'll take a closer look at them here.

Project Plan Execution Tools

Work Authorization System

> The work authorization system is the most important tool for the project plan execution process. It is a formal system for getting the work done at the right time and in the right order. On larger projects, the work authorization system may be formal, requiring the written signoff of functional managers and others, but for some projects, an informal verbal agreement may suffice. The work authorization system allows the project manager to remain in control of project execution, preventing individual team members from completing work out of sequence or skipping necessary steps.

Status Meetings

> Project managers know that status meetings are a common and vital tool. Regularly scheduled meetings held with the team or others to discuss progress on the project can help a project manager foresee and prevent many problems during project execution. These status meetings are often referred to as "performance reviews."

Project Management Information System (PMIS)

> In project plan execution, the project management information system is the tool that the project manager uses to keep up to date on the status

of work being performed on the project. See the project management information system section above under the project plan development process for more information.

Project Plan Execution Outputs

Work Results

It stands to reason that if work is being performed, results should be the output of that work. In this case, as the work packages are executed, work results will happen. These results are used as an input to many of the controlling processes.

Change Requests

When the work is actually performed, change requests are most often generated. Although project plan execution is not the only place a change request may occur, it is the one most frequently associated with change.

Integrated Change Control

Integrated change control is another process in which the project manager is expected to be proactive. Watch for questions related to that fact on the exam. It is here that the project manager manages change and keeps the project on track.

The project manager's job related to project change falls into three categories: [1]

1. Influencing underlying factors that lead to change. This is an exam favorite! The project manager should be proactive about change factors. He should not merely wait around for change requests to come in, but he should make sure wherever possible that unnecessary changes are not even requested.

2. Determining that a change has happened and capturing any change that occurs to the project scope.

3. Coordinating changes across all project areas. If a change is made to the budget, it will almost certainly affect the schedule and scope and possibly other factors such as risk and quality. It is the project manager's job to coordinate and integrate all of this change back into the project plan.

Integrated Change Control Inputs

The inputs to this process are simply the outputs from the other processes, including the project plan, performance measurements, and change requests.

Integrated Change Control Tools

Integrated Change Control System

The change control system refers to the processes put into place to evaluate, capture, and track changes to the project. This system is different from the scope change control system discussed in Chapter 4 in that scope change control is concerned with changes to the *product*, and the integrated change control system is concerned with changes to the *project*. Something can increase the project's scope without affecting the product's scope (for instance, mandatory weekly meetings with the customer), and it is important that the project manager have a system for tracking these changes and for determining which changes will benefit the project.

The change control system is the set of procedures that specify how performance on the project will be evaluated. The change control system should include:

- How change requests should be submitted
- How change requests should be managed
- How change requests should be approved

You will probably see at least one question on the exam asking you how to handle a change request. You should choose the answer that includes adhering to the defined change control system. You should not automatically submit a change to the change control board, since you may or may not even have such a group in actual practice, and it is the project manager's responsibility to handle change and not that of the change control board. The project manager should only submit a change to another group such as the change control board, if he has already evaluated the change and determined that it is an appropriate action.

Configuration Management

There is a lot of confusion about configuration management, even among the "experts." This confusion has led to many different definitions, but configuration management is not overly complex. It is a term that refers to the system of managing documentation, change control, accounting, and auditing. For the test, you should understand three things:

1. Configuration management applies to the physical characteristics of the product.
2. Configuration management is a tool associated with integrated change control.
3. Configuration management is used to make sure that the configuration of the product is in line with the plan.[2] For instance, computer systems and airplanes may be physically configured in different ways from the base product before they are actually delivered. Configuration management takes every element of the project into account, making certain that the product's configuration is reflected in the project plan, the billing, and the project documentation.

Project Management Information System

The PMIS is described previously under project plan execution tools. It is also a tool of integrated change control.

Integrated Change Control Outputs

Project Plan Updates

The primary output here is that changes to the project plan are made. This stands to reason since the process of change control primarily deals with influencing, tracking, and evaluating and managing changes to the project plan.

Corrective Action

Corrective action is just what it sounds like – any action taken to bring the results of the project work closer in line with the project plan. The corrective action that results from integrated change control becomes an input into project plan execution. This flow of outputs and inputs illustrates the concept of project integration that is central to integration management.

Lessons Learned

Documenting lessons learned involves looking at variances on the project and describing how this could be avoided in the future. This information becomes an input into future projects.

Going Deeper

Because the topic of integration management is somewhat specific to PMI, the single best source for information on integration management is the PMBOK 2000.

Integration Management Questions

1.   Producing a project plan may BEST be described as:

    A. Creating a network logic diagram that identifies the critical path.
    B. Using a software tool to track schedule, cost, and resources.
    C. Creating a single document that guides project plan execution.
    D. Creating a plan that contains the entire product scope.

2.   Updates to the project plan are an output of:

    A. Integrated change control.
    B. Project plan development.
    C. Project plan executing.
    D. Project planning.

3.   You are meeting with a new project manager who has taken over a project that is in the middle of executing. The previous project manager has left the company and the new project manager is upset that change requests are streaming in from numerous sources including his boss, the customer, and various stakeholders. The project manager is not even aware of how to process all of these incoming change requests. Where would you refer him?

    A. Scope statement.
    B. Project plan.
    C. The previous project manager.
    D. Project charter.

4.   The purpose of the change control board is:

    A. To guide change.
    B. To evaluate change.
    C. To influence change.
    D. To affect change.

5.   The work authorization system is used:

   A. So that people know when they will be performing the work.

   B. So that senior management may provide input by authorizing work requests.

   C. To ensure that only people authorized on the project are allowed to do the work.

   D. To ensure work gets performed at the right time in the right order.

6.   Your customer has mandated that the schedule be reduced by 10% in order to be first to market with a new software product. As the project manager, what should you evaluate FIRST?

   A. The effect on the stakeholders.

   B. The market impact.

   C. The estimated effects on budget, scope, quality and risk.

   D. The gap between the previous schedule and the requested schedule.

7.   If you are creating a single, coherent document to guide project execution and control, you are creating:

   A. The execution plan.

   B. The project plan.

   C. The integration plan.

   D. The project framework.

8.   The change control system should be created as part of which process group?

   A. Initiation.

   B. Planning.

   C. Executing.

   D. Controlling.

9.   The work authorization system is MOST often:

   A. Created by the functional manager.

   B. Created by the project manager.

   C. Verbal.

   D. Written.

10. Which of the following represents the project manager's responsibility in regard to change on a project:

    A. Influence the factors that cause project change.
    B. Ensure all changes are communicated to the change control board.
    C. Deny change wherever possible.
    D. Prioritize change below execution.

11. The project plan is made up of:

    A. The other planning outputs.
    B. The other planning outputs, tools, and techniques.
    C. The aggregate outputs of all software tools.
    D. Scope verification.

12. When changes are approved and made to the project, they should be:

    A. Tracked against the project baseline.
    B. Incorporated into the project baseline.
    C. Included as an addendum to the project plan.
    D. Approved by someone other than the project manager.

13. The project management information system is:

    A. The sum of all information technology systems on the project.
    B. The system for tracking the status of project items.
    C. The system for configuration management.
    D. The system that supports the project plan.

14. You are a project manager, and your team is executing the work packages to produce a medical records archive and retrieval system. Two of the project's customers have just asked for changes that each says should be the number one priority. What would be BEST to do?

    A. Have the project team meet with the customers to decide which would be easiest and prioritize that one first.
    B. Assign someone from the team to prioritize the changes.
    C. Prioritize the changes without involving the team.
    D. Deny both changes since you are executing.

15. The program manager is asking why your project is scheduled to take sixteen months. He claims that previous projects in the organization were able to complete similar projects in less than half of that time. What would be the BEST thing to do?

   A. Look for historical information on the previous projects to understand them better.
   B. Refer the program manager to the schedule management plan.
   C. Refer the program manager to the project plan.
   D. Explain to the program manager that estimates should always err on the side of being too large.

16. You work for a defense contractor on a project that is not considered to be strategic for the company. Although the project is not the company's top priority, you have managed to secure many of the company's top resources to work on your project. At today's company meeting, you find out that your organization has won a very large, strategic project. What should you do FIRST?

   A. Contact management to find out if you can be transferred to this project because it is strategic to the company.
   B. Contact management to find out how this new project will affect your project.
   C. Hold a team meeting and explain that since the resources have been allocated to your project, they are not eligible to go to the new project.
   D. Fast track your project to accelerate its completion date.

17. The project sponsor requests a change to the project. The project manager calls a meeting of the team and several stakeholders. This demonstrates:

   A. A participatory style of management.
   B. Withdrawal.
   C. No integrated change control system.
   D. No project management information system.

18. Your organization has a policy that any project changes that increase budget by more than 1.5% should be signed off by the project office. You have a change that was requested by the customer that will increase the budget by 3%; however, the customer has offered to pay for all of this change and does not want to slow it down. Which option represents the BEST choice?

   A. Approve the change yourself and take it to the project office after the work is complete.
   B. Ask the customer to take the change to the project office and explain the situation.
   C. Do not allow the change since it increases the budget by over 1.5%.
   D. Take the change to the project office.

19. The person or group responsible for evaluating change on a project is:

   A. The project manager.
   B. The sponsor.
   C. The project team.
   D. The program manager.

20. The output of the project plan execution process is:

   A. The work packages.
   B. The work authorization system.
   C. The work results.
   D. The work breakdown structure.

Answers to Integration Management Questions

1. C. The project plan is a single plan that drives execution (and control). 'A' is incorrect since it is only a part of planning. 'B' is incorrect because that will not make up the entire project plan. 'D' is incorrect since scope may or may not be a part of the project plan, but it does not make up all of it.

2. A. Updates to the project plan are an output of the integrated change control process.

3. B. The project plan would contain the methods for processing changes to the project.

4. B. The change control board is a formal board that evaluates changes to the project.

5. D. The purpose of the work authorization system is to make sure work gets performed in the right sequence and at the right time. 'A' would be referring to the schedule. 'B' is incorrect since senior management should not be involved at that level. That is the job of the functional manager. 'C' is not the purpose of the work authorization system.

6. C. The first thing you should do is understand the effects on the other elements of the project.

7. B. This is the definition of the project plan.

8. B. The change control system is created during a planning process.

9. D. Usually the work authorization is written. 'A' and 'B' are incorrect since the work authorization may be created by either the functional manager or the project manager, or it could be standard across the organization.

10. A. The project manager must be proactive and influence the factors that cause change.

11. A. The project plan consists of many things, but the only one from this list that matches is the outputs from the other planning processes, such as risk, cost, time, quality, etc. 'B' is incorrect because the other tools and techniques do not form part of the project plan.

12.   B. Did this one fool you? Approved changes that are made to the project get factored back into the baseline. Many people incorrectly choose 'A', but the purpose of the baseline is NOT to measure approved change, but to measure deviation.

13.   B. The PMIS is used to keep track of the status of project items. It does not necessarily have anything to do with information technology.

14.   C. Prioritizing the changes is the job of the project manager. 'A' is wrong because you do not want to distract the team at this point – they should be doing the work. 'B' is wrong because it is the project manager's responsibility to help prioritize competing demands. 'D' is incorrect, because changes cannot automatically be denied simply because you are in execution.

15.   A. Historical information may provide an excellent justification for why your project is taking sixteen months, or perhaps it will show you how someone else accomplished the same type of work in less time. Either way, it provides a great benchmark for you to factor in to your project. 'B' is incorrect since the schedule management plan only tells how the schedule will be managed. 'C' is incorrect because the project plan will not tell the program manager why the project is taking longer than he expects. 'D' is wrong because estimates should be accurate with a reserve added on top as needed.

16.   B. Remember the rule that you should evaluate things first! You need to know if your project is going to be affected before taking action. Many people choose 'D', but fast tracking the schedule increases risk, and that would not be necessary until choice 'B' had been performed.

17.   C. Team meetings to evaluate a change are generally a very bad idea and show a lack of a good integrated change control system.

18.   D. Organizational policies MUST be followed! None of the other options presents an acceptable alternative. Choice 'B' would be asking the customer to do the project manager's job.

19.   A. The project manager is primarily responsible for evaluating changes to the project, and he is empowered to act on that evaluation.

20.   C. The work results are an output of project plan execution.

Professional Responsibility

Difficulty	Memorization	Exam Importance	Corresponding PMBOK Chapter
Low	Low	High	Not covered in PMBOK

Questions of professional responsibility have always been on the exam in one form or another, but now this area is represented as its own category on the test. PMI states that there are 29 questions that come directly from professional responsibility[1], but many of them are practically indistinguishable from questions from other process areas.

Pay special attention to PMI's philosophy of project management. Once you have mastered that, you will have little difficulty with the professional responsibility questions on the exam.

Philosophy

This chapter is all about philosophy, and each of the sections below builds upon the philosophical base that drives the questions and answers. The philosophy behind professional responsibility is that the project manager should be a leader, should deal with issues in a direct manner, should act ethically and legally, and should be open and up front. For each of these questions, don't ask "What would I do?" but "What should I do?"

The PMP is expected to be professional, and that means following the processes outlined in the PMBOK.

Hard choices are a favorite tactic for the questions in this chapter. You may be presented with a small ethical violation that will be painful to resolve. Always look for the answer that resolves it quickly, openly, and fairly. You may be given a situation that lets you ignore a problem instead of confronting it. Always look for the choice that will let you deal with the problem openly and directly.

Importance

Nearly 15% of the questions on the exam relate directly to this chapter, and many more questions will relate indirectly. By learning PMI's approach to professional responsibility, you will be able to answer these questions, and perhaps more importantly, eliminate many of the incorrect answers from questions in other sections.

15% represents a large allocation of questions and can make a tremendous contribution toward a passing and failing score on the exam, so invest the time to study and understand this chapter.

Preparation

After studying, most students find these questions among the easiest on the exam. Because it is impractical to try and cover every possible ethical scenario, the preparation in this chapter is focused on a general understanding of the project manager's professional responsibility.

It is important to note that although this topic makes up a significant part of the exam, it does not appear in the PMBOK 2000.

PMI Code of Conduct

Carefully review the code of conduct printed below. PMP applicants sign this statement when applying to take the exam. Most of the questions in this section will pertain to this code, either directly or indirectly.

Responsibilities to the Profession

Compliance with all organizational rules and policies

1. Responsibility to provide accurate and truthful representations concerning all information directly or indirectly related to all aspects of the PMI Certification Program, including but not limited to the following: examination applications, test item banks, examinations, answer sheets, candidate information and PMI Continuing Certification Requirements Program reporting forms.

2. Upon a reasonable and clear factual basis, responsibility to report possible violations of the PMP Code of Professional Conduct by individuals in the field of project management.

3. Responsibility to cooperate with PMI concerning ethics violations and the collection of related information.

4. Responsibility to disclose to clients, customers, owners or contractors, significant circumstances that could be construed as a conflict of interest or an appearance of impropriety.

Candidate/Certificant Professional Practice

1. Responsibility to provide accurate, truthful advertising and representations concerning qualifications, experience and performance of services.

2. Responsibility to comply with laws, regulations and ethical standards governing professional practice in the state/province and/or country when providing project management services.

Advancement of the Profession

1. Responsibility to recognize and respect intellectual property developed or owned by others, and to otherwise act in an accurate, truthful and complete manner, including all activities related to professional work and research.

2. Responsibility to support and disseminate the PMP Code of Professional Conduct to other PMI certificants.

Responsibilities to Customers and the Public

Qualifications, experience and performance of professional services

1. Responsibility to provide accurate and truthful representations to the public in advertising, public statements and in the preparation of estimates concerning costs, services and expected results.

2. Responsibility to maintain and satisfy the scope and objectives of professional services, unless otherwise directed by the customer.

3. Responsibility to maintain and respect the confidentiality of sensitive information obtained in the course of professional activities or otherwise where a clear obligation exists.

Conflict of interest situations and other prohibited professional conduct

1. Responsibility to ensure that a conflict of interest does not compromise legitimate interests of a client or customer, or influence/interfere with professional judgments.

2. Responsibility to refrain from offering or accepting inappropriate payments, gifts, or other forms of compensation for personal gain, unless in conformity with applicable laws or customs of the country where project management services are being provided.

Categories

There are five categories on the exam for professional responsibility. They are listed below with the rough distribution you can expect on the exam:

Subcategory	Approximate # of Questions
Ensure Integrity and Professionalism	8
Contribute to Knowledge Base	3
Enhance Individual Competence	5
Balance Stakeholder Interests	7
Interact with Team and Stakeholders	6

Ensure Integrity and Professionalism

Some of the questions in this section may surprise the PMP applicant who has not thoroughly prepared. Many of the questions may create very difficult situations that would be easier to ignore or dodge in real life; however, PMI requires that Project Management Professionals deal with these situations in a direct and open manner.

If there were one simple phrase that sums up this section of the test, it would be "Do the right thing," even if it is painful or would be tempting to avoid. If a test question offers you an easy way out, beware! If the exam presents you with an option that represents a shortcut, do not take it.

The key subtopics for this section are:

Laws

You should always follow the laws and customs of the state, municipality, or country where you are working.

International law can be a fairly tricky and sometimes ambiguous area, but the questions on the exam are generally straightforward in this regard. The general rule for the exam is this: If you are asked to do something in another country that is not customarily done in your culture, you should first evaluate and investigate it, determine if it is unethical or illegal, and then act accordingly. This may be difficult for those who are not accustomed to international dealings. For instance, if you are asked to make a payment to a city council in another country in order to get a work permit, evaluate whether or not the payment is a bribe. If it is a bribe, do not make the payment. If it is not a bribe, and it is customary, or even the law, then make the payment.

A short way of looking at it is that if it is illegal or unethical in any way, then it's wrong. Otherwise, the custom in the country where the work is being performed may prevail.

There are infinite possibilities as to what may be asked here. Questions of bribery, discrimination, and illegal activity are among the favorites, but by following the thought process previously described, these questions should present no problem. Only make sure that you are not thinking so concretely that you think anything is wrong if it is different from your practices in your home country.

Policies

Your organization's policies must be followed. If you have an interest that conflicts with a policy, the policy is to be considered first. If your organization has a policy that all travel must be booked through the company's travel agency but you find that you can get a cheaper rate through your mother's travel agency, you should adhere to the company policy and use the corporate travel agency.

Integrity

Integrity may be defined as sticking to high moral principles. For the test, the important concept is that you should do what you said you would do, deal with problems openly and honestly, and do not put personal gain ahead of the project.

Company and professional politics may play a prominent role in your life or company, and many project managers learn to be quite adept at them, but they are relegated to a low position on the exam.

Keep in mind that carrying out the right choice for questions in this section of the PMP exam would often involve standing up to the company's president, refusing an order from your boss, telling the customer the whole truth, and many other things that might have unpleasant consequences.

If a choice appears sneaky, underhanded, or dishonest in any way, it is probably not the correct answer. If the behavior is not direct, open, and straightforward, it is probably not the right behavior – even if it would ultimately appear to help the project! This will help you eliminate the wrong choices on many questions.

Professionalism

Questions about professionalism on the exam are testing your knowledge of how a Project Management Professional acts as a professional in the workplace. According to the code of professional conduct, a project manager is to follow the process and act with respect toward others.

Process

The keys for these questions are to take the process outlined in this book and the PMBOK seriously. The PMI process is not just a formality or a theoretical best-case scenario. It is a serious set of processes, inputs, tools and techniques, and outputs that will reduce risk and improve time, cost, and efficiency. That said, the process is not painless. For the exam, however, the process must be followed. If your customer asks you to cut corners on the process in order to save money, you should not agree.

Respect

The project manager shows respect to others. This extends not only to individuals, but to cultures. PMI is a strong advocate of multiculturalism, and questions on the test will often reflect this bias. Just as PMI does not advocate forcing in other areas, the project manager is not to force or impose their culture or personal beliefs upon others. Multicultural and "politically correct" answers are usually good choices for questions related to professionalism.

Another area of respect that often appears on the test is the respect for confidentiality. This covers confidentiality of client information, trade secrets, project information, and any personal information that may be disclosed during the course of the project.

Contribute to Knowledge Base

PMI expects Project Management Professionals to stay engaged and further the profession. The PMP certification was not designed for people to earn and never use. This is reflected on the exam with questions about activities that don't necessarily relate directly to a project.

Any time a project manager has an opportunity to further the project management training or learning of someone else, such as sharing lessons learned, mentoring, teaching, or leading in best practices, there is a very good chance that is the correct choice.

PMPs are encouraged to publish, teach, write, and disseminate the methodology and process as much as they can. Answers that offer a variant of these activities as the choice are often correct.

Enhance Individual Competence

PMI considers the PMP to be quite a milestone in one's career, but it is by no means the end. Project Management Professionals are expected to continue to study, learn, and grow professionally. As you have no doubt seen, any one of the knowledge areas could consume an entire career, so do not assume that you have learned all there is to know. Even one topic, such as quality, or risk, could provide more than a lifetime's worth of material to study and master.

Another favorite key here is that you know your own areas of weakness and continue to develop that. Do you know what your professional weaknesses are? Are you strong at planning but weak in communication? Are you good at planning tasks but poor at leading people? Everyone has strong suits as well as areas that need to be developed. It is important that the Project Management Professional knows what his or her professional growth needs are and pays attention to them.

Additionally, project managers can contribute more to the body of knowledge if they are familiar with their industries. PMPs should study their industries, learn them well, and thus enhance their ability to apply the project management processes to their work.

You should expect to see questions that put you in a situation of taking a hard look at your abilities, or learning where it is that you are weak. In these scenarios, the project manager should strive for continued improvement, growth, and increased proficiency.

Balance Stakeholder Interests

This one is certainly one of the most difficult areas to master in real life. Stakeholders may not care about each other, and thus their interests may collide or conflict.

The project manager must accurately identify the stakeholders, then understand them, and then seek to balance their interests. This can be nearly impossible at times! For the exam, keep these principles in mind:

• Be fair to everyone and respect the differences of the group.
• Resolve stakeholder conflict in favor of the customer.
• Be open and honest about the resolution. Don't hide things from one stakeholder in order to please another.
• Do the ethical thing in all decisions.

Interact with Team and Stakeholders

This section can present difficulties for those who go in to the test unprepared or with the wrong mindset, especially in the area of work ethics. It is tempting for some people to approach questions with a sense of "fairness" about how hard someone should work, but work ethics vary from country to country, and project managers should take that into account. That does not mean that laziness or negligence should be tolerated, but it does mean that different cultures place different values upon work, and it is not the project manager's job to force them to the level of his home country.

As stated previously, cultural differences on the team should be respected (notice how many times the concept of "respect" is mentioned in this chapter), and multiculturalism is something PMI promotes heavily. Your dealings with your team and the many stakeholders on a project should be professional and mindful of their customs.

As in other areas, communication should be open and regular so that people are aware of what is going on with the project.

Social-Economic-Environmental Sustainability

An additional topic included here is that organizations are accountable for social, environmental, and economic impacts to their project. Project managers should factor in the interests of the community, the environment, and society when making decisions.

On the exam, you may encounter a question that poses a situation where the project would benefit but society would suffer. The project manager should avoid all such situations and scenarios. If the situation becomes untenable or unresolvable, the project manager should disclose the situation and as a last resort, resign the project.

Categories

Professional Responsibility Questions

1. You have reviewed the schedule and have discovered that the project is going to be later than originally communicated. Your boss has asked you not to tell this to your customer even though he agrees that there is no way to shorten the schedule. You have an upcoming status meeting with the customer later on that same day. What should you do?

   A. Cancel the status meeting with the customer.
   B. Call the customer and explain your dilemma to them in confidence.
   C. Explain to your boss that it is unethical to knowingly report an incorrect status to anyone on the project.
   D. Ask your boss to put his request to you in writing.

2. You are in a PMP study group when a coworker, who is also a friend, tells you that she has acquired the questions from the actual exam. What would be the MOST appropriate course of action?

   A. Study from the questions, compare them to the questions on the PMP exam and determine if any further action is warranted.
   B. Ask your friend to surrender the questions and turn them over to your boss.
   C. Decline the offer and change to a different study group.
   D. Contact PMI and explain the situation to them.

3. You have started managing a project in a country that observes nearly double the amount of holidays that your home country takes. Additionally, each team member from this country receives three more weeks of vacation each year than you do. What is your MOST appropriate course of action?

   A. Authorize the same amount of vacation time for your team in order to preserve team equality.
   B. Use the other country's vacation and holidays as schedule constraints.
   C. Allow the extra vacation for that country's team, but request that they produce the same or better results as your team.
   D. Try to get this part of the project relocated to a different country with a stronger work ethic.

4. Your customer instructs you that they would like to bypass creating a work breakdown structure in favor of creating a more detailed activity definition list. You have expressed disagreement with the customer on this approach, but they remain insistent. What is the BEST way to handle this situation?

    A. Document your disagreement with the customer and do it their way.
    B. Follow the customer's wishes, but create the activity list so that it is as close as possible to a work breakdown structure.
    C. Have your project sponsor explain the necessity of the work breakdown structure to the customer.
    D. Have PMI call your customer.

5. You are working in a foreign country, trying to procure a piece of expensive industrial machinery. As you evaluate the bids, one of the potential sellers calls you and mentions that he could probably get 25% of the price knocked off his bid, making his by far the most attractive price. In return, he asks you to pay him one fifth of that amount as a show of your appreciation. What should you do?

    A. Do what is necessary to secure the lowest bid for your customer.
    B. Ignore the offer and evaluate the bids as if this had not happened.
    C. Eliminate this seller's bid, and notify the organization.
    D. Ask the seller if he could reduce the price by even more and assure him he will be well rewarded for his efforts.

6. A project manager has confided in you that he is struggling with the whole concept of project management. He is constantly being handed down unreasonable demands by the customer and is trying to balance that with unreasonable and often opposing demands from senior management and stakeholders. He is worried that the two projects he is managing may fail and asks you for help. What is the BEST thing you can do in this case?

    A. Provide your friend with a copy of the PMBOK.
    B. Encourage your friend to get project management training.
    C. Tell your friend that he should not be managing projects.
    D. Have a private talk with your friend's boss about the problem.

7. You have just taken over a project that is executing the work packages. As you review the status of the project, you become aware that the previous project manager reported milestones as being hit that have not been reached. Additionally, the CPI is 0.88 and the SPI is 0.81. Management is unaware of all of these facts. What should you do?

    A. Crash the schedule to try to get things back in line.
    B. Explain the revised status to management.
    C. Refuse to take on this project assignment.
    D. Ask the key stakeholders for direction.

8. Two of your coworkers ask if they can confide in you. They tell you that they have been using the chemical lab that is a part of your project's construction to manufacture illegal drugs. The drugs have made them quite a lot of money, and they want to know if you would like to participate in this venture with them. What should you do in this situation?

    A. Take the opportunity to mentor these resources.
    B. Investigate the situation and determine whether or not it is really illegal.
    C. Report the situation to the authorities.
    D. Insist that they seek help, but do not report them since this was shared in confidence.

9. Two stakeholders have begun fighting over functionality on your project. Who should resolve this conflict?

    A. Senior management.
    B. The sponsor.
    C. The customer.
    D. The project manager.

10.   You discover that a new pipeline project you are managing poses a previously undiscovered threat to the environment. What is the MOST appropriate course of action?

    A. Seek guidance from government officials.

    B. Seek guidance from the media.

    C. Seek guidance from an attorney.

    D. Resign the project.

11.   Your project team has begun execution of the work packages, when you discover that two of the team members do not have all of the skills needed to finish the project. The team members will need to undergo some training in order to complete their tasks. What is the BEST thing you can do?

    A. Help them get the necessary training.

    B. Contact human resources to find out why they did not have necessary training.

    C. Let them learn by doing the work.

    D. Ask the customer to invest in training the resources.

12.   A colleague confesses that he has been posing as a PMP. He says that the prestige is wonderful, but pursuing the certification has never interested him. What should you do in this situation?

    A. Contact the police.

    B. Contact PMI and alert them to the situation.

    C. Ask your colleague to pursue the real PMP Certification.

    D. Report this to your colleague's human resources department.

13.   You are working on a project to construct an office building in another country when you discover that you must obtain a second building permit from the local authority. When you inquire about this, you find out that the local permit will take 6 to 8 weeks to be issued; however, an official mentions that you can speed this up by paying a $500 "rush fee". The fee is within the project's budget, and the need is urgent. What is the BEST thing to do?

   A. Pay the $500.
   B. Do not pay the $500 and wait the 6 to 8 weeks.
   C. Ask the official if he would accept less than $500.
   D. Ask someone on your team to pay the fee for you.

14.   You are employing a subcontractor to complete a critical piece of work when the project manager for that subcontractor asks you out on a date, making it clear that this is a personal engagement and will not affect business. What would be the BEST course of action?

   A. Accept the invitation if you are so inclined.
   B. Politely refuse the invitation.
   C. Ask your manager for permission to go on the date.
   D. Consult your human resource department for guidance.

15.   You have been assigned to a project for a new software product that you do not believe will succeed. You have made these feelings clear to your company, but they wish you to work on the project anyway. What would be the BEST course of action in this case?

   A. Excuse yourself from the project.
   B. Escalate the situation to the customer.
   C. Manage the project.
   D. Resign from the company.

16. As project manager, you have met with the stakeholders and certain high profile stakeholders have provided you with a series of change requests that fundamentally alter the project and raise the risk to an unacceptably high level. The stakeholders have heard your explanation of this, but they remain insistent that the new functionality is needed. Which option below would be MOST appropriate?

   A. Explain to the stakeholders that their request cannot be fulfilled.
   B. Stall the stakeholders until the request becomes irrelevant.
   C. Remove these stakeholders from your list of stakeholders and exclude them from further project correspondence.
   D. Call a meeting with the project team to help resolve the problem.

17. As project manager, you have been asked to serve on a product selection committee. When you join, you find out that one of the products that the company is evaluating is manufactured by the company where your wife works as a sales director. What is the BEST way to handle this situation?

   A. Disclose the situation to the project selection committee.
   B. Quietly excuse yourself from the committee.
   C. Remain completely impartial throughout the product selection.
   D. Vote against the product in the interest of fairness.

18. You and your project team work for a large and well-known consulting company and are compensated based on how many hours you bill. In the make or buy analysis you performed, you find that you can save the project nearly $300,000 if you procure a software module rather than have your consulting team write it. What is the MOST appropriate way to resolve this conflict?

   A. Resolve the conflict in favor of you and your team if you are within budget.
   B. Resolve the conflict in favor of your employer.
   C. Let the team vote on how to resolve the conflict.
   D. Resolve the conflict in favor of the customer.

19.　The project you are currently managing is highly similar to one you worked on for a different customer six months ago. On the previous project, you performed a detailed feasibility study that would save two calendar months if you could use it on this project. You signed a non-disclosure agreement with the previous customer. What is the BEST course of action in this situation?

　　A. Disregard the previous feasibility study and perform a new feasibility study for your current customer.

　　B. Ask your previous customer for permission to use the feasibility study.

　　C. Use the feasibility study from the first project, since such non-disclosure agreements are not legally enforceable.

　　D. Ask your project office for guidance.

20.　A conflict of interest should be:

　　A. Resolved quietly.

　　B. Disclosed openly.

　　C. Monitored carefully.

　　D. Ignored deliberately.

Answers to Professional Responsibility Questions

1. C. The code of professional conduct reads: *"Responsibility to provide accurate and truthful representations to the public in advertising, public statements and in the preparation of estimates concerning costs, services and expected results."* You cannot ethically lie to a customer, management, your boss, or your team, even if ordered to do so.

2. D. The code of professional conduct reads: *"Upon a reasonable and clear factual basis, responsibility to report possible violations of the PMP Code of Professional Conduct by individuals in the field of project management."*

3. B. Professional responsibility questions tend to have a strong multicultural slant. This is because respect for other cultures is highly valued. Any answer other than 'B' does not reflect this value.

4. C. Here is a great example of where the customer is not always right. Did you remember that PMI considers it unethical to deviate from the stated process? Skipping something as foundational as the work breakdown structure would not further the project, your reputation, or the customer's interests. This may make sense, but why should the sponsor explain this to the customer? Because the sponsor can act as a liaison to the customer in difficult circumstances like this.

5. C. This seller wants you to bribe him with a 25% kickback. You cannot ethically do this, even though it may save your customer or your project money. In this case, the best thing to do is avoid the situation and disclose it.

6. B. The best answer here is to encourage your friend to get training in project management. Answer 'A' would not help because the PMBOK would not help your friend be successful. 'C' is not a good answer at all. Just because someone struggles does not mean that they should not be doing the job of managing projects. 'D' is a bad choice because you should confront the problem directly (with your friend).

7. B. Based on these numbers, you know that the schedule and costs are slipping. Any time a status changes you should alert stakeholders (in this case, management). Before any other action, you should report the status. 'A' is incorrect because crashing would only make the cost situation worse. 'C' is incorrect because there is no reason to refuse the project simply because it is not tracking well. A good project manager is exactly what is needed here. 'D' is incorrect because you should be evaluating and giving direction to the project instead of asking the stakeholders to do this.

8. C. You have a responsibility to report any illegal activity to the authorities.

9. D. It is the project manager's responsibility to balance stakeholder's interests. The project manager should attempt to resolve this conflict.

10. A. Because you have a socio-economic-environmental responsibility, you should alert the government officials and seek guidance. They have a vested interest in helping resolve this quickly, and this would deal with the root of the problem. Answers 'B', 'C', and 'D' do not deal directly with the problem.

11. A. You have a responsibility to mentor and help your team get training. Remember that the cost of training is typically born by the performing organization's budget and not by your project's budget, and not by the customer.

12. B. The PMP Code of Professional Conduct states that *"Upon a reasonable and clear factual basis, responsibility to report possible violations of the PMP Code of Professional Conduct by individuals in the field of project management."*

13. A. This does not constitute a bribe. You should pay the fee. If the official wanted you to slip the money under the table, that would be different, but in this case the fee has a legitimate purpose.

14. B. This would be a conflict of interest, and it is the project manager's duty to avoid all conflicts of interest. Consulting the human resources department or your manager would not avoid a conflict of interest.

15. C. This is a difficult scenario, but you cannot always pick and choose projects that appeal to you. The best thing is to manage the project and follow the project management processes. If the project will not be successful, it should become apparent sooner rather than later.

16.   A. It is the project manager's job to balance competing stakeholder interests. It may be tempting to try to accommodate everyone's requests, but some simply must be refused. In this case, you must explain to the stakeholders that their requests cannot be fulfilled.

17.   A. The code of conduct states that conflicts of interest should be clearly disclosed. None of the other choices really satisfies that rule. 'B' might be a tempting choice, but it is not the best choice, since you should be upfront and open about such situations.

18.   D. As a general rule, conflicts should be resolved in favor of the customer. In this case, that is particularly true.

19.   B. You should ask permission from the previous customer. 'A' is incorrect because you are not working in the best interest of your current customer if you do this. It may become necessary to do the work over again, but you should try to negotiate that with your previous customer first rather than rushing to "reinvent the wheel." 'C' is incorrect because even if the non-disclosure agreement was not legally enforceable, it is still agreement between you and your previous customer, and you are *ethically* bound to comply with it. The PMP code of conduct gives specific guidance against improper use of proprietary information. 'D' is incorrect because more guidance is not what is needed here, as the issues are clear. Your project office's approval to use the previous material would not make it acceptable.

20.   B. The PMP Code of conduct states *"Responsibility to disclose to clients, customer, owners, or contractors, significant circumstances that could be considered as a conflict of interest or an appearance of impropriety."*

How To Pass The PMP

Difficulty	Memorization	Exam Importance	Corresponding PMBOK Chapter
Low	Low	High	Not covered in PMBOK

Passing the PMP on your first try has nothing to do with good luck. It is all about preparation and strategy. While the other chapters in this book are all about the preparation, this chapter focuses on the test strategy itself. The following are techniques on how you can be sure to avoid careless mistakes during your exam.

Reading the Questions

A critical step to passing the PMP is to read and understand each question. Questions on the exam may be long and have many twists and turns. They are often full of irrelevant information thrown in intentionally to distract you from the relevant facts. Those who pass the PMP know to read the questions carefully. Many times the only relevant information is contained at the very the end. Consider the following example:

Q: **Mark has a project where task A is dependent on the start and has a duration of 3. Task B is dependent on start and has a duration of 5. Task C is dependent on A and has a duration of 4. Task D is dependent on B and has a duration of 6, and the finish is dependent on tasks C and D. Mark is using his project network diagram to help create a schedule. The schedule for the project is usually created during which process?**

   A. Cost estimating.
   B. Cost budgeting.
   C. Schedule control.
   D. Schedule development.

Questions like the one above are not uncommon on the PMP Exam. If you take the time to draw out a complex project network diagram, you will have wasted valuable time, when the question was only asking you to pick the process (the answer is 'D').

On lengthy questions, the best practice is to quickly skip down to the last sentence for a clue as to what the question is asking. Then read the entire question thoroughly. Most of them have a very short final sentence that will summarize the actual question. Make sure, however, to read the entire question at least once! Don't simply rely on the last sentence.

Just as important as carefully reading the questions is reading each of the four answers. You should never stop reading the answers as soon as you find one you like. Instead, always read all four answers before making your selection.

A Guessing Strategy

By simply reading the material in this book, you will immediately know how to answer many of the questions on the exam. For many others, you will have an instinctive guess. If you have studied the other chapters, you should trust that instinct. It is not there by chance. Your instinct was created by exposing yourself to this material in different ways. Your mind will begin to gravitate toward the right answer even if you are not explicitly aware of it.

Guessing on the PMP does not have to be left purely to chance. If you do not know the answer immediately, begin by eliminating wrong answers, or ones you suspect are wrong. Let's take a fairly difficult question as an example:

Q: **Historical information is used as an input to all of the following processes EXCEPT:**

    A. Activity definition.

    B. Initiation.

    C. Administrative closure.

    D. Quantitative risk analysis.

Unless you have memorized all of the inputs to all of the processes (the PMBOK lists 186 inputs alone), you are going to have to guess at this one. However, if you throw up your hands and pick one, you only have a 25% chance of getting it right. Instead, you should think about what is being asked. Historical information is used as an input in 9 of the processes in the PMBOK, so that only helps a little, but when you stop to consider that it is used primarily in planning processes, suddenly the picture becomes a little clearer. Now you can see that 'A' and 'B' are probably not the right answer. Both of these would be a good fit for historical information. Now you have a 50% chance of guessing between 'C' and 'D'. Look at them more carefully and ask yourself where would historical information most likely be used an input? Quantitative risk analysis is a good guess, since you might use past results (historical information) to help you analyze and quantify risk. So now, you are left

Guessing

with choice 'C' Administrative closure as the one that looks least likely to have historical information as an input. It may be a guess, but it is a very educated one.

The method here is simply to think about each answer and eliminate ones that are obviously wrong. Even if you only knock off one wrong answer, you have significantly increased your odds of choosing the right one. You will find that most times you can knock off at least two, evening your chances of answering the question correctly.

Spotting Tricks and Traps

The PMP does have trick questions. They are designed specifically to catch people who are coming in with little formal process experience, those who have thumbed through the PMBOK a few times and are now going to take the exam. These people try to rely on their work experience, which often does not line up with PMI's prescribed method for doing things. As a result, they typically don't even come close to passing the exam.

At times, however, these trick questions can also fool a seasoned pro! Listed below are some techniques you can use so that you will not fall into these traps.

Follow the Process

This is always the right answer. There will be questions on your exam that give you "common sense" scenarios that will give you a seemingly innocent way to skip the formal process and save time, or perhaps avoid some conflict by not following procedure. This is almost certainly a trap. The right answer is to follow PMI's process! Do not give in to pressure from irate customers, stakeholders, or even your boss to do otherwise.

Don't Take the Easy Way Out

There will often be choices that allow you to postpone a difficult decision, dodge a thorny issue, or ignore a problem. This is almost never the right thing to do for questions on the exam.

Act Directly and Say What You Mean

In PMI's world, project managers communicate directly. They do not dance around the issue, gossip, or imply things, and they do not communicate through a third party. If they have bad news to tell the customer, they go to the customer and tell them the facts – and the sooner, the better. If they have a problem with a team member, they confront the person, usually directly, although at times it may be appropriate to get the team member's functional manager involved.

Study the Roles

By the time you take the exam, you should be confident about the roles of stakeholders, sponsors, customers, team members, functional managers, the project office, and most importantly, the project manager (plus the other roles that are discussed in Chapter 2 – Foundational Terms and Concepts). Expect several "who should perform this activity" type questions. If you have absolutely no clue, guessing the "project manager" is a good idea.

Additionally, understand the difference between the different types of organizations (projectized, matrix, and functional). Most of your questions will pertain to matrix organizations, so focus your study on that one.

Project Manager's Role

Expanding on the previous point, project managers are the ones who make decisions and carry them out. They have the final decision on most points, can spend budget, can change schedules, and can approve or refuse scope. For the test, assume that the project manager is large and in charge!

Another attribute of project managers is that they are proactive in their approach to managing tasks and information. They do not wait for changes to occur. Instead, they are actively influencing the factors that contribute to change. Instead of waiting for information to come to them, they are actively communicating and making certain they have accurate and up to date information.

Don't Get Stuck

You should expect to find a few questions on the exam that you do not know how to answer. You will look at it and see 4 correct answers, making it impossible to pick just 1. In this case, do not agonize. Even using every good technique, you will still have to make an educated guess at some questions. Some test takers can get quite upset at this, and it can undermine their confidence. If a question stumps you, simply mark it for review and move on. Never spend 15 minutes staring at a single question unless you have already answered all the others. One question is only worth one half of one percent on the exam, so if you do not know the answer, do not worry about it.

You may even discover that a block of questions seem especially difficult to you. This experience can be discouraging and may cause your confidence to waver. Don't be alarmed if you happen upon several difficult questions in a row. Keep marking them for review and keep moving, until you come to more familiar ground. You may find that questions later in the test will offer you hints or jog your memory, helping you with those you initially found difficult.

Exam Time Management

You will have a few minutes at the beginning to go through a tutorial. You probably won't find much value in the actual tutorial; however, you absolutely should take it. After going through it, you will be given a chance to wait before taking the test. Use that time to write down essential formulae and processes on your scratch paper.

Scratch Paper

You will be given five sheets of blank paper when you walk into the exam. You may not carry your own paper into the test. When you sit down to begin the exam, you should write down a few key things. Regardless of how well you know this material, at a minimum, write the following on your first sheet of scratch paper.

1. Earned Value formulae (EV, PV, AC, CPI, SPI, CV, SV, BAC, EAC, ETC) from Chapter 6. You will probably need to refer to these several times during the exam, and it will save time and improve your accuracy if you have written them out.
2. The time management formulae for PERT estimates and standard deviation.
3. The communication channels formula described in Chapter 9.

Even if you are tempted to skip this step, don't! When you come to a lengthy and confusing question that requires you to calculate several different values, you will be glad that you already have your formulae written down for review. This will free your mind to concentrate on the specific question rather than on recalling a formula.

Budgeting Your Time

Going into the exam, you may be fast, or you may be a slower test taker. Everyone should walk into the exam with a strategy for managing their time, based on their own pace. Do not underestimate how hard it is to sit for a 200 question, 4 hour exam. The test-taking process is strenuous and mentally and physically taxing.

If you have a test time management strategy that has served you well in the past, you should use that. If not, here is a generic strategy that many people have used "as is" to take and pass the PMP.

1. Sit for the tutorial and download your information to your scratch paper.
2. When the exam begins, take the first 75 questions, pacing yourself to take approximately 45 minutes.
3. Take your first break. Spend 5 minutes stretching and get a bite of food from your locker.
4. Take the next 75 questions, again pacing yourself to take 45 to 50 minutes.
5. Take your 2nd break. Spend approximately 10 minutes, go to the bathroom, and get a snack.
6. Answer the final 50 questions and then return to answer any ones you did not answer the first time. Budget approximately 45 minutes for this as well. You may not take that long, but it is normal for your pace to slow down as the test wears on.
7. Take a bigger break 15 minutes, (relishing the fact that you have now answered all the questions on the PMP).
8. At this point, you should be at about three hours into the test or less.
9. Perform a review of the first 100 questions. Pace yourself to finish this in about 25 minutes.
10. Take a short 5 minute stretch break if needed.
11. Review last 100 questions and any other ones in your remaining time.

Managing Your Review

When you make a review pass through the exam, you will come across questions that you missed the first time but that are apparent when you look at them again. This is normal, and you should not hesitate to change any answers that you can see you missed. Many people change as many as

10% of the answers on their review. If you catch yourself changing more than that, be careful! You may be second guessing yourself and actually do more harm than good.

When you go through your review pass on the exam, do not take the whole test over again. Instead, employ three rapid fire steps:

1. Did you read the question correctly the first time?
2. Did your selected answer match what was being asked?
3. Perform a complete check of your math where applicable.

Difficulty

Everyone wants to know what the hardest topic on the exam is. That is a difficult question to answer for two reasons:

1. The PMBOK and the test are divided differently. There are 9 knowledge areas in the PMBOK 2000, each given their own chapter. But all of this material also fits into one of 5 processes (plus professional responsibility). To make it more confusing, the PMBOK 2000 is arranged by knowledge area, but the test is arranged by process. This can heighten the confusion when evaluating your test results!

2. The other reason that difficulty is hard to predict is that everyone's experience will differ. No two tests are alike just as no two people have identical backgrounds. If you have heavy finance and accounting experience, time and cost may be easy subjects for you. If you have a strong legal background or have worked for the government then questions about procurement may be easy for you. If you have human resources or psychology training, human resources management may be easiest.

Based on a typical profile of someone who had earned an undergraduate degree in management and had non-industry specific experience managing projects, the material would roughly rank as shown below:

Framework	1	
Foundational Concepts	2	
Cost	3	Harder
Time	4	
Risk	5	
Integration	6	
Procurement	7	Medium Difficulty
Scope	8	
Quality	9	
Human Resources	10	
Communication	11	Easier
Professional Responsibility	12	

This scale is relative, since very little of the material on the exam is considered "easy" to everyone. Ultimately, your professional experience and study can significantly change the order of this list for you.

Also note that many test resources identify integration management as the hardest section; however, that is because they throw everything (including the kitchen sink) into that topic. Integration as a standalone topic is not overly difficult.

Managing Anxiety

Finally, if test-taking has always been a fear-inducing activity for you, there is one simple strategy that may help you manage the physical symptoms of anxiety so that your thinking and memory are not impaired: Take a deep breath. This may sound like obvious advice, but it is based on sound research. Studies in the field of stress management have shown that feelings of anxiety (the "fight or flight" response") are linked with elevated levels of adrenaline and certain brain chemicals. One way to bring your brain chemistry back into balance is to draw a deep breath, hold it for about 6 seconds, and slowly release it. Repeat this breathing pattern whenever you begin to feel panicky over particular questions. It will help to slow your heart rate and clear your mind for greater concentration on the task at hand.

Another thing to remember is that many people who take the exam do not pass – especially on their first attempt. While no one wants to fail the test, you can turn around immediately and apply to take it again (at a reduced rate). If this happens to you, use it as a learning experience. You will have a much higher chance for success on your next attempt, and you will have your score sheet that gives you a breakdown of where you need to study. As the inspired Jerome Kern once penned to music, "Take a deep breath; pick yourself up; dust yourself off; start all over again."

Managing Anxiety

Final Exam

Difficulty	Memorization	Exam Importance	Corresponding PMBOK Chapter	A
Low	Low	High	Not covered in PMBOK	

Instructions

This simulated PMP Exam may be used in several ways. If you take it as a final, you will get a very good idea how you would do if you walked right in to take the PMP Exam. In that way, it can be a very good readiness indicator.

Perhaps the best way to use this exam is to take it again and again, reviewing the answers that go with each question. The answers and explanations will give you insight into the formation of each question and the thought process you should follow to answer it.

Prior to taking the PMP, the best strategy is to take this exam repeatedly, reviewing the answers, until you can make a score of 85% or better.

If you are taking this as a final exam, you have 4 hours (240 minutes) to complete the following 200 questions, including any breaks you may take.

Each question has only one best answer. Mark the one best answer on your answer sheet by filling in the circle next to A, B, C, or D.

A passing score on this test, like the PMP Exam, is 137 correct out of 200.

1. During testing, multiple defects were identified in a product. The project manager overseeing this product's development can best use which tool to help prioritize the problems?

    A. Pareto diagram.
    B. Control chart.
    C. Variance analysis.
    D. Order of magnitude estimate.

2. You are the manager of an aircraft design project. A significant portion of this aircraft will be designed by a subcontracting firm. How will this affect your communications management plan?

    A. More formal verbal communication will be required.
    B. Performance reports will be more detailed.
    C. More formal written communication will be required.
    D. Communication channels will significantly increase.

3. What officially creates the project?

    A. The project initiation document.
    B. The kickoff meeting.
    C. The project charter.
    D. The statement of work.

4. **Refer to the table at the right. What is the critical path?**

    A. Start-A-B-C-I-Finish.
    B. Start-A-B-H-I-Finish.
    C. Start-D-E-H-I-Finish.
    D. Start-F-G-I-Finish.

Task	Dependency	Duration
Start	None	0
A	Start	3
B	A	2
C	B	2
D	Start	4
E	D	1
F	Start	5
G	F	7
H	B, E	3
I	C, G, H	4
Finish	I	0

5.   The Delphi technique is a way to:

    A. Analyze performance.

    B. Gather expert opinion.

    C. Resolve conflict.

    D. Estimate durations.

6.   The work authorization system makes sure that:

    A. All the work and only the work gets performed.

    B. Work gets performed in right order and at the right time.

    C. Work is done completely and correctly.

    D. Functional managers are allowed complete control over who is assigned and when.

7.   Your team is hard at work on their assigned project tasks when one team member discovers a risk that was not identified during risk planning. What is the FIRST thing to do?

    A. Halt work on the project.

    B. Update the risk management plan.

    C. Look for ways to mitigate the risk.

    D. Assess the risk.

8.   The activity duration estimates should be developed by:

    A. The person or team doing the work.

    B. The project manager.

    C. Senior management.

    D. The customer.

9.   The project plan should be all of the following EXCEPT:

    A. A formal document.

    B. Distributed to stakeholders in accordance with the communications management plan.

    C. Approved by all project stakeholders.

    D. Used to manage project execution.

10.   You have been asked to take charge of project planning for a new project, but you have very little experience in managing projects. What will be the best source of help for you?

   A. Your education.
   B. Your on-the-job training.
   C. Historical information.
   D. Your functional manager.

11.   The majority of the project budget is expended on:

   A. Project plan development.
   B. Project plan execution.
   C. Integrated change control.
   D. Project communication.

12.   **Corrective action is:**

   A. Fixing past anomalies.
   B. Anything done to bring the project's future performance in line with the project plan.
   C. The responsibility of the change control board.
   D. An output of project plan execution.

13.   **Outputs of project plan execution include:**

   A. Work results and performance reports.
   B. Work results and corrective action.
   C. Work results and change requests.
   D. Performance reports and change requests.

14.   **Your original plan was to construct a building with six stories, with each story costing $150,000. This was to be completed in four months; however, the project has not gone as planned. Two months into the project, earned value is $400,000. What is the budgeted at completion?**

   A. 450,000
   B. 600,000
   C. 800,000
   D. 900,000

15.　Project integration is primarily the responsibility of:

　　A. The project team.
　　B. The project manager.
　　C. Senior management.
　　D. The project sponsor.

16.　One of your team members has discovered a way to add an extra deliverable to the project that will have minimal impact on the project schedule and cost. The project cost performance index is 1.3 and the schedule performance index is 1.5. The functionality was not included in the scope. How should you proceed?

　　A. Conform to the project scope and do not add the deliverable.
　　B. Deliver the extra work to the customer since it will not increase their costs.
　　C. Reject the deliverable because you are behind schedule.
　　D. Ask senior management for a decision.

17.　If a project manager is unsure who has the authority to approve changes in project scope, she should consult:

　　A. The customer.
　　B. The scope statement.
　　C. The sponsor.
　　D. The scope management plan.

18.　An end user has just requested a minor change to the project that will not impact the project schedule. How should you, the project manager, respond?

　　A. Authorize the change quickly to ensure that the schedule can truly remain unaffected.
　　B. Deny the change to help prevent scope creep.
　　C. Evaluate the impact of the change on the other project constraints.
　　D. Submit the change request to the change control board.

19.   Which of the following tools is used in initiating a project?

    A. Product analysis.

    B. Stakeholder analysis.

    C. Expert judgment.

    D. Decomposition.

20.   You overhear a casual conversation between two team members in which one confides to the other some problems he is having in completing his part of the project work. You realize that the work being discussed is on the project's critical path and that the information you overheard could mean a significant delay for your project. What should you do?

    A. Let the team member know that you heard his conversation and discuss the work problems with him immediately.

    B. Begin analyzing ways to compress the project schedule in anticipation of the potential delay.

    C. Ask a third team member to get involved immediately and encourage the two other team members to come to you with the delay.

    D. Ask human resources for help in resolving the problem.

21.   In which group of processes should the project manager be assigned his or her role in the project?

    A. Initiating.

    B. Planning.

    C. Executing.

    D. Controlling.

22.   A project charter should always include:

    A. Historical information.

    B. The business need underlying the project.

    C. The work breakdown structure.

    D. The scope management plan.

23. Your project team has just received the sponsor's approval for the scope statement. What is the NEXT step that needs to be taken?

    A. Develop the product description.
    B. Create a work breakdown structure.
    C. Hold the kickoff meeting.
    D. Create the network diagram.

24. Which of the following is NOT an input into scope definition?

    A. Product description.
    B. Historical information.
    C. Scope statement.
    D. Constraints.

25. The key function of the project manager's job in project integration is:

    A. Minimizing conflict to promote team unity.
    B. Making key decisions about resource allocation.
    C. Communicating with people of various backgrounds.
    D. Problem-solving and decision making between project subsystems.

26. In which of the following documents could the sponsor find work package descriptions?

    A. The work breakdown structure dictionary.
    B. The project charter.
    C. The scope management plan.
    D. The scope statement.

27. The process in which project deliverables are reviewed and accepted is called:

    A. Scope planning.
    B. Scope verification.
    C. Initiation.
    D. Scope change control.

28.   A statement of work is:

A. A type of contract.

B. A description of the project's product.

C. Necessary for every project.

D. A description of the part of a product to be obtained from an outside vendor.

29.   A commercial real-estate developer is planning to build a new office complex. He contracts with a construction firm to build one of the buildings for the actual cost of providing the materials and services plus a fixed fee for profit. What type of contract does this scenario represent?

A. Independent vendor.

B. Fixed price.

C. Cost-reimbursable.

D. Time and materials.

30.   You and your spouse both work for large companies in different industries. However, one day you learn that your company will be soliciting bids for a project and your spouse's company intends to bid. Your spouse will not be involved in the bidding process or any of the work it might produce if won. What should you do?

A. Request to be transferred off the project.

B. Inform management of the situation.

C. Say nothing and go on with the bidding process.

D. Say nothing but set up a system of checks and balances to ensure that your team selects the contractor impartially.

31.   Which of the following is NOT a purpose that scope definition serves?

A. To increase the accuracy of estimates.

B. To help facilitate roles and responsibilities.

C. To document the relationship between the product and the business need.

D. To define a baseline for project performance.

32. You are assigned to replace a project manager on a large software project for a telecommunications company in the middle of project execution. Portions of the software are being supplied by subcontractors working at your company's offices. You would like to know how performance reporting for these contract workers is to be carried out. Where could you find such information?

    A. The project charter.

    B. The procurement management plan.

    C. The work breakdown structure.

    D. The organizational chart.

33. Which of the following is NOT a type of contract?

    A. Cost-revisable.

    B. Fixed-price.

    C. Cost-reimbursable.

    D. Time and materials.

34. Your team has identified a component that they need for a project. There is some concern that they have never constructed a component like this one, but there are similar components available from sellers. Which of the following procurement activities would be MOST appropriate to perform?

    A. Solicitation.

    B. Make or buy analysis.

    C. Benefit/cost analysis.

    D. Source selection.

35. The activity list serves as an input to:

    A. The work breakdown structure.

    B. Activity definition.

    C. Activity duration estimating.

    D. Resource planning.

36. The person or group that formally accepts the project's product is:

    A. The quality team.
    B. The customer.
    C. The project team.
    D. Senior management.

37. The project activity list:

    A. Serves as an extension of the work breakdown structure.
    B. Is synonymous with the work breakdown structure.
    C. Is used to create the scope statement.
    D. Is included in the project charter.

38. Float refers to:

    A. A method for decreasing risk on a project.
    B. How long an activity can be delayed without affecting the critical path.
    C. A time lapse between a project communication and the response that follows.
    D. The difference between the budgeted cost and actual cost.

39. If a project scope requires goods or services that must be obtained outside the project organization, what management process will be used in obtaining them?

    A. Project contract management.
    B. Project solicitation management.
    C. Project procurement management.
    D. Project source management.

40. You are producing a training video for your company's human resource department. After the project is underway, a member of senior management requests that you use a copyrighted piece of music as background in the video. This video will not be sold or viewed outside of your company. As the project manager, you should:

    A. Use the song as requested by management.
    B. Investigate obtaining permission from the music publisher to use the song.
    C. Submit the request to the change control board.
    D. Produce the video without the song as specified in the project plan.

41. What is the most important function the project manager serves?

    A. Staffing.
    B. Motivating.
    C. Team building.
    D. Communicating.

42. If a task has been estimated at O = 4 days, P = 9 days, and M = 7, what is the standard deviation?

    A. 5/6 of a day.
    B. 6.83 days.
    C. 1/3 of a day.
    D. 1/2 of a day.

43. Refer to the table at the right. If task H were increased from 3 to 7, what impact would this have on the project?

    A. The project would finish later.
    B. The project would finish earlier.
    C. The schedule risk would decrease.
    D. The critical path would change, but the finish date would not change.

Task	Dependency	Duration
Start	None	0
A	Start	3
B	A	2
C	B	2
D	Start	4
E	D	1
F	Start	5
G	F	7
H	B, E	3
I	C, G, H	4
Finish	I	0

44. All of the following are needed for creating the project budget except:

    A. Cost estimates.
    B. Risk management plan.
    C. Schedule.
    D. Organizational policies.

45. Your company's CIO has requested a meeting with you and two other project managers for a status update on your various projects. What is the BEST document you can bring with you to this meeting:

    A. The milestone chart for this project.
    B. The network diagram for this project.
    C. Copies of the most recent status reports from the team members.
    D. The project charter.

46. Resource requirements should be developed to:

    A. The highest level within the work breakdown structure.
    B. The lowest level within the work breakdown structure.
    C. The most refined cost estimates available.
    D. The level set by the project office

47. Analogous estimating uses:

    A. Estimates of individual activities rolled up into a project total.
    B. Actual costs from a previous project as a basis for estimates.
    C. Computerized estimating tools.
    D. Parametric modeling techniques.

48. If the optimistic estimate for an activity is 15 days and the pessimistic estimate is 25 days, what is the most likely estimate?

    A. 19 days.
    B. 20 days.
    C. 21 days.
    D. Unknown.

49.   What does the standard deviation tell about a data set?

A. How diverse the population is.

B. The mean of the population as it relates to the median.

C. The specification limits of the population.

D. The range of data points within the population.

50.   Quality management theory is characterized by which of the following statements:

A. Inspection is the most important element for ensuring quality.

B. Planning for quality must be emphasized.

C. Contingency planning is a critical element of quality assurance.

D. Quality planning quantifies efforts to exceed customer expectations.

51.   Which of the following is NOT emphasized in project quality management?

A. Customer satisfaction.

B. Team responsibility.

C. Phases within processes.

D. Prevention over inspection.

52.   Benefit/cost analysis, benchmarking, flowcharting, and design of experiments are all techniques of what quality process?

A. Quality assurance.

B. Quality control.

C. Quality execution.

D. Quality definition.

53.   Which of the following is NOT an input to quality planning?

A. Organizational quality policies.

B. Scope statement.

C. Project schedule.

D. Standards and regulations.

54. The procurement management plan provides:

    A. Templates for contracts to be used.
    B. A formal description of how risks will be balanced within contracts.
    C. A description of procurement options.
    D. The types of contracts to be used for items being procured.

55. Ultimately, responsibility for quality management lies with the:

    A. Project team.
    B. Quality team.
    C. Project manager.
    D. Functional manager.

56. All of the following are tools used in quality control EXCEPT:

    A. Fishbone diagram.
    B. Pareto charts.
    C. Control charts.
    D. Trend analysis.

57. Control charts are:

    A. Used in product review.
    B. Used to chart a project's expected value.
    C. Used to determine if a process is in control.
    D. Used to define a statistical sample.

58. Which of the following statements regarding stakeholders is TRUE?

    A. They have some measurable financial interest in the project.
    B. Their needs should be qualified or quantified.
    C. Key stakeholders participate in the creation of the stakeholder management plan.
    D. They may either be positively or negatively affected by the outcome of the project.

59.   A risk rating matrix is useful for:

    A. Risk identification.
    B. Qualitative risk analysis.
    C. Quantitative risk analysis.
    D. Risk response planning.

60.   Your company must choose between two different projects. Project X has a net present value of $100,000. Project Y has a net present value of $75,000. What is the opportunity cost of choosing Project X?

    A. $100,000
    B. $75,000
    C. $25,000
    D. $50,000

61.   A risk database is produced during:

    A. Risk management planning.
    B. Risk identification.
    C. Risk assessment.
    D. Risk monitoring.

62.   A workaround is:

    A. A technique for conflict management.
    B. An adjustment to the project budget.
    C. A response to an unplanned risk event.
    D. A non-critical path on the network diagram.

63. You are managing a team developing a software product. You have contracted out a portion of the development. Midway through the project you learn that the contracting company is entering Chapter 11. A manager from the subcontracting company assures you that the state of the company will not affect your project. What should you do FIRST?

A. Perform additional risk response planning to control the risk this situation poses.

B. Stop all pending and future payments to the subcontractor until the threat is fully assessed.

C. Contact your legal department to research your options.

D. Meet with senior management to apprise them of the situation.

64. In a functional organization:

A. Power primarily lies with the project manager.

B. Power primarily lies with the functional manager.

C. Power is blended between functional and project managers.

D. Power primarily lies with the project office.

65. The process of identifying, documenting, and assigning roles, responsibilities, and reporting relationships for a project is called:

A. Project interfacing.

B. Organizational breakdown.

C. Staff management planning.

D. Organizational planning.

66. A Responsibility Assignment Matrix (RAM) does NOT indicate:

A. Who does what on the project.

B. Job roles for team members.

C. Job roles and responsibilities for groups.

D. Project reporting relationships.

67. A manager who follows Theory X believes:

    A. Employees can be trusted to direct their own efforts.
    B. Project success requires that project objectives must align with company objectives.
    C. Workers must be closely supervised because they dislike work.
    D. Effective quality management requires the use of performance measurements.

68. Which of the following is NOT a constructive team role?

    A. Withdrawer.
    B. Information seeker.
    C. Clarifier.
    D. Gate keeper.

69. If a project team is experiencing conflict over a technical decision that is negatively affecting project performance, the BEST source of power the project manager could exert to bring about cooperation would be:

    A. Legitimate.
    B. Penalty.
    C. Referent.
    D. Expert.

70. You have asked a team member to estimate the duration for a specific activity, and she has reported back to you with three estimates. The best case scenario is that the activity could be completed in 18 days; however, her most likely estimate for the task is 30 days. She has also indicated that there is the possibility the task could take as long as 60 days. What is the PERT estimate for this task?

    A. 4 days.
    B. 7 days.
    C. 33 days.
    D. 49 days.

71. Which of the following types of conflict resolution provides only a temporary solution to the problem?

    A. Withdrawal.
    B. Compromising.
    C. Forcing.
    D. Problem-solving.

72. The communications management plan:

    A. Should be formal.
    B. Should be highly detailed.
    C. Should include the project's major milestones.
    D. Should detail what methods should be used to gather and store information.

73. When communication links are undefined or broken:

    A. The communications management plan should be rewritten.
    B. Conflict will increase.
    C. The project manager's power will decrease.
    D. Project work will stop.

74. For two days you have been asking a member of your team for a status report on one of the key deliverables of your project. You finally get the report thirty minutes before you are to meet with senior management for a project update. A quick review of the status report reveals some information that you know is incorrect. What action should you take?

    A. Fix what you can in the report before the meeting starts and try to steer discussion away from the areas you don't have time to fix.
    B. Bring your team member with you to the meeting and confront her with the inaccuracies in her report.
    C. Reschedule the meeting for a later date and have the team member rewrite the report.
    D. Cancel the meeting, fix the report yourself, and circulate the new report to senior management in lieu of the original meeting.

75. There were 10 people on your project, and 5 more people were added last week. How many additional paths of communication were created?

    A. 10.
    B. 45.
    C. 60.
    D. 105.

76. A project manager is having difficulty getting resources from a functional manager. Which of the following would be the MOST appropriate to help resolve this problem?

    A. Senior management.
    B. The customer.
    C. Key stakeholders.
    D. The sponsor.

77. Communicating via email is considered:

    A. Formal written communication.
    B. Informal written communication.
    C. Formal electronic communication.
    D. Informal non-verbal communication.

78. Smoothing, forcing, and withdrawing are all forms of:

    A. Organizational power.
    B. Communication.
    C. Conflict resolution.
    D. Schedule compression.

79. You have a team member who is habitually late to meetings with the customer. The customer has expressed dissatisfaction with the situation and has asked you to resolve it. Your BEST course of action is:

    A. Issue a formal written reprimand to the team member
    B. Meet with the team member to discuss the problem and ask for solutions.
    C. Meet with the team member and the customer to promote further understanding.
    D. Email the team member to bring the situation to his attention.

80. You are midway through managing a project with a sponsor-approved budget of $850,000. Using earned value management, you have determined that the project will run $125,000 under budget. You have also determined that if the project is delivered that far under budget you will not make your bonus since you are compensated for the hours you bill. What is your BEST course of action?

    A. Add extra features to the project scope that take advantage of the available budget, and increase customer satisfaction.

    B. Meet with the project sponsor to inform him of your findings.

    C. Maintain current project activities, and bill for the original amount.

    D. Ask the sponsor to approve additional features, given the available budget.

81. The most important factor in project integration is:

    A. A clearly defined scope.

    B. Timely corrective action.

    C. Team buy-in on the project plan.

    D. Effective communication.

82. You are a project manager for a software development firm. You are in the final stages of negotiation with a third party vendor whose product your company is considering implementing. You discover by chance that one of your employees has scheduled a product demonstration with herself, the vendor, and your boss, but you have not been notified about the meeting. What do you do?

    A. Show up at the meeting unannounced and discuss the situation with the employee later in private.

    B. Report this employee's actions to your boss using the company's formal reporting procedure.

    C. Discuss the employee's actions with her before the meeting.

    D. Report the employee's actions to her functional manager.

83. Your team has encountered recent unanticipated problems. After extensive earned value analysis you determine that the project has a schedule performance index of .54 and a cost performance index of 1.3. Additionally your customer has just requested a significant change. What should you do?

    A. Alert management about the schedule delays.
    B. Alert management about the cost overruns.
    C. Alert management about the scope change.
    D. Reject the requested change.

84. You are in the middle of bidding on a large and complex project that will produce a great deal of revenue for your company should you win the bid. The buyer has specified several conditions that accelerate some of the key dates and milestones. You have done extensive planning with your team and have determined that there is no way that your organization can perform the required scope of work under these new deadlines. Your boss, however, is not convinced that you are right and is also concerned that if you don't agree to the new dates you will lose the contract. What should you do?

    A. Appeal to the buyer for additional time to estimate.
    B. Ask your boss to make the commitment on behalf of the team.
    C. Adhere to the estimates your team has made.
    D. Agree to the dates the customer has requested.

85. Your company is soliciting bids from advertising firms for the marketing of the product your project will produce. A sales representatives from one of the bidding firms calls to invite you to attend a sporting event with him at his expense so that he can ask you some questions about the product to help him put together his bid. How should you respond?

    A. Attend the event and discuss the project with the representative.
    B. Accept his offer but tell him in advance that you cannot answer questions about the project.
    C. Attend the event and answer all questions, but then write a report on the questions and answers and submit the FAQ to the other bidders.
    D. Reject the offer and invite the sales representative to pose his questions at the bidders' conference.

86.   Analogous estimating is also called:

    A. Vendor bid analysis.

    B. Bottom-up estimating.

    C. Scalable model estimating.

    D. Top-down estimating.

87.   You are beginning construction of a bridge in another country, when you discover that this country requires that one of its licensed engineers sign off on the plans before you break ground. Your senior engineer on the project is licensed in your own country and is probably more qualified than anyone to sign off on this, and their engineer is not available to review the plans for another three weeks. The customer has stressed that this project must not be delayed. What do you do?

    A. Have your engineer sign off on the plans, forward them to the other engineer and begin construction.

    B. Have your engineer sign off on the plans since he is licensed in your country and begin construction.

    C. Wait to begin construction until the country's engineer signs off on the plans.

    D. Forward the plans to the country's engineer for their signature and start construction.

88.   **Refer to the table at right. What is the length of the critical path?**

    A. 16

    B. 21

    C. 22

    D. 23

Task	Duration
Start-A	1
A-B	3
B-C	4
A-E	3
E-F	1
C-D	6
E-C	0
B-F	7
F-G	7
G-Finish	5
D-Finish	2

89. You are managing the installation of a new oil well pump in a very productive well. Due to very efficient management and significant personal effort, the project is completed several days ahead of schedule. The customer is ecstatic and offers you a $2,500 "appreciation fee". What should you do?

    A. Accept the fee, but notify management.
    B. Do not accept the fee and notify management.
    C. Put the gift into the project's reserve fund.
    D. Donate the gift to charity.

90. Decomposition is a technique used in:

    A. Activity definition
    B. Activity duration estimating
    C. Activity sequencing
    D. Schedule development

91. A fixed-price contract offers the seller:

    A. A higher risk than the buyer.
    B. A risk level equal to that of the buyer.
    C. A lower risk than the buyer.
    D. Reimbursement of actual costs.

92. The individual on a project with limited authority who handles some communication and ensures that tasks are completed on time is:

    A. The project manager.
    B. The project leader.
    C. The project coordinator.
    D. The sponsor.

93. At what point in project planning would you decide to change the project scope in order to avoid certain high-risk activities?

    A. Risk identification.
    B. Risk qualification.
    C. Risk monitoring.
    D. Risk response planning.

94. Which of the following techniques is used in scope planning?

    A. Project selection methods.
    B. WBS templates.
    C. Benefit/cost analysis.
    D. Inspection.

95. Which of the following statements is NOT TRUE of integration management?

    A. Integration is primarily concerned with making sure various elements of the project are coordinated.
    B. Integration is a discrete process.
    C. The project management information system is used to support all aspects of the project.
    D. The project manager must make tradeoffs between competing project objectives.

96. Maslow's Hierarchy of Needs theory concludes that:

    A. Higher needs cannot be realized until the lower needs are satisfied.
    B. Hygiene factors are those that provide physical safety and emotional security.
    C. Psychological needs for growth and fulfillment are ineffective motivators.
    D. The greater the financial reward, the more motivated the workers will be.

97. A project is all of the following EXCEPT:

    A. Progressively elaborated.
    B. Has never been done by this company before.
    C. Interrelated activities.
    D. Strategic to the company.

98. Your manager has asked to review the quality management plan with you to ensure that it is being followed appropriately. In which process is your boss involved?

    A. Quality control.
    B. Quality management.
    C. Quality planning.
    D. Quality assurance.

99. Variance analysis is a tool used to:

    A. Measure variance between actual work and the baseline.
    B. Measure variance between planned value and schedule variance.
    C. Measure variance between earned value and actual cost.
    D. Measure variance between earned value and cost variance.

100. In a strong matrix organization:

    A. More power is given to the functional manager.
    B. More power is given to the project manager.
    C. More power is given to the project expeditor.
    D. More power is given to the project coordinator.

101. A "performance review" is another name for:

    A. Program stress test.
    B. Scope verification.
    C. Status meeting.
    D. Employment review.

102. The Scope Statement is typically:

    A. A definitive list of all the work and only the work to be done on the project.
    B. Issued by senior management.
    C. Progressively elaborated.
    D. Defined before the functional specifications.

103. Which of the following is a negative team role?

    A. Initiator.
    B. Information seeker.
    C. Devil's advocate.
    D. Gate keeper.

104. During project plan execution your project team should be:

    A. Focused on making sure earned value is equal to planned value.
    B. Communicating work results to the stakeholders.
    C. Ensuring that all project changes are reflected in the project plan.
    D. Executing the work packages.

105. When is the project management information system used MOST?

    A. Initiation processes.
    B. Planning processes.
    C. Executing processes.
    D. Controlling processes.

106. In a typical project, most of the resources are utilized and expended during:

    A. Initiation processes.
    B. Planning processes.
    C. Executing processes.
    D. Controlling processes.

107. A project manager is taking the product of his project to his customer for verification that it meets the scope. The customer and the project manager are working together to carefully compare the product to the project's scope to ensure that the work was done to specification. The tool that the customer and the project manager are using is:

    A. Inspection.
    B. Quality assurance.
    C. Quality control.
    D. User acceptance testing.

108. Which of the following is NOT a project quality management process?

    A. Quality assurance.
    B. Quality planning.
    C. Quality improvement.
    D. Quality control.

109. Schedule constraints should include all of the following EXCEPT?

    A. Imposed dates.
    B. Key events.
    C. Major milestones.
    D. Leads and lags.

110. Which of the following choices fits the definition for benchmarking?

    A. Comparing planned results to actual results.
    B. Comparing actual or planned results to those of other projects.
    C. Statistical sampling of results and comparing them to the plan.
    D. Comparing planned value with earned value.

111. The activity list should include:

    A. The activities on the project that are on the critical path.
    B. A subset of all project activities.
    C. All of the activities defined on the project.
    D. A superset of the project activities.

112. Administrative closure should be performed:

    A. At the end of each phase or the end of the project.
    B. Before formal acceptance of the project's product.
    C. As a safeguard against risk.
    D. By someone other than the project manager.

113. Project resources should be released as part of which process?

    A. Team development.
    B. Contract closure.
    C. Administrative closure.
    D. Resource closure.

114. Which of the following is NOT an input into activity definition?

    A. The work breakdown structure.
    B. Historical information.
    C. Assumptions.
    D. The activity list.

115. A project to lay 10 miles of a petroleum pipeline was scheduled to be completed today, exactly 20 weeks from the start of the project. You receive a report that the project has an overall schedule performance index of 0.8. Based on this information, when would you expect the project to be completed?

    A. 2 weeks early.
    B. In 2 more weeks.
    C. In 5 more weeks.
    D. In 10 more weeks.

116. The term "slack" is also known as:

    A. Lag.
    B. Lead.
    C. Float.
    D. Free float.

117. Which of the following BEST describes the project plan?

    A. A formal, approved document used to guide project execution, control, and closure.
    B. The aggregate of all work performed during planning.
    C. The work breakdown structure, schedule management plan, budget, cost management plan, and quality management plan.
    D. The document that outlines all of the work and only the work that must be performed on a project.

118. Which of the following is NOT a primary goal of integrated change control?

    A. Influencing factors that cause change.
    B. Determining that a change has occurred.
    C. Managing change as it occurs.
    D. Denying change whenever possible.

119. You are providing project management services in a foreign country. In an attempt to improve employment, this country has enacted a law limiting the number of hours foreigners may work per week. You are behind schedule on the project and need to work overtime. What is the BEST way to handle this situation?

    A. Work the overtime only if you own country's laws do not prohibit this.
    B. Work the overtime if it is not constituted overtime by your country's definition.
    C. Do not work the overtime since it is prohibited by law.
    D. Speak with legal representation to find out if the law is enforceable.

120. "The features and attributes that characterize a product" describes which of the following?

    A. The product scope.
    B. The project scope.
    C. The work breakdown structure.
    D. The critical success factors.

121.   You have assumed responsibility for a project that has completed planning and is executing the work packages of the project. In one of your first status meetings, a member of the project team begins to question the validity of the duration estimates for a series of related tasks assigned to her. What action should you take FIRST?

    A. Remind the team member that planning has been completed and ask her to do her best to adhere to the estimates.

    B. Temporarily suspend execution and ask the team member for updated estimates.

    C. Review the supporting detail for the estimates contained in the project plan to understand how the estimates were originally derived.

    D. Ask another team member with expertise in this area to perform a peer review on the estimates to validate or invalidate the concern.

122.   Approved budget changes should be:

    A. Added to the schedule management plan.

    B. Added to the project's cost baseline.

    C. Added to the project's reserve fund and used only if needed.

    D. Added to the lessons learned.

123.   An organization where the project manager is in charge of the projects and has primary responsibility for the resources is:

    A. Functional.

    B. Projectized.

    C. Matrix.

    D. Hierarchical.

124.   Based on the table at the right. Which path listed below represents the LEAST schedule risk?

    A. Start-A-B-C-I-Finish

    B. Start-A-B-H-I-Finish

    C. Start-D-E-H-I-Finish

    D. Start-F-G-I-Finish

Task	Dependency	Duration
Start	None	0
A	Start	3
B	A	2
C	B	2
D	Start	4
E	D	1
F	Start	5
G	F	7
H	B, E	3
I	C, G, H	4
Finish	I	0

125. As part of your project, your customer needs a software module to handle credit card payments. Senior management informs you that they already own the rights to such a module and would like for you to use this piece of software on the project; however, upon investigation, you determine that your company's software is not a good match for this customer's needs. After informing your senior management, they maintain their request that you use their software. How should you resolve this conflict?

    A. Look to build or procure another solution for the customer.
    B. Act in favor of the performing organization.
    C. Use your company's software module as requested as long as it does not jeopardize the project.
    D. Involve an objective outside party to help resolve the dispute.

126. Leads and Lags are used as an input into which process?

    A. Activity sequencing.
    B. Cost estimating.
    C. Performance reporting.
    D. Schedule development.

127. You have received a report showing that your overall schedule performance index is 1.5. How should you interpret this information?

    A. You are earning value into your project at 1.5 times the rate you had planned.
    B. You are spending $1.50 for every dollar you planned to spend at this point in the schedule.
    C. You are earning $1.50 of value back into your project for every $1.00 you spend.
    D. You are earning $0.67 of value back into your project for every $1.00 you planned to earn.

128. The organizational chart produced on the project should include which of the following:

    A. The performing organization's organizational structure.
    B. A representation of all identified stakeholders.
    C. The reporting structure for the project.
    D. The organizational structure for all entities related to the project.

129. Cost estimating should be performed:

    A. Before the work breakdown structure is created and before the budget is developed.

    B. Before the work breakdown structure is created and after the budget is developed.

    C. After the work breakdown structure is created and before the budget is developed.

    D. After the work breakdown structure is created and after the budget is developed.

130. A list of the risks that could affect the project is an output of which process?

    A. Risk management planning.

    B. Risk identification.

    C. Risk response planning.

    D. Risk monitoring and control.

131. Which process focuses on producing a list of the activities needed to produce the deliverables and sub-deliverables described in the work breakdown structure?

    A. Activity definition.

    B. Activity sequencing.

    C. Activity list.

    D. Activity duration estimating.

132. Whose job is it to resolve competing objectives and goals between parties on the project?

    A. The stakeholders.

    B. The project manager.

    C. Senior management.

    D. The sponsor.

133.   As project manager, you have made the decision to outsource a part of your project to an outside organization with whom you have never previously worked. You are ready to begin negotiating the contract. What should be your goal in the contract negotiations?

   A. Having a lawyer or the legal department review each clause in the proposed contract prior to sharing it with any outside entity.
   B. Negotiating the best possible price for your customer or organization.
   C. Arriving at mutually agreeable terms for the contract between your organization and the subcontracting organization.
   D. Shifting as much of the project risk to the subcontracting organization as possible.

134.   You have been working under contract on a very large automotive project that has spanned several years. As part of this project, you have been privileged to practically all of the project information. As you are transitioning off of the project, you would like to use the extensive work breakdown structure as an input into future projects. You were never asked to sign a non disclosure agreement with the current organization. What is the appropriate thing to do in this case?

   A. Use the work breakdown structure as you are not bound by any agreement not to.
   B. Use the work breakdown structure, but do not share it with others.
   C. Do not use the work breakdown structure without the organization's permission.
   D. Do not use the work breakdown structure because it would still be illegal.

135.   Which of the following is NOT an output of cost control?

   A. Corrective action.
   B. Lessons learned.
   C. Budget updates.
   D. Cost baseline.

136. If the schedule variance = $0.00, what must also be true?

    A. Earned value must be equal to planned value.

    B. The cost performance index must be equal to 1.

    C. The schedule performance index must be greater than 1.

    D. The estimate at complete must be equal to budgeted at complete.

137. Activities are a further decomposition of which of the following:

    A. The statement of scope.

    B. The work packages.

    C. The project network diagram.

    D. The functional specification.

138. Which statement is TRUE regarding the staffing management plan?

    A. It is used as an input into organizational planning.

    B. It becomes part of the project plan.

    C. It should name every human and material resource who will be working on the project.

    D. It should contain an organization chart for the performing organization.

139. Jeremy is a project manager who is asking his team to identify the risk triggers on his project. As part of this process, he has divided the project team into seven sub-teams, each focusing on a separate area of the project. He has asked that the risk triggers be delivered by each sub-team no later than one week from today. Which statement below BEST applies to risk triggers?

    A. They are actions that may cause risk events.

    B. They are warning signs that a risk event may be occurring.

    C. They are mechanisms for creating a positive risk on the project.

    D. They are mechanisms for controlling risk on the project.

140. You have a friend in another organization who has shared with you that he is having difficulty understanding the value of doing a scope statement. Your friend's boss is not familiar with formal project management processes and does not want to waste time on the project performing unnecessary activities. What is your MOST appropriate response?

    A. Do not get involved since this is not within your organization.
    B. Pay a visit to your friend's project office and educate them on the value of a scope statement.
    C. Mentor your friend on the value of project management processes.
    D. Encourage your friend to change organizations.

141. You are managing a project to construct 25 miles of highway at an estimated cost of $1.2 million per mile. You have projected that you should be able to complete the project in 5 weeks. What is your planned value for the end of the 3rd week of the project?

    A. $12,000,000
    B. $18,000,000
    C. $24,000,000
    D. $30,000,000

142. Which term below describes the amount of time a task may be delayed before it affects the early start date of a subsequent task?

    A. Float.
    B. Slack.
    C. Free float.
    D. Lead.

143. Why is earned value analysis used during risk monitoring and control?

    A. To calculate the positive or negative value of a risk event.
    B. To ensure that the project is delivered on budget.
    C. To avoid risk.
    D. To monitor whether or not a financial risk is occurring or has occurred.

144. You have an unfavorable project status to report to your customer at a weekly meeting; however, you are reasonably certain that you can correct the situation by next week's meeting. The customer will not be pleased to hear the current status and based on past history, will likely overreact. How should you handle this situation?

    A. Report the current status to the customer.

    B. Report your anticipated project status for next week to the customer.

    C. Omit the information from your meeting and cover it next week when the news improves.

    D. Ask you project office for guidance.

145. What type of process is source selection?

    A. Planning.

    B. Executing.

    C. Controlling.

    D. Closing.

146. Who is responsible for providing funding for the project?

    A. The qualified financial institution.

    B. Senior management.

    C. The sponsor.

    D. The project manager.

147. The project has been successfully completed when:

    A. All of the work has been completed to specification within time and budget.

    B. The customer is happy.

    C. The sponsor signs off on the project.

    D. Earned value equals planned value.

148. What is the PRIMARY objective of the project manager?

    A. To follow PMI's processes.

    B. To deliver maximum value for the organization.

    C. To deliver the agreed upon scope of the project within the time and budget.

    D. To delight the customer.

149. Graphical Evaluative Review Technique is an example of:

    A. Performance review.
    B. Arrow diagramming method.
    C. Precedence diagramming method.
    D. Conditional diagramming method.

150. After your customer has accepted the product of your project, you discover a small, but important piece of functionality that was overlooked. The project was performed under contract, and the customer has already signed off. What is the MOST appropriate course of action?

    A. Take no action since this is a legal issue and the customer has signed off.
    B. Report the oversight to the customer and perform the work.
    C. Report the oversight to the customer and ask them to issue a change request if they still want the component.
    D. Ask the sponsor for his opinion on how this should be handled.

151. What is indicated by an activity's late finish date?

    A. The latest the activity can finish without delaying a subsequent activity.
    B. The latest the activity can finish without delaying the project.
    C. The latest probable date that the activity will finish.
    D. The worst-case or pessimistic estimate for an activity.

152. A speech given at a tradeshow is an example of which kind of communication?

    A. Informal written.
    B. Formal written.
    C. Informal verbal.
    D. Formal verbal.

153. Requests for payment would typically be performed in which process?

    A. Formal closure.
    B. Scope verification.
    C. Contract administration.
    D. Solicitation.

154. Herzberg's theory of motivation states that:

    A. Hygiene factors must be present for motivational factors to work.
    B. Motivation to work on the project must be related back to the individual's need.
    C. An individual's higher needs will not emerge until the lower needs are met.
    D. Individuals are motivated by a desire to reach proficiency.

155. If there are multiple critical paths on the project, which of the following must also be true?

    A. Only one path will ultimately emerge as the true critical path.
    B. The schedule risk will be higher with multiple critical paths than with one.
    C. The schedule should be crashed in order to resolve the conflict.
    D. The schedule should be fast-tracked in order to resolve the conflict.

156. Which projected payback period below is the MOST desirable?

    A. 24 months.
    B. 52 weeks.
    C. 3 years.
    D. 1000 days.

157. Which of the following would be an output of activity sequencing?

    A. Mandatory dependencies.
    B. An activity on arrow diagram.
    C. Discretionary dependencies.
    D. External dependencies.

158. While executing the project plan, you discover that a component was missed during planning. The project schedule is not in danger, but the component is not absolutely critical for go-live. What should you do?

    A. Treat the component as a new project.
    B. Reject the component as it would introduce unacceptable risk.
    C. Appeal to the project sponsor for guidance.
    D. Return to planning processes for the new component.

159.   The goal of duration compression is to:

    A. Reduce time by reducing risk on the project.

    B. Reduce cost on the project.

    C. Reduce the scope by eliminating non-critical functionality from the project.

    D. Reduce the schedule without changing the scope.

160.   You are managing two projects for two different customers. While meeting with one customer, you discover a sensitive piece of information that could help your other customer, saving them a significant percentage of their project budget. What should you do?

    A. Act in accordance with any legal documents you have signed.

    B. Disclose your conflict of interest and keep the information confidential.

    C. Share the information with the other customer if it increases project value.

    D. Excuse yourself from both projects if possible.

161.   What is the difference between a standard and a regulation?

    A. A standard is issued by ANSI, and a regulation is issued by the government.

    B. A standard is an input into quality planning, while a regulation is an input into initiation.

    C. A standard usually should be followed, and a regulation must be followed.

    D. There is no appreciable difference between a standard and a regulation.

162.   Evaluation criteria are used to:

    A. Select a qualified seller.

    B. Measure conformance to quality.

    C. Determine if a project should be undertaken.

    D. Evaluate performance on the project.

163. Richard is a project manager who is looking at the risks on his project and developing options to enhance the opportunities and reduce the threats to the project's objectives. Which process is Richard performing?

    A. Risk management planning.
    B. Risk identification.
    C. Qualitative risk analysis.
    D. Risk response planning.

164. If you are soliciting bids for a project, which of the following would be an appropriate output from this process?

    A. Proposals from potential sellers.
    B. Change requests.
    C. Contracts.
    D. Qualified seller lists.

165. The work results of the project:

    A. Are always products.
    B. Are products, services, or results.
    C. Are only considered work results if quality standards have been met.
    D. Are an output of the work authorization system.

166. You have been directed by your customer, your sponsor, and senior management to manage a project that you believe will have a very negative impact on the economy and society. You have shared your concerns, but all parties continue to insist that you proceed. What should you do?

    A. Manage the project because all parties agree.
    B. Refuse to manage the project.
    C. Manage the project, but document your objections.
    D. Contact PMI.

167. The quality policy is an important input into quality planning because:

    A. It defines the performing organization's formal position on quality.
    B. It helps benchmark the project against other similar projects.
    C. It provides specific quality standards that may be used to measure the output of the project.
    D. It details the constraints and assumption the project must take in to consideration.

168. During execution, regular project team meetings should PRIMARILY be used to:

    A. Discuss the project and give the team a chance to voice any concerns.
    B. Evaluate new change requests.
    C. Review the status and progress of work completed.
    D. Meet with the customer to evaluate and enhance satisfaction.

169. A project manager has a problem with a team member's attendance, but every time the project manager schedules a meeting to discuss the problem, the team member comes up with a reason they cannot attend at the last minute. Which conflict management technique is the team member exhibiting?

    A. Passive-aggressive
    B. Covering up
    C. Diverting
    D. Withdrawing

170. In which of the following organizations is the project manager MOST likely to be part time?

    A. Weak matrix
    B. Strong matrix
    C. Functional
    D. Projectized

171. What is the output used to show project roles and responsibilities on the project?

    A. The resource histogram.
    B. The organization chart.
    C. The responsibility assignment matrix.
    D. The staffing management plan.

172. Kim is managing a multi-million dollar construction project to that is scheduled to take nearly two years to complete. During one of the planning processes, she discovers a significant threat to her project's budget and schedule due to the fact that she is planning to build during the hurricane season in a high-risk area. After carefully evaluating her options, she decides to build earlier in the season when there is less of a risk of severe hurricane damage. This is an example of:

    A. Risk avoidance.
    B. Risk transference.
    C. Risk acceptance.
    D. Risk mitigation.

173. You are managing the development of a software project to be created under procurement. The team will span three countries and five time zones, and because of the size of the project, you are very concerned about cost. Which of the following types of contract would BEST help keep cost down?

    A. Time and materials.
    B. Cost plus fixed fee.
    C. Cost plus incentive fee.
    D. Variable conditions.

174. If there were 16 people on the project, and that number increases to 25, which of the following must also be true?

    A. The development of the communications management plan will be more difficult.
    B. Stakeholder analysis will be more difficult.
    C. Information distribution will be more difficult.
    D. Controlling communication will be more difficult.

175.   You are a PMP, and PMI has contacted you regarding an investigation of your best friend who is also a PMP at your company. How should you proceed?

   A. Cooperate fully with PMI.
   B. Protest that this is conflict of interest.
   C. Protect your friend.
   D. Find out why PMI thinks your friend should be investigated.

176.   A project is scheduled to last for 6 months and cost $300,000. At the end of the 1st month, the project is 20% complete. What is the Earned Value?

   A. $50,010.
   B. $60,000.
   C. $100,020.
   D. $120,000.

177.   Which of the following roles typically has the LEAST power?

   A. Project coordinator.
   B. Project expeditor.
   C. Project manager.
   D. Project director.

178.   Configuration management is:

   A. A technique used in project plan development.
   B. Used to ensure that the product scope is complete and correct.
   C. Formally defined in initiation.
   D. A procedure to identify and document the functional and physical characteristics of an item or system.

179.   Organizational planning is often tightly linked with:

   A. Scope planning.
   B. Communications planning.
   C. Schedule planning.
   D. Resource planning.

180. A company in the middle of a new product development merges with another company in the middle of the project. The project is terminated because the new company already offers a similar product. What is the FIRST thing the project manager should do?

A. Make sure your lessons learned are communicated to the manager of the existing product.

B. Obtain a written project termination.

C. Perform a comparative product analysis.

D. Enter administrative closure.

181. A benefit-cost ratio of 1.5 tells you that:

A. The payback period will be one and one half years.

B. The project cannot pay for itself.

C. The project will yield revenue that is 1.5 times its cost.

D. The project will cost 1.5 times the revenue it produces.

182. The MOST important input into resource planning is:

A. The work breakdown structure.

B. The historical information.

C. The project charter.

D. The constraints and assumptions.

183. Life-cycle costing involves:

A. Determining what physical resources will be needed to complete a project.

B. Considering the overall costs of a project during and after its completion.

C. Assigning a value to each activity on the project.

D. Calculating the internal rate of return.

184. A construction company is building a new office complex and has contracted with a computer hardware firm to install computer networking cables throughout the buildings. The contract states that the construction company will buy the materials and pay an hourly rate to the computer firm to cover their time on the project. Who is assuming the primary cost risk in this contract?

    A. The companies share the risk equally.
    B. There is not enough information given to answer the question.
    C. The seller.
    D. The buyer.

185. Linda is managing a multi-national project that utilizes several sub-project teams. Before the last team meeting, the sponsor asked her to bring a Control Account Plan for him to review. Which of the following statements is MOST correct regarding the Control Account Plan?

    A. It is used to plan for and predict future project costs.
    B. It is used to measure cost, and schedule for a point on the WBS.
    C. It is used to relate costs back to the chart of accounts.
    D. It is used as a contingency account for activities that have been identified as high risk.

186. Stakeholder analysis is performed as part of:

    A. Project initiation.
    B. Scope planning.
    C. Communications planning.
    D. Risk management planning.

187. Alex is a project manager who wants to motivate his team by offering them a week of paid vacation if the project is delivered on time. When presenting this to the team, he spends extra time convincing the team that this goal is very achievable. What theory BEST explains Alex's behavior?

    A. Expectancy theory.
    B. Contingency theory.
    C. Achievement theory.
    D. Stimulus/Response theory.

188. All of the following are needed for creating the project budget except:

    A. Cost estimates.
    B. Schedule.
    C. Risk management plan.
    D. Organizational policies.

189. The fact that a software program must be written before it can be tested is an example of a:

    A. Mandatory dependency.
    B. Discretionary dependency.
    C. External dependency.
    D. Milestone dependency.

190. What is the difference between a Gantt chart and a milestone chart?

    A. A Gantt chart is a project plan and a milestone chart is not.
    B. A milestone chart is a project plan and a Gantt chart is not.
    C. A milestone chart shows interdependencies between activities.
    D. A milestone chart shows only major events.

191. Your team has created a scope statement and a work breakdown structure. What is the NEXT step that needs to be taken?

    A. Create a network diagram.
    B. Develop the schedule.
    C. Determine the critical path.
    D. Create the activity list.

192. Authorization of a new project or project phase is part of:

    A. The work authorization system.
    B. Scope initiation.
    C. Scope management.
    D. Project plan integration.

193. A cable company is installing new fiber optic cables in a community. You are the project manager and you will be using subcontractors to provide some of the installations. You have completed the procurement management plan and the statement of work, and you have gathered and prepared the documents that will be distributed to the sellers. What process should happen next?

    A. Scope planning.
    B. Source selection.
    C. Solicitation planning.
    D. Solicitation.

194. Evaluating overall project performance on a regular basis to ensure that it meets established quality standards takes place in which process group of project management?

    A. Planning.
    B. Executing.
    C. Controlling.
    D. Closing.

195. The MAIN use of a project network diagram is to:

    A. Create the project plan.
    B. Show activity percentages complete.
    C. Show activity sequences and dependencies.
    D. Create paths through the network.

196. Who issues the quality policy?

    A. The performing organization.
    B. The stakeholders.
    C. The project manager.
    D. A standards body.

197. You are managing a project when an unplanned risk event occurs. You meet with experts and determine a workaround to keep the project on track. In which process are you engaged?

    A. Qualitative risk analysis.
    B. Quantitative risk analysis.
    C. Risk response planning.
    D. Risk monitoring and control.

198. Bribes may:

    A. Result in a lower overall cost on the project.
    B. Result in jail time for the parties involved.
    C. Result in increased project risk.
    D. Be acceptable only if there is no law against the practice.

199. A project is scheduled to last 6 months and cost $300,000. At the end of the 1st month, the project is 20% complete. What is the schedule performance index?

    A. 0.94
    B. 1.02
    C. 1.18
    D. 2.15

200. Bringing the entire project team and the customer on site to work together is an example of:

    A. Communication control.
    B. Collocation.
    C. Active participation.
    D. Collective team distribution.

Final Exam Answers

1. A. Pareto charts are column charts that rank defects based on the number of occurrences from highest to lowest. Because this tool is based on frequency, it prioritizes the most common causes. 'B' is used to determine whether or not a process is in control. 'C' is used to measure the difference between what was planned and what was done, and 'D' is a type of estimate used in cost management.

2. C. Because this is being done under contract, you will need to use more formal, written communication. Many people incorrectly guess 'D' on this one, but actually the opposite is true. Communication channels will most likely decrease since you are using another company and will probably have a single point of contact as opposed to your own team of many people doing the work. 'B' is not correct, since performance reports should be detailed regardless of who is doing the work.

3. C. The charter is the document that officially creates the project, names the project manager, and gives him authority on the project.

4. D. This problem should be solved in 3 steps. First, draw out the network diagram based on the table. Your representation should resemble the one below:

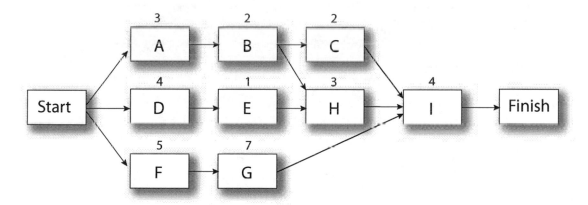

The next step is to list out all of the possible paths through the network. In this example, they are:

Start-A-B-C-I-Finish

Start-A-B-H-I-Finish

Start-D-E-H-I-Finish

Start-F-G-I-Finish

The last step is to add up the values associated with each path. Using the paths above, they are:

Start-A-B-C-I-Finish = 11 units

Start-A-B-H-I-Finish = 12 units

Start-D-E-H-I-Finish = 12 units

Start-F-G-I-Finish = 16 units

The critical path is the longest one, in this case, Start-F-G-I-Finish.

5.   B. The Delphi technique is a way to solicit expert opinion by hiding the identities of group members from each other. This prevents the group from forming a single opinion or from letting one person dominate the group.

6.   B. The work authorization system (WAS) is a system used during project integration management to ensure that work gets done at the right time and in the right sequence.

7.   D. Typically you should assess, investigate, understand, and evaluate before acting. There may be exceptions to this rule, but in general you probably want to select the answer that lets you get all of the information. If there is a series of answers and you are asked what to do FIRST (as in this example), selecting the answer that allows you to be fully informed is usually best. 'A' is incorrect because halting work would probably send risks skyrocketing. 'B' is a good thing to do, but not until you have fully evaluated the risk. 'C' is something you may or may not choose to do, but you should not take action until you have fully assessed the risk.

8.   A. This is frequently missed because people do not fully understand the role of the team in planning. The team should help estimate and should support those estimates. If possible, the person who will be doing the work should have a say in the estimate. 'B' is incorrect because the project manager cannot possibly estimate all of the activities on the project, nor should he even try. 'C' and 'D' are incorrect since management and the customer are probably not aware of all of the low-level details needed, and their estimates would not be accurate.

9.   C. The stakeholders do not have to approve the project plan. They may be very interested in the final product, but the actual plan cannot undergo approval by all stakeholders. Some stakeholders may never approve of the plan since they may be against the project! 'A' is incorrect because the project plan must be a formal. 'B' is incorrect because the communications management plan will specify to whom you should communicate the plan. 'D' is incorrect since the purpose of the project plan is to guide execution and control.

10.   C. Your best source of help would be the information you can use from past projects. 'A' is incorrect since education may or may not be applicable to this project, and although it is good, education is principally theoretical, while historical information contains practical, hard data. 'B' is incorrect, since much practical experience only reinforces bad practices. 'D' is incorrect since functional managers have expertise in domains but not necessarily in the management of projects.

11.   B. The majority of a project's budget is expended in the execution of the work packages. You may have guessed 'A' due to the number of processes that occur as part of planning, but most projects do not involve as many people or resources in planning as they do in execution. Choice 'D' is incorrect because, while a project manager spends 90% of their time communicating, that does not take most of the team's time or the project budget.

12.   B. This is a very important definition. Corrective action is making adjustments to avoid future variances. 'A' is more in line with the definition of rework. 'C' is incorrect since there may or may not be a change control board, and their job would be to approve or reject change requests that have been forwarded by the project manager. 'D' is incorrect because corrective action does not come out of execution, but out of various control processes.

13.   C. This is the only one where both parts of the answer fit the definition. 'A' is incorrect since performance reports do not come out of the execution process. 'B' is incorrect since corrective action comes out of control processes. 'D' is incorrect on both parts of the answer.

14.   D. This type of question often appears on the PMP. It is easier than it first appears. Did you think the question was asking for the estimate at completion (EAC)? It is the originally budgeted amount, or budgeted at completion (BAC) that the question wants. That is calculated simply by taking 6 stories and multiplying it by $150,000/story. This yields the total project amount, which is $900,000.

15.   B. This is an important point. The project manager is the one responsible for integration. 'A' is incorrect because the team should be doing the work. 'C' is incorrect since senior management is not involved in integration management. 'D' is incorrect since the sponsor pays for the project but is not directly involved in integration.

16.   A. You should not add the deliverable. The reason is that this represents "gold plating", or adding functionality over and above the scope. It is not a good idea since this introduces risk and a host of other potential problems on the project. 'B' is incorrect because you do not know how it will affect risk, quality, or other factors. 'C' is incorrect, because you are ahead of schedule with an SPI of 1.5. 'D' is incorrect because it is the project manager's job – not the role of senior management to deal with this kind of change request.

17.   D. The scope management plan is the document that specifies how changes to the scope will be managed.

18.   C. Any of the words "evaluate", "investigate", "understand", or "assess" should automatically put that answer at the top of your list to evaluate. 'D' is incorrect because you may or may not have a change control board.

19.   C. Expert judgment is one of the tools used in initiating a project. 'A' is not a tool defined by PMI (if you were thinking of product description, it is an input – not a tool'. 'B' is used in communication planning. 'D' is a tool used in activity definition – not in initiation.

20.   A. Another bias of PMI's is that you should confront situations directly whenever possible. If you see a choice that represents things like confront, problem-solve, or deal with the situation directly, that is a good hint that you may be on the right answer. In this case, all of the other choices do not deal with the actual problem. Although the first choice may not be pleasant in real life, you should deal with the situation head on and solve the problem.

21.   A. The project manager is officially named, or assigned in the project charter, which is one of the outputs of scope initiation.

22.   B. The project charter is a document, and that document should include the business need behind the project. This is a general description of why the project was undertaken.

23.   B. The scope statement is an output of scope planning. The next step is the scope definition process, and the output of that is the work breakdown structure (WBS).

24.   A. The product description is an input into scope initiation. It is a higher level document and is created before the scope definition process is performed. All of the others are inputs into scope definition.

25.   D. The project manager's job during integration is to solve problems and make decisions. It is not the team's job to do this! Their job should be to execute the work packages. The project manager should be fixing the problems that come up and keeping the team focused on the work.

26.   A. Work package descriptions are contained in the WBS dictionary.

27.   B. Scope verification is where the customer and sponsor verify that the deliverables match what was in the scope.

28.   D. The statement of work (SOW) describes the pieces of the project that are to be performed by an outside vendor. It often starts off general and is revised as the project progresses. 'A' is incorrect because the SOW does not meet the strict qualifications of a contract. 'B' is incorrect because it is too broad – the SOW is only about the pieces that will be outsourced. 'C' is incorrect because an SOW is not needed for all projects – only those that will be procuring parts.

29.   C. This meets the definition of a cost-reimbursable contract. 'A' is a made-up term. 'B' is incorrect since the price is not fixed. 'D' is also incorrect. If you selected this one, you should review the difference between the time and materials and cost-reimbursable contracts.

30.   B. In the code of conduct, PMPs are instructed to avoid conflicts of interest. Your strategy in selecting answer 'B' should have been to look for the one choice that both solved the problem and avoided the conflict of interest. 'A' is incorrect because leaving the project represents avoidance and does not deal with the issue directly. 'C' is incorrect because the conflict of interest remains. 'D' is incorrect because by saying nothing, you are not dealing with the situation directly.

31.   C. Documenting the relationship between the product and the business takes place before scope definition. A justification of the business need is included in the project charter. 'A', 'B', and 'D' all fall under the definition of scope definition.

32.   B. The procurement management plan includes performance reporting specifications. If one of the choices had been "the communications management plan", that might have been a better selection, but given the choices provided, 'B' was the best one.

33.   A. Cost-revisable is not a valid choice (and from the sound of the name, it does it sound particularly safe to either party)! Choices 'B', 'C', and 'D' are all valid contract types.

34.   B. In this case, make or buy analysis is the most appropriate. It is where you decide whether your organization should create the product or whether you should go through procurement. Choice 'A' would be an activity that was performed later in the process. Choice 'C' is a tool for measuring whether a project is worth pursuing and is performed in initiation. Choice 'D' is also an activity performed after the decision has been made to go through procurement.

35.   C. With activities, the important order is define – order – estimate. The activity list is an input in activity duration estimating.

36.   B. Many people may formally accept the product, but in this list, the customer is the only one that fits the definition.

37.   A. The activity list is a decomposition of the WBS. It takes the work packages and breaks them down into activities that can be sequenced, estimated, and assigned.

38.   B. Float is how long an activity may be delayed without delaying the project. Choice 'B' is the only one that fits this definition.

39.   C. Procurement management is used when you go outside of the project for components of the project.

40.   B. This best choices here may be narrowed down to 'B' and 'D'. Think of this senior management request as a change request. Why would you simply ignore it without investigating further? 'B' is the better of the two answers since it solves the problem. If 'D' appears to be a better choice, consider that it actually represents conflict avoidance, which is almost never a good choice.

41.   D. Communication is the most important activity because the project manager spends an estimated 90% of their time communicating.

42.   A. The formula for standard deviation on a PERT estimate is (P-O) ÷ 6. This equates to 5/6. If you guessed 'B', you were probably thinking of the formula for a PERT estimate.

43.   D. At first glance, many people think that the wording of answer 'D' is impossible, but it is the correct choice. This problem should be solved in the usual 3 steps with one additional step at the end. (Did you notice that this was the same project network diagram as shown earlier? This is not uncommon on the PMP) First, draw out the network diagram based on the table. Your representation should resemble the one below:

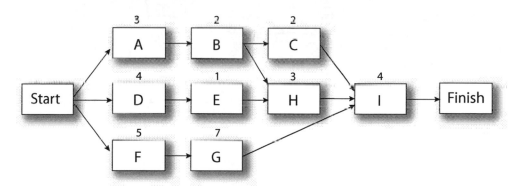

The next step is to list out all of the possible paths through the network. In this example, they are:

Start-A-B-C-I-Finish

Start-A-B-H-I-Finish

Start-D-E-H-I-Finish

Start-F-G-I-Finish

The third step is to add up the values associated with each path. Using the paths above, they are:

Start-A-B-C-I-Finish = 11

Start-A-B-H-I-Finish = 12

Start-D-E-H-I-Finish = 12

Start-F-G-I-Finish = 16

The final additional step is to increase the value of H from 3 to 7 and evaluate the impact. That would change the list to:

Start-A-B-C-I-Finish = 11

Start-A-B-H-I-Finish = 16

Start-D-E-H-I-Finish = 16

Start-F-G-I-Finish = 16

The answer, therefore, is that the critical path would change (there are now 3 critical paths), but the end date remains the same.

Moving from 1 critical path to 3 increases the schedule risk considerably, invalidating choice 'C'.

44. D. Although organizational policies may be useful in a number of scenarios, it is the only choice that is not formally defined as part of the budgeting process.

45.   A. Milestone charts are useful for communicating high-level status on a project. This represents the best of the 4 choices. 'B' would be far too much detail for an executive status meeting. 'C' would not be a bad thing to bring, but it would not be the best document for showing status. 'D' would not provide the status that the CIO seeks.

46.   B. Resource requirements should be developed against the work packages, which are lowest detail of the WBS.

47.   B. Analogous estimates, also called top-down estimates, use previous project costs as a guideline for estimating.

48.   D. You cannot calculate the PERT estimate without knowing values for optimistic, pessimistic, and realistic. In this case, you are only provided with 2 of the 3 numbers, therefore the answer is unknown.

49.   A. The standard deviation measures how diverse the population is. It does this by averaging all of the data points to find the mean, then calculating the average of how far each individual point is from that mean. For a very diverse population, you will have a high standard deviation. For a highly similar population, your standard deviation will be low.

50.   B. This is the best answer. Modern quality management stresses planning and prevention over inspection. This is based on the theory that it costs less to prevent a problem than it does to fix one. 'A' is incorrect, since prevention is stressed over inspection. 'C' is incorrect since contingency planning is part of risk management – not quality management. 'D' is incorrect since quality planning seeks to satisfy the quality standards. It is not focused on exceeding customer expectations.

51.   C. Phases within processes is a made-up term and is not stressed in quality management. Many people mistakenly select 'A' for this; however, quality management does stress that the customer's specifications should be taken into account (the implication being that if the customer's specifications are satisfied, the customer should be satisfied with the product). 'B' is incorrect because Demming's TQM philosophy stresses that the entire team has a responsibility toward quality. 'D' is incorrect because prevention over inspection is a big thrust of quality management, stressing that it costs less to prevent a problem than it does to fix one.

52.   A. Quality assurance is the process that uses these tools.

53.   C. Policies, the scope statement, and standards and regulations are all used as inputs into quality planning. The project schedule is not used.

54.   D. Contract type selection is a tool used in procurement planning. The type(s) of contract(s) used are included in the procurement management plan.

55.   C. The project manager is ultimately responsible for the quality of the product. If you guessed 'A', you were on track because Demming said that the entire team is responsible, but the word "ultimately" is the key here. The person ultimately responsible is the PM. 'B' is incorrect, because the quality team is not a team identified by PMI. 'D' is incorrect because functional managers may be very involved in the quality management process, but they are not ultimately responsible.

56.   A. This one is tricky because all of these tools are used in quality management! 'B', 'C', and 'D' are all used in quality control, but 'A' is used in planning. Fishbone diagrams (also known as Ishikawa diagrams or cause and effect diagrams) are used to evaluate potential quality problems and their root causes.

57.   C. The purpose of a control chart is to statistically determine if a process is in control.

58.   D. Stakeholders may want the project to succeed or fail! They may benefit or lose if the project succeeds. This is contrary to the way the word is used in many circles, and it is hard for many people to think of a stakeholder as potentially being hostile to the project.

59.   B. A risk rating matrix is an output of qualitative risk analysis, and it is used to rank risks qualitatively, that is, based on their characteristics as opposed to numerically.

60.   B. The opportunity cost is what you missed – not the difference between them. Because you invested in Project X, you missed out on the net present value of Project Y, which equals $75,000.

61.   D. A risk database is an output of risk monitoring and control. It allows you to collect, maintain, and analyze all of the data related to risk, and eventually it feeds into the lessons learned.

62.   C. When an anticipated risk event occurs, the plan for addressing that is followed; however, some risks cannot be anticipated. In that case, a workaround is needed.

63.   A. The first thing you should do is to plan for the new risks this situation presents. Remember that you should look for a proactive approach to almost everything. 'B' is incorrect because you cannot simply decide to withhold payment if you are in a contractual relationship. 'C' is incorrect because even though that may be something you would do, it is not the FIRST thing you should do. 'D' is also not the FIRST thing you should do, because this problem should be dealt with by the project manager. Running off to apprise senior management of the situation would not be the first thing a project manager does. It would be far better to do that after the project manager had assessed the situation and planned thoroughly for it.

64.   B. In a functional organization, most of the power rests with the functional manager. 'A' is incorrect since that describes a projectized organization. 'C' is incorrect because that describes a matrix organization. 'D' is incorrect since there is no explicit model in which power rests with the project office.

65.   D. Organizational planning is the process of understanding and identifying the reporting relationships on a project. An output of this process is the project's organizational chart.

66.   D. The responsibility assignment matrix (RAM) does not include reporting relationships. Those are included in the project's organizational chart. 'A' is incorrect because the RAM does show who is responsible for what on the project. 'B' is incorrect because it shows roles on the project for the various team members. 'C' is incorrect because the RAM can be for either individuals or for groups (e.g. engineering, or information technology).

67.   C. McGregor's Theory X manager distrusts people and believes that they must be watched every moment. 'A' is incorrect because that is more descriptive of the opposite, Theory Y manager. 'B' is incorrect because that is more descriptive of the practice of MBO (management by objectives). 'D' is incorrect because Theory X is not directly related to quality management.

68.   A. The withdrawer is someone who does not participate in the meeting and therefore is not a constructive role. 'B' is incorrect because someone who is trying to gather more, good information is contributing in a positive way. 'C' is incorrect because a person who clarifies communication is adding to the meeting as well. 'D' is tricky, but it is incorrect. In project management terminology, a gate keeper is someone who helps others participate and draws people out. Gate keepers would help withdrawers become active participants.

69.   D. In this case, the conflict is of a technical nature, so the best way the project manager could solve the problem is by using his or her technical expertise. 'A' is incorrect because legitimate power might stop the fight, but it wouldn't solve the problem. 'B' is incorrect because it also might stop the fight, but would not solve the problem. 'C' would probably be the least effective approach to solving this particular problem, since referent power is relying on personality or someone else's authority.

70.   C. The PERT estimate is calculated by adding the pessimistic estimate + 4 X realistic estimate + the optimistic estimate and dividing by 6. In this case, it is

$$\frac{60 + (4 \times 30) + 18}{6}$$

This reduces down to $198 \div 6 = 33$.

71.   C. Forcing does do away with the conflict… but only temporarily. It is when the manager says "This is my project, and you will do things my way. Period, end of discussion." The root of the problem is not addressed by this approach, thus the solution is only temporary.

72.   D. Did you guess 'A' or 'B' on this one? The communication plan may be either formal or informal, highly detailed or general, depending on the organization. 'C' is incorrect, because it does not include the project's major milestones. 'D' is the right answer in this case because it details how you are going to gather and store information on the project.

73.   B. One of the main reasons conflict arises on a project is over communication, and one of the results of a project's communication lines being broken is that conflict increases.

74.   C. To answer this one, you should have asked "which choice solves the problem?" The problem is that an employee is giving you incorrect information, and you cannot ethically pass that information on. The only choice that directly deals with the problem and fixes it is 'C'. The solution is not painless, but it is the best choice of the four.

75.   C. If there were 10 people on your project, that would yield 45 communication paths. Add 5 more, and you now have 15 people, which yields 105 communication paths. The question asks how many more paths would you have, thus the answer is $105 - 45 = 60$.

76.   A. It is the role of senior management to resolve organizational conflicts, and to prioritize projects, and either of those may be at the root of this problem. 'B' is incorrect since this is a matter internal to the organization, and the customer should be buffered from it. 'C' is incorrect since the stakeholders cannot always bring influence to bear inside the organization. 'D' is incorrect since the sponsor functions much like a customer internal to the organization. The sponsor does not prioritize projects and would not be the best person to go to in order to sort out an organizational conflict.

77.   B. E-mail is informal written communication. Formal written communication involves such things as changes to the project plan, contract changes, and official communication sent through channels such as certified mail. As e-mail evolves in its usage and protocol, test takers should be aware that although they may use e-mail in a formal manner, it is not considered to be formal communication.

78.   C. These are all considered to be forms of conflict resolution, even though none of these is considered to be an effective way to resolve conflict.

79.   B. Again, as yourself "what is the choice that solves the problem?" In this case, 'B' is the best choice that solves the problem. Before you do anything else, you would want to meet with the person directly and discuss the problem. 'A' may be appropriate at some point but would not be considered best in this case. 'C' is not a good choice, since it is your job to resolve the problem and not the customer's job. 'D' is incorrect since it is too passive a choice and does not really deal with the problem.

80.   B. This question is not only difficult, but there is a lot of information here to distract you. In this case, you should go to the sponsor and let him know, since he has approved the budget. If the project stands to deviate significantly (over or under), then the person paying for it should know as soon as possible. 'A' is incorrect because you are supposed to conform to the scope – not increase it! 'C' is also incorrect. You are working for the sponsor here, and it would not be wise to bill them more than the project costs. 'D' is incorrect, since you do not want to gold plate the scope by adding more than was originally planned.

81.   D. Communication is important at all points in the project, but it is critical during integration. The project manager's job becomes primarily to communicate during this part of the project.

82.   C. Focus on direct, polite confrontation over practically any other method of conflict resolution. In this case, you are the one who needs to resolve the conflict, so you should take the initiative. Discussing the employee's actions with her before the meeting should actually produce a resolution to the problem. 'A' appears direct at first, but it is not really a direct way to deal with the problem. 'B' is simply making the problem someone else's problem – in this case, your boss's. 'D' is incorrect for the same reason 'B' is. This is a problem that you, the project manager, should solve.

83.   A. With an SPI this far below 1, you have a significant schedule delay, and you should report this to management. 'B' is incorrect because you are doing quite well on cost, and there is no overrun. 'C' is incorrect since it is your job to deal with scope change – not management's. 'D' is incorrect because you cannot simply reject changes on the project. They must be evaluated thoroughly and fairly and sent through the scope change control system.

84.   C. The team should be involved in the estimating process, and once they have bought into those estimates, you should resist pressure to automatically slash them. 'A' is incorrect since additional estimating is not what is needed here. 'B' is incorrect since this is just delaying the inevitable and perhaps making matters much worse. 'D' is incorrect since the dates need to come from your estimates and schedule development and not from the client.

85.   D. To answer this, you should consider two things: 1. You need to avoid all conflicts of interest. 2. The solicitation process is supposed to keep all potential sellers on a level playing field. With these facts in mind, 'D' should emerge as the only choice that makes sense.

86.   D. Another name for analogous estimating is top-down estimating, because it looks at projects as a lump sum and not broken down into pieces (which is known as bottom-up estimating).

87.   C. This is a no-win situation, but you must obey laws in the country where you are performing the work, and 'C' is the only option that fully complies with the law. Refer to the PMI code of conduct and you will see that you cannot bend or break laws just to get the project done on time.

88.   D. Critical path questions are solved in 3 steps. First, draw out the project network diagram. Your diagram should look similar to the one depicted below (did you notice that this is activity on arrow?).

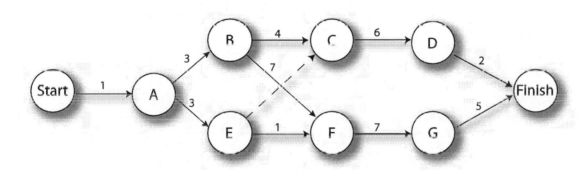

The next step is to list out all of the possible paths in the network. They are:

Start-A-B-C-D-Finish

Start-A-B-F-G-Finish

Start-A-E-C-D-Finish

Start-A-E-F-G-Finish

Finally, add up the length associated with each of those paths:

Start-A-B-C-D-Finish = 16

Start-A-B-F-G-Finish = 23

Start-A-E-C-D-Finish = 12

Start-A-E-F-G-Finish = 17

The critical path emerges as 23, represented by choice 'D'.

89. B. PMI's code of conduct states that you have a "responsibility to refrain from offering or accepting inappropriate payments, gifts, or other forms of compensation for personal gain." The best thing to do in this case is refuse the gift and let management know of the situation.

90. A. Activity definition uses the technique of decomposition to produce the activity list.

91. A. In a fixed price contact, the seller is the one who bears the risk. If the cost runs high, the seller must deliver at the original cost. The buyer's costs are set (fixed), thus offering a measure of security. 'B' is incorrect since the seller has higher risk. 'C' is incorrect since the seller's risk is higher than the buyer's. 'D' is incorrect since cost reimbursable is another form of contract separate from this.

92. C. A project coordinator is someone who is weaker than a project manager but may have some limited decision making power. 'A' is incorrect since a project manager does not have "limited authority" on a project. 'B' is a made up term, and 'D' refers to the sponsor whose role on the project is to pay for the project, receive the product at the end, and give the project good visibility in the organization.

93. D. Risk response planning would be the point at which you determine an appropriate response to the risks that have been identified, qualified, and quantified. Only after the risks are fully understood and analyzed would you make a change to the scope.

94. C. Even though there are a lot of them, it is important to learn to recognize these inputs, tools, and outputs. Benefit/cost analysis is a tool used in scope planning. 'A' is a tool used in scope initiation. 'B' is a tool used in scope definition, and 'D' is a tool used in quality control.

95.   B. Integration (in addition to most of the other processes) is not discrete. In other words, it isn't performed in a vacuum, but instead it is performed with all of the other processes in mind. That is even more pertinent for integration than any of the other knowledge areas. Also keep in mind that the word "integrated" has nearly the opposite meaning of the word "discrete". 'A' is incorrect because that is exactly what integration does. 'C' is also a purpose of integration, because the PMIS is the tool that the project manager uses to know what is going on with the project. 'D' is incorrect because that is also a definition of integration. The project manager is supposed to keep people focused on the work while he solves problems.

96.   A. Maslow's hierarchy is based on the fact that your basic needs, like food and water must be satisfied before higher needs, such as esteem, will become important. 'B' is incorrect because Herzberg's theory of hygiene factors is a different theory of motivation. 'C' is incorrect because this is a different motivational theory. 'D' is related to another theory of scientific management not covered in PMI's materials.

97.   D. Definitions are very important, and this definition question is missed by many people. Understand that projects may or may not be strategic to the company. Although everyone wants their project to be exciting and strategic, more mundane projects also must be undertaken. 'A', 'B', and 'C' are all part of the core definition of a project.

98.   D. In this case, your manager is auditing the process, and audits are performed in quality assurance. Audits are performed primarily to make sure that the process is being followed. 'A' is incorrect because quality control is inspecting specific examples and is not focused on the overall process. 'B' is incorrect because quality management is too broad a term to fit the definition of this process. 'C' is incorrect because quality planning is the process where the quality management plan is created.

99.   A. Variance analysis looks at the difference between what was planned and what was executed. Choice 'A' is the one that correctly identifies this.

100.   B. In a matrix organization, power is shared between the project managers and functional managers. In a strong matrix, the project manager is more powerful, while in a weak matrix, the functional manager has more power. In no circumstances would 'D' be correct, as the project coordinator is, by definition, weaker than a project manager.

101. C. The term "performance review" is another word for a status meeting. The reason for this is that during status meetings, the project manager should be reviewing work performed against what was planned.

102. C. The scope statement typically starts off general and becomes more specific as the project progresses. Progressive elaboration is a term that describes the way in which the details of the scope are discovered over time.

103. C. A devil's advocate is considered to be a negative team role. 'D', a gate keeper, is incorrect because in project management terminology a gate keeper is someone that draws non-participants and withdrawers into the process.

104. D. In project plan execution, the team is executing the work packages and creating the product of the project. Your job as project manager is to keep them focused on this. 'A' is incorrect because that may be your focus, but it is not the team's focus. 'B' is incorrect, because that is the project manager's job and not the team's focus. 'C' incorrect for the same reason. It is the job of the project manager and not the team.

105. C. The project management information system is used primarily during project plan execution. It helps the project manager manage information across the whole project.

106. C. Most of the resources (both human resources and material resources) are expended during executing processes.

107. A. Inspection is a tool of scope verification, which is the process being described in the question. In inspection, the product of the project is compared with the documented scope.

108. C. Quality improvement is an output of quality assurance and quality control. It is not a process.

109. D. Schedule constraints would not contain leads and lags for activities. 'A', 'B', and 'C' would all make sense to include as schedule constraints.

110. B. Benchmarking is a tool of quality management for both the quality planning and quality assurance processes. It takes the results of previous projects and uses them to help set standards for other projects. 'A' and 'C' are incorrect because they would be more closely aligned with quality control. 'D' is unrelated to quality.

111.   C. The activity list should include every activity defined on the project. These activities are then used to create the project network diagram.

112.   A. Administrative closure should be performed at the end of each phase or at the end of the project. It is the process where the project is formally accepted, the project records are created, and ultimately the team is released from the project. It is important to understand that administrative closure may happen several times throughout the project.

113.   C. Resources are released during administrative closure.

114.   D. The activity list is the output of the activity definition process. 'A', 'B', and 'C' are all inputs into activity definition.

115.   C. There are many ways to mathematically solve this problem, but perhaps the simplest is to divide the schedule performance index against the length of the project. 20 weeks ÷ 0.8 = 25 weeks. Therefore, we would expect the project to be 5 weeks late. 'A' should have been eliminated because with a schedule performance index less than 1, there is no way the project should be finished early.

116.   C. The term slack is synonymous with float.

117.   A. The project plan is a formal document. It is created during planning, and is used to guide the execution processes, controlling processes, and closure processes. 'B' is incorrect because that would be closer to the definition for the product. 'C' is close to correct, although it is an incomplete list of what makes up the project plan and the question specifically asks for the BEST description. 'D' is incorrect because this is closer to the definition of the work breakdown structure than it is to the project plan.

118.   D. As part of integrated change control, the project manager will need to know when change has occurred, manage the changes, and influence the factors that cause change, but the project manager should not take on the attitude of denying change whenever possible. Some change is inevitable, and all change requests should be evaluated and not automatically rejected.

119. C. Another no win situation. You cannot bend or break laws just to stay on schedule. The end does not justify the means! You have to obey laws and observe customs in the country where you are performing the work. In this situation, you should look at options that do not involve working overtime.

120. A. There is a difference between the product scope and the project scope. The scope of the project may be much larger than the scope of the product! This question defines the product scope. 'B' would have a much broader definition than this. 'C' is the work that needs to be done to complete the project, but it does not deal with the attributes of a product. 'D' is a phrase often used in project management, but it is unrelated to this definition.

121. C. The supporting detail should be included with the estimates, and that supporting detail is included for situations just like this one. It will help you and the team member understand how the estimates were derived in the first place. 'A' is incorrect since the team member may well have a valid point. 'B' is incorrect because there is no reason to either stop work on the project or to send the team member scrambling for new estimates. 'D' is not a bad choice, but it isn't the FIRST thing you would do. As a starting point, go back and check the facts first. Then if it would be helpful to get another expert involved, you may elect to do that.

122. B. The term "baseline" causes grief for many test takers. Memorize that the baseline (whether it is the scope baseline, schedule baseline, or cost baseline) includes the original plan plus all approved changes.

123. B. Although it is unusual in the real world, a projectized organizational structure gives the project manager near total control of the project and the resources. 'A' is a structure where the functional manager is in charge of projects and resources. 'C' is a structure where the project manager runs the projects and the functional manager manages the people, and 'D' is not a real term for organizational structures.

124.   A. This problem should be solved in the usual 3 steps with one small bit of reasoning applied at the end. First, draw out the network diagram based on the table. Your representation should resemble the one below:

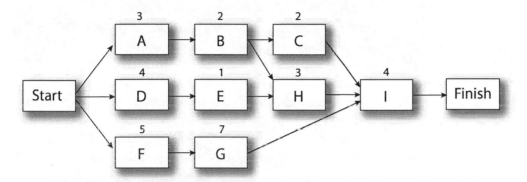

The next step is to list out all of the possible paths through the network. In this example, they are:

Start-A-B-C-I-Finish

Start-A-B-H-I-Finish

Start-D-E-H-I-Finish

Start-F-G-I-Finish

The last step is to add up the values associated with each path. Using the paths above, they are:

Start-A-B-C-I-Finish = 11 units

Start-A-B-H-I-Finish = 12 units

Start-D-E-H-I-Finish = 12 units

Start-F-G-I-Finish = 16 units

The question has asked for the path with the LEAST schedule risk, and that is represented by the shortest path (the one with the highest amount of float). The reason this path has the least risk is that tasks could slip the most here witout affecting the critical path. In this case, it is Start-A-B-C-I-Finish, which corresponds to choice 'A'.

125.   A. When a conflict of interest arises, it should be resolved in favor of the customer. In this case, your company's module has been determined not to be a good fit, so another solution is needed. 'B' is incorrect, because conflicts should be resolved in favor of the customer. 'C' is incorrect because it is has already been determined that it is not best for the project. 'D' is not correct because that is the project managers' job – not that of an outside party.

126.   D. The schedule development process uses leads and lags as inputs.

127.   A. Just as important as understanding the formulae is being able to interpret them. That is what this question is calling on you to do, and it can be quite hard. The schedule performance index (SPI) = EV ÷ PV. Studying the formula, you can see that it compares how much value you actually earned (EV) and divides that by how much you planned to earn (PV). In this case, you have earned value at 1.5 times the rate you had planned.

128.   C. The organizational chart, an output from the organizational planning process, shows the reporting structure for the project.

129.   C. Most of the planning processes have a logical order to them, and this question relies on an understanding of that. The work breakdown structure has to be created before cost estimates are performed, and the cost estimates have to be created before the budget. This should make sense when you stop to consider it.

130.   B. The list of risks is an output of the risk identification process.

131.   A. Activity definition is the process where the work breakdown structure is further decomposed into individual activities.

132.   B. A good rule is that if in doubt, select the "project manager." For this question, that would be correct. It is the project manager's job to resolve competing stakeholder requests and goals.

133.   C. Your goal is to create a win-win situation in the negotiations. A win-lose agreement will usually not let you win in the long-term.

134.   C. The project manager's professional code of conduct instructs you to keep customer information confidential. You should ask permission before using or reusing any part of the project that is not owned by you or your organization.

135. D. The cost baseline is an output of cost budgeting. 'A', 'B', and 'C' are outputs of the cost control process.

136. A. The way to approach this question is to remember how to calculate the schedule variance. It is EV-PV. If the schedule variance = 0, then EV must be equal to PV.

137. B. Activities are a further decomposition of the work breakdown structure, and work packages exist at the lowest levels of the work breakdown structure.

138. B. This one is easier than it first appears. All "management plans," including the staffing management plan, become part of the project plan. 'A' is incorrect because it is an output of organizational planning. 'C' is incorrect because it describes the approach to staffing and not every detail. 'D' is incorrect because the organization charge is a separate output of organizational planning.

139. B. Risk triggers are symptoms or warning signs that risks are about to occur or that a risk has just occurred.

140. C. You have a responsibility to help mentor others in the field of project management. 'A' would be inappropriate, because your responsibility extends to the profession – not just to your organization. 'B' is incorrect because the best place to start is with your friend. 'D' is incorrect because a job change would represent withdrawal and would not solve the problem in any way.

141. B. Planned value is the value of the work you planned to do at a given point in time. The first step is always to calculate your budgeted at completion. It is 25 miles * 1,200,000 / mile = $30,000,000. Now you want to calculate the planned value for 3 weeks of the 5 week project. Simply multiple the budgeted at completion by 3 and divide by 5. This yields $18,000,000. The interpretation of this is that you planned to earn $18,000,000 worth of value back into your project after 3 weeks of work.

142. C. Read this one carefully. It is the definition of free float. 'A' and 'B' were synonyms, which should have thrown up a red flag for you. Those terms tell you how long a task may be delayed before it changes the finish date of the project.

143. D. Earned value management can be used to monitor whether or not a risk is occurring or has occurred. If the schedule performance index or cost performance index slips, that could be the indication of a risk trigger and might require corrective action.

144. A. Even when news is unpopular or unpleasant, you must deliver accurate statuses. 'B' and 'C' attempt to cover up or hide the news. Choice 'D' is unnecessary since you should report the current and accurate status to the customer.

145. B. Source selection is an executing process of procurement, and yes, it is important that you know this type of information for the exam. In this process, the buyer evaluates the responses and chooses a seller.

146. C. Know the roles of each person or group on the project. It is the sponsor provides funding for the project.

147. A. Most importantly, the project should satisfy the scope, schedule, and budget. These are the principal factors of success. 'B' is important in many organizations, but you cannot control happiness as a project manager. The best you can do is to satisfy the scope of work. 'C' may be good to have, but it does not make the project successful. 'D' is also good in that you did what you planned to do when you planned to do it, but it is only an ingredient of project success.

148. C. Your primary objective is to satisfy the scope of work on the project within the agreed upon cost and schedule. 'A' is the means to your end goal of a successful project, but it is only the way you go about it. 'B' is a great goal, but there are other parties here that need to be considered – not just the performing organization. 'D' is good, but you should focus on doing so by delivering what you promised on time and on budget.

149. D. Graphical Evaluative Review Technique (GERT) is a type of conditional diagram that shows loops and logical branches on the project.

150. B. This is the most appropriate answer. Your job is to deliver all of the work that was promised, and 'B' is the only choice that satisfies this.

151. B. A task's late finish date is the latest atask can finish without delaying the project. If it exceeds the late finish date, the critical path will change, ultimately resulting in the finish date slipping. Choice 'A' is close to the definition of free float.

152. D. Speeches such as this one are examples of formal verbal communication.

153. C. Requests for payment (invoices), and payments are activities typically performed during contract administration.

154. A. Herzberg stated that hygiene factors must be present in order for motivational factors to work; however, hygiene factors do not motivate by themselves. They only enable the motivation factors to work.

155. B. The critical path represents the highest schedule risk on the project. If there is more than one critical path, schedule risk is increased. 'A' is not necessarily true. Two or more paths could be the critical path on the project all the way from beginning to end. 'C' and 'D' are ways to "resolve the conflict" when there is no conflict. There will always be at least 1 critical path, and having 2 or more critical paths by no means represents a conflict.

156. B. With a payback period, the shorter the time the better. The hardest thing about this problem is to reduce all of the times to a common denominator so you can see which one is the shortest! B is 1 year, and that is the shortest period of time of the 3 choices.

157. B. A project network diagram (like activity on arrow) is an output of activity sequencing. The other 3 types of dependencies represented in choices 'A', 'C', and 'D' are all inputs to activity sequencing.

158. D. The processes are not set in stone so that once you have finished planning you can never return. Remember that projects are progressively elaborated, and that often times you will need to revisit processes again and again. There is no reason not to return to planning in the example given here.

159. D. The goal of duration compression is to accelerate the due date without shortening the scope of the project.

160. B. Conflicts of interest should be disclosed and avoided. 'A' is not a good choice, because you are not only bound to act legally, but ethically! 'C' is not correct because you would not be keeping information confidential. 'D' would not be a rational choice. Resigning from both projects would cause more problems and solve nothing.

161. C. A standard usually should be followed, while a regulation has to be followed.

162. A. The evaluation criteria are created in the solicitation planning process. In the source selection process the evaluation criteria are used to select a qualified seller after responses have been received.

163. D. Richard is performing risk response planning. After the risks have been identified, qualified, and quantified, they should be responded to. Risk response planning looks at how to make the opportunities more likely and better and the threats less likely and less severe. Remember that a risk is an uncertainty that could be good or bad.

164. A. In order to answer this question, you must first be able to identify in which process you solicit bids. It is the solicitation process, and the output of solicitation is a proposal.

165. B. The work results of the project may be products, services, or results. 'A' is incorrect because work results could be a product, a service, or a result. 'C' is incorrect because the work results don't have to meet quality to be considered work! 'D' is incorrect because the output of the work authorization system is not the work itself, but that a resource is authorized to do the work.

166. B. You have a responsibility to society, the environment, and the economy, and this comes higher than your responsibility to your boss. You are not to just follow orders, but you should think for yourself to ensure that the project does not do harm. Note that this is not merely a disagreement over the probability success of the project.

167. A. Some companies rest their reputation on the high quality of their product. Others do not. The quality policy defines how important quality is on this project from the performing organization's perspective.

168. C. Status meetings, also known as performance reviews, were never meant to be a time where everyone sits around discussing the project. The purpose of these meetings is to discuss progress and performance on work that has been completed.

169. D. By not facing the problem The team member is withdrawing. 'A', 'B', and 'C' are not terms regularly used in project management circles.

170. C. In a functional organization, the project manager has little formal power and may even be part time! It is the functional manager who is more powerful in this structure.

171. C. The responsibility assignment matrix, created during organizational planning, is a chart that can show roles and responsibilities on the project. 'A' is incorrect because it shows resources usage levels across the project. 'B' is incorrect because it shows reporting relationships but not specific responsibilities. 'D' is incorrect because this general document tells how you are going to approach staffing the project.

172. D. Risk mitigation is when you try to make the risk less severe or less likely. By accelerating the construction, Kim is mitigating the likelihood of a hurricane damaging her project.

173. C. The answer "fixed price" would have been the best here, but it was not in the list of choices! Of the ones listed, cost plus incentive fee would provide the seller with an incentive to keep their costs down. 'A' provides no incentive at all for the seller to keep costs down. 'B' would not provide the same incentive since the seller gets a fixed fee regardless of the project costs. 'D' is not a real contract type.

174. D. The more channels of communication on a project, the more difficult it is to control communications. 'A', 'B', and 'C' are probably not true because these people are internal to the project, and the creation of the plan and analysis of the stakeholders, and communication with them would not necessarily be more difficult.

175. A. Here is an example where you should ignore the trigger words "find out." You have a responsibility to comply fully with PMI in an investigation. 'B', 'C', and 'D' may be tempting, but you should cooperate with PMI.

176. B. Earned value is what you have actually done at a point in time. In this case the budgeted at completion for the project is $300,000, and you have completed 20% of that. All of the other facts in the problem are irrelevant. The answer is $300,000 * 20% = $60,000.

177. B. The project expeditor is the weakest role here. This person is typically a staff assistant to an executive who is managing the project. 'C' is the most powerful, and 'A' would be next. 'D' is not a term identified within PMI's processes.

178. D. This is a definition of configuration management. 'A' is incorrect because it is part of the integrated change control process and not project plan development. 'B' is incorrect because that is more descriptive of inspection – a tool of scope verification. 'C' is incorrect because this is performed after initiation.

179. D. Organizational planning, a process of human resource management, and resource planning, a process of cost management, are often tightly linked. The two processes both deal with resources on the project.

180. D. When a project ends or is cancelled, the project manager should enter administrative closure. 'A' would come out of administrative closure. 'B' is not defined as part of the closure process. 'C' might be correct in some cases, but there is not reason to assume a there was any contract in this example.

181. C. The interpretation of this is important. A benefit-cost ratio indicates how much benefit you expect to receive for the cost expended. In this example you could to get $1.50 profit for every dollar of cost.

182. A. The work breakdown structure is the cornerstone of the project, and it is the most important input to resource planning. Out of the other choices, only 'B' is an input to this process, but the most important input is the work breakdown structure because it contains all of the work to be done on the project.

183. B. Life-cycle costing takes a broad look at the project, considering such things as operational costs, scrap value, etc. It doesn't just ask how much it costs to make a product, but it looks at the total cost of ownership.

184. D. The buyer is primarily assuming the risk here because they are in a time and materials contract. The seller gets paid for every hour they work.

185. B. A Control Account Plan (also known as either a CAP or a Cost Account Plan), is a control point, placed on the WBS, that aids in the measurement of scope, time, and cost. It helps the project manager measure how much a package of scope cost, and how long it took to complete.

186. C. Stakeholder analysis is done as part of communications planning so that you know with whom you will be communicating.

187.   A. Expectancy theory says that reward motivation will work if the team believes that the goal is achievable.

188.   D. Organizational policies are not directly used in creating the project budget. 'A', 'B', and 'C' are all inputs to the cost budgeting process.

189.   A. There is no way to get around that dependency, so it is a mandatory dependency.

190.   D. A milestone chart only shows major events (milestones) on the project's timeline. 'A' and 'B' are incorrect because neither a Gantt chart nor a milestone chart are project plans. 'C' is incorrect because milestones are high level representations that do not show interdependencies between activities.

191.   D. After the scope statement and the work breakdown structure, you should move into activity definition. 'A' cannot be done before the activity list since the activity list is used to create the network diagram. 'B' and 'C' cannot be done until the network diagram is completed. The correct order of these choices listed would be: 'D', 'A', 'C', 'B'.

192.   B. Authorization for a new project or project phase is part of the scope initiation process.

193.   D. This is not the easiest question on the exam! You must first determine what you have done and then determine what is next. Look carefully at what you have created, and you will see that you have just finished the procurement planning process and the solicitation planning process. The next process to be performed should be solicitation.

194.   C. Generally, any time you are looking at past performance, you are in a controlling process.

195.   C. The primary purpose of the project network diagram is to show the sequence of activities and their dependencies. 'A' is incorrect because the project plan is made up of all planning output. 'B' is incorrect because the percentage complete is not reflected on the network diagram. 'D' is incorrect because the project network shows the paths through the network, but it does not create them.

196. A. The quality policy is a document issued by the performing organization that describes their attitude regarding quality. As different companies place different values on quality, the quality policy will differ. For instance, the quality policy for a pharmaceutical company will almost certainly have a stricter quality policy than a maker of novelty toys.

197. D. Did you guess 'C' for this one? The risk would have been planned in risk response planning, but if it was unforeseen and it occurred then you would have caught that in risk monitoring and control. That is the process where workarounds are created.

198. B. Accepting or offering a bribe can land you in jail. As a project manager, you cannot accept or offer bribes to anyone. 'A', 'C', and 'D' are all designed to trap people who don't see bribes as clearly inappropriate and illegal.

199. C. The formula for the schedule performance index is earned value ÷ planned value (EV÷PV). To get EV, we need to know how much we have completed to date. The budgeted at complete is $300,000, and we are 20% complete. Therefore, EV = $300,000 * 20% = $60,000. Planned value is what we had planned to complete at this point. We are 1 month into a 6 month project, or 1/6 of the way through. 1/6 = .17 (17%), and our budgeted at completion of $300,000 * 17% = $51,000. Now that we have EV ($60,000) and PV ($51,000), we can calculate the schedule performance index. It is EV÷PV, or $60,000 ÷ $51,000 = 1.18. The interpretation of this number is that the project is earning value 1.18 times as fast as was planned, and any index that is 1 or greater is a good thing!

200. B. Collocation is a tool used in the team development process where the team is brought together in a single location.

Endnotes

Introduction

1   The PMBOK is the trademarked term that is short for the Project Management Institute's Guide to the Project Management Body of Knowledge. The book is an ANSI specification, providing an overview of PMI's processes. PMI points out in the PMBOK itself that it is not a study-guide for the exam. Its purpose is to define the theories and practices within project movement that are widely accepted.

Chapter 1   The Exam

1   Project Management Professional Examination Details, March 4, 2002, online at www.pmi.org.

2   Although the first five categories listed in the table are PMI Processes, the sixth category is relatively new to PMI. It is not a project management process, but a category of questions related to the project manager's responsibility and integrity. Project Management Processes are covered in depth in chapter 10, while Professional Responsibility is covered in Chapter 12.

Chapter 2   Foundational Concepts

1   Pinto, Jeffrey K. *The Project Management Institute: Project Management Handbook.* Jossey-Bass Publishers, 1998, p. 117.

2   Kerzner, Harold. *Project Management : A Systems Approach to Planning, Scheduling, and Controlling.* John Wiley & Sons, 2000, p. 133.

3   IBID, pp. 14-16.

Chapter 3   Framework

1   PMBOK 2000, p. 32.

Chapter 4   Scope Management

1   Pinto, Jeffrey K.; Rouhiainen, Pekka. *Building Customer-based Project Organizations.* New York: John Wiley & Sons, 2001, pp. 9-10.

2 PMI, Practice Standard for Work Breakdown Structures, Project Management Institute, 2001, p 1.

3 Knutson, Joan; Bitz, Ira, Project Management: How to Plan and Manage Successful Projects, New York, AMACOM, 1991, p

4 Rasiel, Ethan M.; Friga, Paul N. *The McKinsey Mind: Understanding and Implementing the Problem-solving Tools and Management Techniques of the World's Top Strategic Consulting Firm.* Chicago, IL, McGraw-Hill Professional, 2001, pp 6 – 11. This book provides an excellent treatment of how to build MECE trees. The principles for creating these trees can be easily applied to the creation of Work Breakdown Structures, which are similar in nature.

5 Kerzner, p 576.

6 Pinto, Jeffrey K. The Project Management Institute: Project Management Handbook, Jossey-Bass Publishers, 1998, p 179.

7 Kerzner, p 826.

8 IBID, p 611.

9 Pinto, p 159.

10 IBID, pp. 578-579.

11 PMI, Practice Standard for Work Breakdown Structures, Project Management Institute, 2001, p 15.

Chapter 6 Cost Management

1 It should be noted that many resources use slightly different terminology for some concepts. The PMP Exam may also use both terms. Example, some of the books listed above will speak of Actual Costs (AC) as Actual Cost of Work Performed (ACWP), Earned Value (EV) is often Budgeted Cost of Work Performed (BCWP), and Planned Value (PV) is referred to as Budgeted Cost of Work Scheduled (BCWS). Although the terms are different, the concepts are the same.

Chapter 7 Quality Management

1 PMBOK, p. 97.

2 Hodgetts, Richard M. *Implementing TQM in Small & Medium-sized Organizations: A Step-by-step Guide.* Amacom, 1996. p. 41.

3 Hodgetts, p. 38.

4   Eckes, George. *The Six Sigma Revolution: How General Electric and Others Turned Process Into Profits.* New York: John Wiley & Sons, Inc. (US), 2001, p. 93.

5   Kerzner, p 1106.

6   Ryan, Thomas P. *Statistical Methods for Quality Improvement.* New York: John Wiley & Sons, Inc. (US), 2000, p. 341.

Chapter 8   Human Resources Management

1   Kotter, John P. *A Force for Change: How Leadership Differs from Management.* New York: The Free Press.

2   IBID.

3   Kerzner, p 475.

4   Pinto, p 9.

5   Kerzner, p 475.

6   Pinto, p. 247.

7   Stuckenbruck, Linn; Marshall, David. *Team Building for Project Managers.* Project Management Institute, 1990, pp 48-49.

8   IBID, p. 48.

9   Kerzner, p. 67.

10   The author once reported on a project to the CIO of a Fortune 500 company who was a notorious and infamous topic jumper. The negative net effect of this was empirically demonstrated time and again and ultimately led to meetings being scheduled in secret in obscure locations so as to avoid the errant CIO.

11   The author also has many stories about this from yet another project at another public company, where the Vice President, again coincidentally the author's boss, was such a strong dominator that his name was ultimately coined into a verb. Daily exclamations from team members that they had a meeting which had been overrun by the overbearing VP were commonplace, and turnover within this particular department became legendary in the industry.

12   Thamhain, Hans J, and Wilemon, David L. *Conflict Management in Project-Oriented Work Environments*, PMI, 1974, p 87.

13   Maslow, A. H. *Motivation and Personality.* 2d ed. New York: Harper & Row, 1970.

14   McGregor, Douglas. *The Human Side of Enterprise.* New York: McGraw-Hill, 1960.

15   Gray, Jerry L., and Frederick A. Starke. *Organizational Behavior: Concepts and Applications.* Columbus, OH: 1988.

16   Lewis, James P. *Project Planning, Scheduling & Control: A Hands-on Guide to Bringing Projects in On Time and On Budget.* pp. 289-293.

17   Herzberg, Mausner, and Snyderman. *The Motivation to Work.* New York: John Wiley, 1959.

18   Pinnington, Ashly; Edwards, Tony. *Introduction to Human Resource Management,* p 130.

19   Pinto, p 295.

Chapter 9   Communication Management

1   Mina, Eli. *The Complete Handbook of Business Meetings.* New York: AMACOM, 2000, p 32.

2   Pinto, p. 245.

3.   Stuckenbruck, Linn C., *Team Building for Project Managers,* Pennsylvania: PMI, 1990, p. 32

Chapter 10   Risk Management

1   PMBOK 2000, p. 131.

2   PMBOK 2000, p. 135.

Chapter 11   Procurement Management

1   PMBOK 2000, p. 147

2   PMBOK 2000, p. 148

3   PMBOK 2000, p. 151

4   Pinto, p. 79

5   PMBOK 2000, p. 153

6   Article 2 of the United States Uniform Commercial Code Section 2 § 2-206

Chapter 12   Integration Management

1   PMBOK 2000, p. 47.

2   Pinto, p. 16.

Chapter 13   Professional Responsibility

1   Project Management Professional Examination Details, March 4,

Index

Index

Index

Index

N

Negative Float 89
Negotiation 167, 182, 237, 246, 247, 314
Network Logic Diagram 66, 68, 69, 72, 74, 85, 86, 90, 91, 94, 99, 101, 104, 105, 108, 253, 260, 285
Network Paths 71, 74, 79, 91, 93, 94, 106, 108
Net Present Value (NPV) 45–46, 126, 129, 133, 136
NPV. *See* Net Present Value

O

Obligation (contract) 239, 269
Obligation (contracts) 239
Ongoing Education 5
Opportunity Cost 45, 134, 137
Order of magnitude estimate 132, 136, 296
Organizational Alignment. *See* Alignment of Goals
Organizational planning 164–166, 181, 182, 183, 184, 185, 310, 337, 353, 370
Organization (types of) 9, 18–22, 162, 165, 169, 178, 180, 182, 183, 184, 185, 255, 265, 288
Outputs (process) 28, 43, 53, 114, 141, 166, 214, 216, 217, 237, 255, 256, 258, 298

P

Parametric Modeling 114, 133, 137
Pareto's Law 150
Pareto Diagram 141, 149–150, 154, 158, 296, 308, 343
Passing (exam) 2, 267, 287, xvi
Paths. *See* Network Paths
Payback Period 46, 126, 129
PDM. *See* Precedence Diagramming Method
Performance Reporting 195, 201, 205
Performance Reports 53, 195, 200, 205, 296, 298, 343, 346
Performance reviews 255, 360, 368
Personal Alignment. *See* Alignment of Goals
PERT. *See* Program Evaluation and Review Technique
Planned Value 117, 118, 119, 120, 121, 127, 128, 129, 134, 135, 136, 137, 254, 289, 374
Planning Process 27, 30, 32, 42, 43, 47, 49, 53, 68, 70, 113, 115, 140, 141, 145, 147, 153, 156, 157, 158, 159, 164, 183, 184, 189, 210, 214, 216, 227, 236, 243, 261, 373, 376
PMBOK , 3, 15, 28, 29, 36, 39, 44, 66, 116, 161, 209, 211, 230, 251, 259, 267, 268, 276, 282, 286, 287, 291, 373, 374, 376, xvi
PMI. *See* Project Management Institute
PMIS. *See* Project Management Information System
Portfolio 13–14
Power 9, 19, 162, 165, 169–170, 170, 177, 178, 180, 183, 184, 185
Precedence Diagramming Method 90
Present Value 45–46, 136
Problem Solving 21, 180. *See* Confrontation
Process Groups 29–36
Procurement Documents 235–236
Procurement Management 205, 229–250
Procurement Management Plan 235, 245, 253
Professional Responsibility 1, 4, 267–284, 291

Index

Index